The NOOK® Book

An Unofficial Guide Sixth Edition

Patrick Kanouse

nook

800 East 96th Street, Indianapolis, Indiana 46240

Trademarks

Warning and Disclaimer

Special Sales

For information about buying this title in bulk quantities, or for special sales opportunities (which may include electronic versions; custom cover designs; and content particular to your business, training goals, marketing focus, or branding interests), please contact our corporate sales department at corpsales@pearsoned.com or (800) 382-3419.

For government sales inquiries, please contact governmentsales@pearsoned.com.

For questions about sales outside the U.S., please contact international@pearsoned.com.

Editor-in-Chief
Greg Wiegand

Acquisitions Editor
Michelle Newcomb

Development Editor
Brandon Cackowski-Schnell

Managing Editor
Kristy Hart

Senior Project Editor
Betsy Gratner

Copy Editor
Apostrophe Editing Services

Senior Indexer
Cheryl Lenser

Proofreader
Kathy Ruiz

Technical Editor
Christian Kenyeres

Editorial Assistant
Cindy Teeters

Cover Designer
Mark Shirar

Compositor
Nonie Ratcliff

Table of Contents

Introduction   vii

PART I   **Samsung Galaxy Tab 4 NOOK**

  1 Getting Started with Your Samsung Galaxy Tab 4 NOOK   1

  2 Customizing and Configuring Your Samsung Galaxy
     Tab 4 NOOK   15

  3 **Reading on Your Samsung Galaxy Tab 4 NOOK and Beyond**   **51**

  4 Using Highlights, Bookmarks, and Annotations   89

  5 Reading and Using NOOK Books for Kids Features   99

  6 Lending and Borrowing Books with LendMe on Your
     Samsung Galaxy Tab 4 NOOK   107

  7 **Playing Music, Audiobooks, and Podcasts**   **111**

  8 Watching Videos on Your Samsung Galaxy Tab 4 NOOK   119

  9 Using NOOK Apps and Surfing the Web   129

 10 Creating and Using Profiles on Your Samsung
     Galaxy Tab 4 NOOK   141

 11 **Using the Social Features of Your Samsung Galaxy
     Tab 4 NOOK**   **153**

 12 Shopping and Visiting B&N on Your Samsung Galaxy
     Tab 4 NOOK   161

 13 Using the Google Play Store and Google Apps   173

 14 Using the Samsung Galaxy Tab 4 NOOK Camera
     and Google Hangouts   183

PART II   **NOOK GlowLight**

15   Getting Started with Your NOOK GlowLight   **193**

16   Customizing and Configuring Your NOOK GlowLight   199

17   Reading on Your NOOK GlowLight and Beyond   209

18   Lending and Borrowing Books with LendMe
     on Your NOOK GlowLight   221

19   Using Highlights, Bookmarks, and Annotations   **225**

20   Using the Social Features of Your NOOK GlowLight   229

21   Shopping and Visiting B&N on Your NOOK GlowLight   233

PART III   **Beyond the NOOKs**

22   Reading Beyond Your NOOK: Mobile Apps   239

23   Reading Beyond Your NOOK: Desktop Apps   **297**

24   Managing Your ebooks with Calibre   335

25   Using My NOOK Library   345

26   Using NOOK Press to Sell Your ebooks   355

27 Reading Beyond Your NOOK: NOOK App for Windows 8   **371**

A   Understanding ebook Formats   385

B   Sources for ebooks Other than B&N   389

C   Can I Read This Here?   393

     Index   **395**

About the Author

Patrick Kanouse works as the director of workflow services for Pearson Education. Always a bookworm, he has gladly adopted ebook reading technologies, while still appreciating and valuing the printed book.

Patrick also teaches technical communications at IUPUI. Outside of teaching about writing, reading on his NOOK®, and writing about his NOOK, he writes fiction and poetry, having published a NOOK Press™ book at BN.com that you can read on your NOOK. You can find him online at patrickkanouse.com and on Twitter at @patrickkanouse.

Patrick lives in Westfield, Indiana, with his wife and two Yorkies.

Dedication

This book is dedicated to my wife, Gina, who has always supported my every endeavor, even if it is immersed in some ancient history reading or volumes of poetry or dragging her to the latest science fiction movie. Without her support and encouragement, nothing that I attempt would be possible.

Acknowledgments

Thanks to Loretta Yates for asking me to revise and write this book many editions ago and thank you to Michelle Newcomb for asking me to update this edition. Given the pace of writing this edition, I must give substantial thanks to the book team for taking my initial words and making them much better, finding places I could improve, making obscurities clear—that is, making me look good: Brandon Cackowski-Schnell, Kristy Hart, Betsy Gratner, San Dee Phillips, and everyone in production.

We Want to Hear from You!

As the reader of this book, *you* are our most important critic and commentator. We value your opinion and want to know what we're doing right, what we could do better, what areas you'd like to see us publish in, and any other words of wisdom you're willing to pass our way.

We welcome your comments. You can email or write to let us know what you did or didn't like about this book—as well as what we can do to make our books better.

Please note that we cannot help you with technical problems related to the topic of this book.

When you write, please be sure to include this book's title and author as well as your name and email address. We will carefully review your comments and share them with the author and editors who worked on the book.

Email: feedback@quepublishing.com

Mail: Que Publishing
            ATTN: Reader Feedback
            800 East 96th Street
            Indianapolis, IN 46240 USA

Reader Services

Visit our website and register this book at quepublishing.com/register for convenient access to any updates, downloads, or errata that might be available for this book.

Introduction

Congratulations on your purchase of the Samsung Galaxy Tab® 4 NOOK® or NOOK GlowLight™, Barnes & Noble's (simply B&N from here on) ebook readers.

The Samsung Galaxy Tab 4 NOOK represents a shift by B&N in its approach to devices and digital content. Although B&N remains committed to manufacturing the NOOK GlowLight, it decided to partner with Samsung for tablets. Samsung is the hardware maker, and B&N focuses on the software. The B&N software—NOOK Reader, NOOK Library, NOOK Store™, and others—is embedded into the device much more so than just installing an app on another tablet. The Samsung Galaxy Tab 4 NOOK is a full-featured Android tablet with extra NOOK software as a continuous part of the experience. This gives you the ability to download many more apps from the Google Play Store while using the device to read and watch content you purchase from B&N.

This book is intended to give you all the information you need to get the most from your Samsung Galaxy Tab 4 NOOK, NOOK GlowLight, NOOK mobile apps, NOOK desktop apps, NOOK for Web, and NOOK for Windows 8, whichever version you have, and the associated supporting applications. You not only learn how to use your NOOK, but you also learn all the best places to get books and other content as well as using a free tool called Calibre to help you manage your ebook library.

By the time you finish this book, you'll be comfortable with all aspects of your NOOK. Following are some of the many things you can learn how to do in this book:

- ▶ Add your own pictures for use as a wallpaper or screensaver.

- ▶ Use B&N's unique LendMe® feature to lend and borrow books.

- ▶ Play music, audiobooks, podcasts, and more.

- ▶ Watch video, including NOOK Video™, Netflix, and Hulu Plus.

- ▶ Read your ebooks on your iPhone, iPod Touch, iPad, Android tablet, Android phone, and computer.

- ▶ Get books (many free) from many sources on the Internet, and load them onto your NOOK.

- ▶ Manage all your ebooks, and update author and title information if needed.

- ▶ Automatically download full-color covers for your books that display on your NOOK.

▶ Use your Samsung Galaxy Tab 4 NOOK to browse the web.

▶ Use your Samsung Galaxy Tab 4 NOOK to read enhanced books and children's books. You can even record your own readings of your child's favorite books.

▶ Use highlights, annotations, and bookmarks.

▶ Use the Google Play Store to find more apps.

▶ Set up profiles.

▶ Use the NOOK Store to find more digital content to read and watch.

▶ Learn how to publish your books using B&N's NOOK Press website.

This book is divided into three parts:

▶ Part I, "Samsung Galaxy Tab 4 NOOK," focuses exclusively on using the Samsung Galaxy Tab 4 NOOK.

▶ Part II, "NOOK GlowLight," focuses on using the NOOK GlowLight. This part is also useful for NOOK Simple Touch® owners.

▶ Part III, "Beyond the NOOKs," focuses on using the NOOK-related apps, Calibre, and B&N's NOOK Press.

Mixed in with all this, you can find plenty of tips and tricks to help you get the most from your NOOK.

NOTE: Writing this book presents a unique challenge. The E Ink NOOK has some limitations with images. Although the images do appear, complex images or images with a lot of information can be tedious to see. The Samsung Galaxy Tab 4 NOOK, however, present images in a much better fashion, as do the related NOOK Reading Apps™. Therefore, for all aspects of the Samsung Galaxy Tab 4 NOOK and NOOK Apps, the use of images will be more substantial than with the NOOK GlowLight chapters.

NOTE: Throughout this book, you encounter the terms ebook and NOOK Book®; ebook will be used generically. NOOK Books is what B&N calls its version of ebooks that it sells through B&N. These are still ebooks, and NOOK Book is more of a marketing device, but the distinction is useful because only NOOK Books sync between devices and support social features. Also, only NOOK Books are visible in My NOOK® Library on BN.com.

NOTE: If you're looking for coverage of the NOOK® HD or NOOK® HD+, take a look at the fifth edition of *The NOOK Book*.

NOTE: If you're looking for coverage of the NOOK Color™ or NOOK Tablet™, take a look at the third edition of *The NOOK Book*.

It's my hope that you don't have any questions about using your NOOK after reading this book, but if you do, don't hesitate to send me an email at NOOK@patrickkanouse.com. I'll gladly help if I can. You can also find me on Twitter at @patrickkanouse. Finally, my blog, http://patrickkanouse.blogspot.com/, has a section devoted to updates as I get them related to this book, so check in every so often.

Thank you for buying *The NOOK Book*!

CHAPTER 1

Getting Started with Your Samsung Galaxy Tab 4 NOOK

Before getting into the details of using your Samsung Galaxy Tab 4 NOOK, let's take a look at some of the basics: gestures, setup, and basic navigation. With these basics in place, you can then discover all the other incredible things your Samsung Galaxy Tab 4 NOOK can do.

> NOTE: From here on, I'll simply refer to this device as the NOOK.

> NOTE: Barnes & Noble uses a lowercase *n* when it spells *NOOK* and for the NOOK's logo.

> NOTE: Two Samsung Galaxy Tab 4 NOOKs are available: the Samsung Galaxy Tab 4 NOOK 7.0 and the Samsung Galaxy Tab 4 NOOK 10.1. The software of the two devices are identical, though the physical buttons are located differently on each device and the 10.1 is a larger device. This book uses images from the 7.0 version of the device. But all functionality is identical.

Understanding NOOK Gestures

You control the NOOK, excepting the Power button, Home button, Back key, Recent key, and volume controls, by gestures:

▶ **Tap**: This is the most common gesture. Just press your finger to the screen and raise it. Usually, you use this gesture with buttons and covers.

▶ **Press and hold**: This is the same as the tap gesture, but instead of raising your finger, you hold it to the screen for a couple of seconds. This often opens an additional menu from which to choose by a tap, but you can encounter other results from a press and hold.

▶ **Dragging**: Much like press and hold, you press an item on the screen and hold it. You can then drag it to a different location. (This gesture is often used for rearranging your Home screen icons.)

▶ **Swipe left/swipe right**: The gesture is mostly for turning pages. Like a tap, touch your finger on the screen and quickly drag it to the left (or right) and lift your finger up.

▶ **Scroll**: Essentially the vertical version of the swipe gesture. You can control the speed of the scroll by swiping up or down more rapidly. You can slow down or stop the scroll by tapping the screen to stop or pressing and holding to slow the scroll.

▶ **Sweep**: Use this gesture to take screen shots of what's on your NOOK. Use the side of your palm and swipe it from the right edge to the left edge. You'll know you've done it successfully when the borders of the screen flash white briefly.

▶ **Pinch and zoom in/pinch and zoom out**: This is a method to zoom in or out on pictures, PDFs, web pages, and so on. To zoom in or show part of the screen more closely, you place your index finger and thumb closely together on the screen (that is, pinch) and then spread them apart. To zoom out or show more of the screen, you do the pinch and zoom in gesture in reverse — this is also called unpinch.

Setting Up and Registering Your NOOK

When you first turn on your NOOK, you get a welcome screen with access to Accessibility options. If you need to adjust these, tap Accessibility, make any adjustments, and tap Next. If you don't need to make such adjustments, tap Start.

The next step is to set up the Wi-Fi access (see Figure 1.1). If you don't see your network ID but should, tap Scan. Tap the network you want to join and enter the required information. Tap Next. If the network is hidden or you cannot see it in the list, tap Add Wi-Fi Network, enter the necessary information, and tap Connect.

FIGURE 1.1   Pick your Wi-Fi network.

NOTE: Want Wi-Fi access on the go? Many wireless companies such as Verizon offer mobile Wi-Fi hotspots at reasonable prices. A mobile hotspot uses the 3G or 4G cellular network but treats it as a Wi-Fi connection, so you never need to be without wireless access.

For more information on connecting your NOOK to a Wi-Fi hotspot after your initial set up, **see** "Using Wi-Fi Hotspots," later in this chapter.

The next screen enables you to set your time zone. Your NOOK defaults to your network information, but if you want to change the time zone, choose Your Time Zone, and select a different one. Tap Next.

The next screen relates to the end-user license agreement (EULA). Agree to the EULA and Diagnostic Data agreement by tapping the I Understand check box—you must do this to continue to use the device. If you want to share diagnostic data, tap Yes. Basically, if software fails to update, your NOOK sends the error logs directly to Samsung. You can choose No Thanks. Tap Next.

You are asked if you have a Google account. If you do not, you can tap No and get an account now. If you have a Google account and want to connect it to your NOOK, tap Yes and enter your Google account credentials. Your NOOK will sign in.

Regardless if you have a Google account, you see the Google and Your Location screen. You can select all, none, or a subset of these options (see Figure 1.2).

FIGURE 1.2   The Google and Your Location screen.

These options allow you to control how accurately your device will locate you in time and space. The more you agree to, the more your device will know your precise location. This is important because if you post to Facebook or other social media sites on your NOOK device, you may be communicating your location to the world, so consider carefully how much information you want to share.

Tap Next after you make your decisions for Google and Your Location.

Then identify who the tablet belongs to by entering your first and last name. Tap Done when complete.

The Samsung Account screen appears next. If you have an existing Samsung account, tap Sign In. If you do not have a Samsung account and want to create one, tap Create One, complete the information on the next screen, and then tap Sign Up. You can skip creating a Samsung account as well.

You then have an option of creating or connecting your existing Dropbox account to this NOOK. Dropbox is a cloud service for file storage. You can also skip this step. If you sign in to your existing Dropbox account, your NOOK will ask you to allow it to connect with Dropbox. Tap Allow.

After you decide what to do about Dropbox, the NOOK portion of the device begins.

If you have an existing B&N account, tap Sign In and enter your account information. Tap Sign In. If you don't have an account, you can create one by tapping Create an Account. Fill out the form and tap Submit.

> NOTE: You can also set up a B&N account on your computer by visiting barnesandnoble.com, clicking Sign In, and then clicking No, Register Now in the pop-up window.

To register your NOOK, you also need to provide a default credit card with a valid billing address to be associated with your B&N account.

Your NOOK then gives you a chance to enter a device name (which makes it easier to identify online if you have several NOOKs or Samsung devices). Adjust the name as you want and tap Done. Then tap Finish.

You are then taken to the Home screen, and your NOOK is now set up for use.

Orienting Yourself to Your NOOK

Now orient yourself to the NOOK and the basic navigational features. You won't get the details about putting items on it and so on in the following sections, but you'll get there eventually. This is simply to orient you to common locations you revisit often in this book.

The Lock Screen

After you set up your NOOK, whenever it goes to sleep or powers off, whenever you wake it up or power it back on, you must unlock it. This occurs on the Lock screen. If the NOOK is asleep, pressing the Home button brings up the Lock screen. If you power the NOOK on, after it completes the start sequence, you go to the Lock screen.

From the Lock screen, you can select the profile in the top right you want to start using (profiles are covered in Chapter 10, "Creating and Using Profiles on Your Samsung Galaxy Tab 4 NOOK"). Click the icon of the profile you want to use. (The current profile has a white circle at the edge of the image.) Depending on how you lock your NOOK (covered in "Lock Screen" in Chapter 2, "Customizing and

Configuring Your Samsung Galaxy Tab 4 NOOK"), unlock the device. The screen that appears is the Home screen.

Home Screen

This is the screen that appears after you unlock the NOOK. The Home screen is a central location, and you interact with it a lot. The screen is divided into several sections (see Figure 1.3):

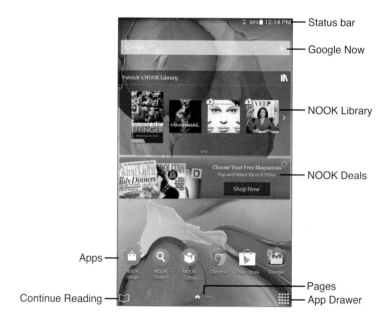

FIGURE 1.3   The Home screen.

▶ **Status bar**: The status bar rests at the top of the screen. On the right side, you see the Wi-Fi connectivity, battery monitor, and current time. Also, you see notifications on the left side of the status bar. If you press and hold the status bar and then drag down, you can open up the Notifications pane, which has a lot more than notifications. Here you can turn on and off Wi-Fi, GPS location services, and Bluetooth, control brightness and volume, turn off screen rotation or Multi Window as well as access all the other settings.

▶ **Google Now**: This is the light gray box at the top of the screen below the status bar. You can begin typing in here to begin a Google search. The first time you tap this, you are asked if you want to use Google Now, which can do some awesome things, like give you weather information, link into apps you use, and present information about it. For example, I am a baseball nut, so I have MLB's At Bat installed and my favorite teams indicated. Google Now lets me know about upcoming games, scores, and so on without ever opening the MLB At Bat app.

▶ **NOOK Library**: This widget shows you the most recent items you've accessed from your NOOK Library. Tap the right and left arrows to scroll through the most recent 12 items. Tap the Books icon in the top right of the widget to access your full NOOK Library (**see** "The Library" section in Chapter 3, "Reading on Your Samsung Galaxy Tab 4 NOOK and Beyond," for more information about using your NOOK Library).

▶ **NOOK Deals**: This widget presents a series of deals available from the NOOK Shop. Tap the Refresh button to update the widget with new deals. **See** Chapter 12, "Shopping and Visiting B&N on Your Samsung Galaxy Tab 4 NOOK," for more information about shopping on your NOOK.

▶ **Pages**: You can set up your Home screen to have multiple pages. (It begins with two by default.) The page you are currently looking at is colored white. On these pages, you can add apps, widgets, and more for quick access.

▶ **Apps**: By default, you have the NOOK Shop, NOOK Search, NOOK Today, Chrome, Play Store, and Google apps. Tap them to open the app you want to use. These are covered later in Part I, "Samsung Galaxy Tab 4 NOOK."

▶ **Continue Reading**: You can tap this icon to continue reading or watching whatever NOOK book, magazine, or newspaper you last read on your NOOK.

▶ **Apps Drawer**: Tapping this gives you access to all your apps as well as available widgets.

If you press and hold an empty area of the Home screen, the Home screen pop-up appears. From here, you have a variety of options for accessing your content, including setting wallpaper and adding items to the pages.

Recent Key

If you press the Recent key, the bottom third of the Home screen presents a scrollable list of the most recently used and accessed apps and so on (see Figure 1.4)—the Recent Drawer. You have several options on this screen. First, you can tap any of the apps and make that the active app. You can tap Close All to close all the apps at once. Or you can tap Task Manager, which opens the Task Manager app, where you can close individual apps.

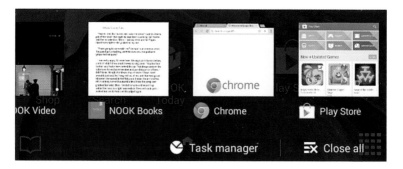

FIGURE 1.4   The Recent Drawer.

If you press the Recent key again, it closes the Recent Drawer and returns you to the screen you were previously on. Use the Recent Drawer to quickly and easily access recent items without having to press the Home button and navigate where you want to go.

TIP: You can also swipe up or down on the app to close just that app as well.

Back Key

If you press the Back key, the NOOK takes you back to what you were doing just prior. For example, if you were reading a book, pressed the Home key, and then opened Gmail to check your mail, if you tap the Back key, you'll go back to the Home screen. The Back key is most useful in the NOOK Shop. As you browse deeper and deeper into categories, the Back key can take you back up through your browsing.

Modifying the Home Screen

You can add more pages to your Home screen as well as add or remove apps and widgets that appear on each page.

To add a page to the Home screen, pinch and zoom on a page of the Home screen. All your pages shrink to a smaller version, and you see a "ghost" page with a plus sign on it. Tap the plus sign to add a page.

To delete a page, pinch and zoom on a page of the Home screen, press and hold a page and then drag it to the Remove or trash can at the top of the page.

To move pages around, pinch and zoom on a page of the Home screen, press and hold a page and then drag it between, before, or after any of the existing pages and lift your finger.

To designate a new page as the primary page on the Home screen, pinch and zoom on a page of the Home screen. When the pages are visible in their thumbnail form, tap the house icon on the page you want to be the new primary page.

To move icons or widgets around, press and hold the app's icon or widget. The page shrinks a bit, and you can then drag the icon or widget around on that page. You can move it to another page by dragging the icon or widget down to the bottom of the screen, where thumbnail versions of existing pages are. The page you drag the icon onto will become visible, and you can drop the icon there. If you drag the icon to the small page with a plus sign, a new page is created.

If you drag the icon to the App Info item at the top of the page, a detailed screen of the app appears. If you drag the icon to the Remove or trash can icon at the top of the page, the app or widget is removed from the Home screen. However, it is not removed from the device.

If you have apps you want to group together, you can create a folder. Drag an icon to the Create Folder icon at the top of the page. When you drop it, you are asked to give the folder a name and it appears on page. From there on, you can drag to that folder and drop the icon there. To access it from the folder, tap the folder and then tap the app.

If you want to move an app from the App Drawer to a page, the process is identical, except you tap the App Drawer and then press and hold the icon until you can drag it to where you want. However, you can also drag the app there to the Uninstall icon at the top of the screen, and the app is removed from the device. If you don't like your options, drag the icon to the Cancel button.

From the App Drawer, you also have access to widgets. Tap the App Drawer and then tap Widgets at the top of the screen. You can then browse the widgets. To add them to a page, follow the same actions as an app icon.

Using Wi-Fi Hotspots

Your NOOK can connect to Wi-Fi networks other than the one you initially set up. B&N offers free Wi-Fi access in all B&N stores. If you take your NOOK to a B&N store, it can automatically connect to the Wi-Fi hotspot in that store.

For more information on using your NOOK in a B&N store, **see** Chapter 12.

To connect your NOOK to a Wi-Fi hotspot other than one in a B&N store, follow these steps:

1. From the Notifications pane, tap the Settings icon (**see** Figure 1.5).

2. In the Connections tab, tap Wi-Fi. If Wi-Fi is off, tap the "switch" to turn it on. (The slider turns green and moves to the right.)

3. Tap the Wi-Fi hotspot you want to use. Your NOOK displays the SSID for all Wi-Fi hotspots in range.

4. If required, enter the password for your Wi-Fi hotspot.

5. Tap Connect.

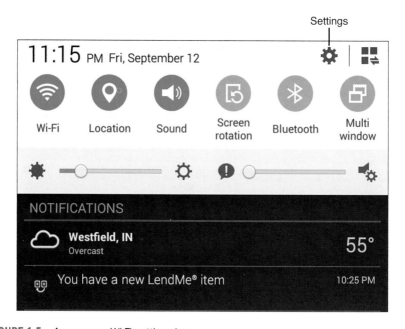

FIGURE 1.5   Access your Wi-Fi settings here.

Your NOOK should now indicate that it is connected; you should see the Wi-Fi signal indicator on the status bar on the top right next to the battery indicator.

If your Wi-Fi hotspot isn't listed after you turn on Wi-Fi or is not in the list of Wireless Networks, follow these steps:

1. From the status bar, tap the Settings icon.

2. In the Connections tab, tap Wi-Fi and then tap Add Wi-Fi Network. If Wi-Fi is off, tap the "switch" to turn it on. (The slider turns green and moves to the right.)

3. Enter the network service set identified (SSID), select the type of security (if the Wi-Fi is secured), and enter the password for your Wi-Fi hotspot if necessary. If you don't know this information, ask the person who set up the Wi-Fi network.

Your NOOK can connect to a Wi-Fi hotspot that requires you to browse to a web page to authenticate yourself. For example, many hotel Wi-Fi hotspots require you to enter a room number or other information to connect. You can connect to a Wi-Fi hotspot that has this requirement by tapping the Web Launch Button from the Home screen after you join the Wi-Fi network.

Disconnecting and Forgetting a Wi-Fi Hotspot

If you want to stop using a Wi-Fi hotspot, you have two options: disconnect or forget. Disconnect just prevents your NOOK from connecting to that Wi-Fi hotspot. Forgetting the hotspot removes the information about the hotspot from your NOOK. If you later want to reconnect to that hotspot, you must set it up again. To disconnect or forget a Wi-Fi hotspot, follow these steps:

1. From the status bar, tap the Settings icon.

2. In the Connections tab, tap Wi-Fi.

3. If Wi-Fi is turned off, turn it on.

4. Tap the Wi-Fi hotspot. This displays a pop-up window.

5. Tap Forget to disconnect from the Wi-Fi hotspot.

For more information on configuring the settings on your NOOK (including turning off the Wi-Fi card), **see** "Your NOOK's Settings" in Chapter 2.

Charging and Caring for Your NOOK's Battery

Your NOOK uses a high-tech battery called a lithium polymer battery. You can charge your NOOK's battery by plugging your NOOK into a wall outlet using the supplied AC adapter.

TIP: Just like any electronic device, your NOOK is susceptible to power spikes and other electrical anomalies. If you want to ensure that your NOOK is protected from electrical problems, plug it into a surge suppressor when charging the battery.

Some basic rules can help you maximize the life of your battery:

▶ Try to avoid fully discharging your battery. Recharge it when it gets down to approximately 20% or so. Although charging it repeatedly is not necessarily a bad thing, the battery seems to function optimally if you charge it only when it drops down toward that 20% area.

▶ To maximize battery life, turn off Wi-Fi, and leave it off whenever you don't need it. Same goes with Bluetooth.

▶ Avoid high heat. Reading in sunlight is fine, but avoid storing your NOOK near a heat source.

▶ If storing your NOOK for a long period (a week or more), charge the battery to approximately 50% rather than giving it a full charge. The battery, even off, slowly loses its charge—very slowly, but loses nonetheless. By charging it to 50% only and then powering it off for a long time, it mimics how it was initially packaged and shipped. The 50% will go away slowly, and when you power it on again, it may have a low charge, but it is more like what the "factory" setting would have been.

> NOTE: Your NOOK charges only when plugged into an outlet. It will not charge when plugged via the USB cable into a computer.

By following these instructions, your NOOK's battery should last years. If you do need to replace the battery, contact B&N Customer Service.

When You Are Not Reading

When you finish reading, you should let your NOOK go to sleep instead of turning it off. You can force the NOOK to sleep by pressing and quickly letting go of the Power button.

By leaving your NOOK on with Wi-Fi on, it will occasionally download content from B&N such as subscription content and any books that you purchase from the B&N website. When you're ready to start reading again, simply press and release the power switch at the top of your NOOK to wake it up. Alternatively, you can press the Home button.

Your NOOK's Controls

Before you enjoy content on your NOOK, let's go over the controls on your NOOK (see Figure 1.6). In general, you can interact with your NOOK using the touch controls of tapping, pressing and holding, and swiping. The few physical buttons are minimal but provide some tactile controls. The most frequent button you are likely to use is the Home button.

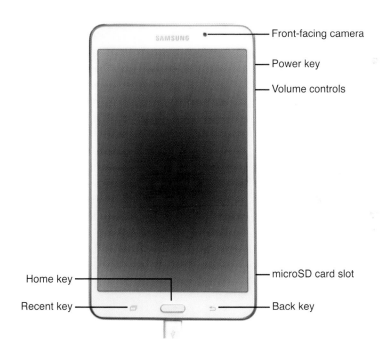

FIGURE 1.6 Your NOOK's controls.

The Power Button

The Power button is the sole button on the top-right side of the NOOK. In addition to powering your NOOK on and off, the Power button can wake your NOOK when it's sleeping or put it to sleep when you finish reading.

To put your NOOK to sleep or wake it using the Power button, press and release the Power button quickly. To turn off your NOOK, press and hold the Power button for 5 seconds. To turn on your NOOK again, press and release the Power button quickly.

The Home Button

The Home button is identified by the NOOK logo (a lowercase n) and is located in the center of the black bar along at the bottom of the touchscreen display. Like the Power button, the Home button performs more than one function.

You can wake your NOOK by pressing the Home button. If the touchscreen is already illuminated, pressing the Home button takes you to your NOOK's Home screen.

The Volume Buttons

These two buttons on the top of the NOOK control the volume. If no videos, music, or other sounds are playing, the Volume buttons control the Notification volume (that is, when something new arrives such as subscription content). When video, music, or other sounds are playing, the Volume buttons control the sound of the media.

How Should I Clean My NOOK's Touchscreen?

Your NOOK's touchscreen is going to get dirty and covered in fingerprints. The best way to clean it is using a dry, microfiber cloth like the one you would use to clean eyeglasses. If you must use a cleaning fluid, spray it lightly on the cloth and then wipe the touchscreen. Use only cleaning sprays designed for cleaning LCD screens.

CHAPTER 2

Customizing and Configuring Your Samsung Galaxy Tab 4 NOOK

Your NOOK has many features that enable you to easily customize it and make it your own. There are also many settings that control how your NOOK operates. In this chapter, you examine how to customize and configure your NOOK.

Using Custom Wallpaper

You can customize your NOOK by using custom wallpaper images. Wallpaper appears on the Home pages when you are on the Home screen. (One image appears on all pages.) Basically, it's the background that you always see when you press the Home button, so something nice is desirable. You also encounter the term *live wallpapers*, which are images that change over time—for example, a set of waves that a whale comes riding through.

If you do a Google search for **NOOK wallpaper**, you receive many results for where you can obtain wallpapers. You can also load them to your NOOK with the necessary images.

Choosing a Wallpaper

The easiest place to change your NOOK's wallpaper is to go to the Home screen and do so. Here's how:

1. Make sure your NOOK is at the Home screen by pressing the Home button.

2. In an area of the Home page where a cover does not appear, press and hold until the Add to Home screen pop-up appears (see Figure 2.1).

3. Tap Set Wallpaper.

4. Tap Home screen, Lock screen, or Home and Lock screens depending on what you want to set the wallpaper for.

5. Tap either Gallery, Wallpapers, or Live Wallpapers. Wallpapers consists of images provided by Samsung or images you have loaded into the Gallery. Gallery displays any photographs in JPG, PNG, or GIF formats you have placed on your NOOK. Live Wallpapers are those that Samsung has provided and others you have installed from the Google Play Store.

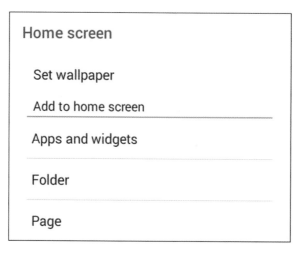

FIGURE 2.1   The Add to Home Screen appears when you press and hold on a blank area of the Home page.

NOTE: Live Wallpapers are images that change over time (some quickly, some slowly). You can purchase (or many are free) Live Wallpapers from the Google Play Store—just type **Live Wallpapers** in the search box (**see** Chapter 13, "Using the Google Play Store and Google Apps"). Live wallpapers are sold as apps and automatically appear in the Live Wallpapers options.

6. If you chose Wallpapers, choose the wallpaper you want. The screen shows you the image. Set Wallpaper. If you chose Gallery, choose the photo you want. It opens with some outlined boxes and two buttons: Cancel and Done.

The outside box controls the sizing of the two interior boxes. Those two boxes represent the landscape and portrait layouts—basically making a nice image regardless of how you hold your NOOK (see Figure 2.2). Whatever is *inside* the interior boxes will be used for the wallpaper. To adjust the cropping size, press and hold one of the squares, and then drag it around to wherever you want it. Tap Done to make it the wallpaper and return to the Home screen, or tap Cancel to exit to the Home screen.

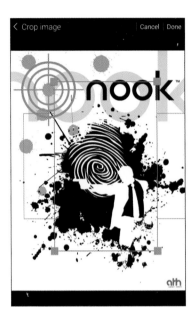

FIGURE 2.2   Pick the area of the image you want to use for your Home screen.

If you chose Live Wallpapers, choose the Live Wallpaper you want. The screen shows you the animation. Tap Set Wallpaper. You may also have a Settings option. If you tap this, you are provided settings specific to that Live Wallpaper. Adjust as you see fit. To set the wallpaper with those configuration options, tap Set Wallpaper.

Should You Use a Specific File Format for Images?

Your NOOK supports JPEG, GIF, and PNG files. For images, using either JPEG or PNG is your best option. GIF isn't a good option for photographs, but if your image is line art or text, GIF can work fine. If you're unsure, stick with JPEG.

Your NOOK's Settings

Your NOOK offers configurable settings for controlling many of its features, which are broken into three large categories: quick settings, NOOK-specific settings, and NOOK-general tablet settings. Let's look at the quick settings first (see Figure 2.3).

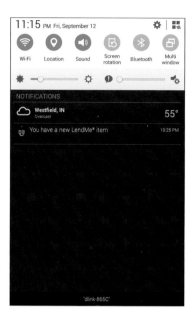

FIGURE 2.3   Quick settings provide ready access to popular settings.

If you tap the Setting icon in the Notifications pane, you can gain access to the settings (see Figure 2.4). You can also access the settings by tapping the Apps button on the Home screen and tapping Settings in the Apps page that appears.

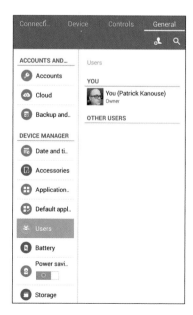

FIGURE 2.4   Beyond the Quick settings.

The general settings are broken into four large categories or tabs: Connection, Device, Controls, and General. For simplicity's sake, the following sections deal with all settings.

Quick Settings

When you open the Notifications pane, you see a number of settings options (refer to Figure 2.3):

- ▶ **Wi-Fi**: Tap this to turn off or on Wi-Fi.

- ▶ **Location**: Tap this to turn on or off location tracking.

- ▶ **Sound**: Tap this to mute or unmute your NOOK.

- ▶ **Screen Rotation**: Tap this to turn on or off screen rotation. You might want to ensure that a book you are reading stays in portrait mode, and this is the setting you can use to ensure that the screen does not rotate with the device. If the screen is in landscape mode, when you turn off screen rotation, it will stay in landscape mode—same for portrait mode.

- ▶ **Bluetooth**: Tap this to turn on or off Bluetooth.

- ▶ **Multi Window**: Tap this to turn off the NOOK's Multi Window™ feature, which allows you to see two or more apps on the same screen (so long as the apps support that feature). To use Multi Window if it's available, swipe from the right corner toward the left, which slides a list of apps (see Figure 2.5). Tap the second app you want to open and it opens at the bottom of the screen (see Figure 2.6).

- ▶ **Brightness**: Tap and drag to set the brightness of the screen.

- ▶ **Volume**: Tap and drag to adjust the volume—this is the same as pressing the volume control buttons.

FIGURE 2.5   Picking a second window to open.

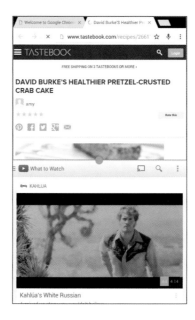

FIGURE 2.6   Using the Multi Window feature on your NOOK.

At the top of the Notification pane, you also have the All Settings button (gear icon) and More Quick Settings button (three squares and back and forth arrows icon). Tap All Settings to get to the general settings. Tap the More Quick Settings button to see a few more quick settings:

▶ **Sync**: If you leave this on, any apps you have update automatically when a new update become available. This means that your NOOK is occasionally querying a remote server for updates. If you turn it off, you'll save some power.

▶ **Smart Stay**: If the conditions are appropriate (that is, not too dark), your NOOK will stay powered on so long as you are looking at it if Smart Stay is turned on. The NOOK uses the front-facing camera to determine if you are looking at the device. If you are, your NOOK will ignore the power off settings and stay on.

▶ **Power Saving**: Tap this to turn on this feature, which will adjust screen brightness according to the ambient conditions.

▶ **Blocking Mode**: Are notifications interrupting your reading? Stop them by turning on Blocking mode.

▶ **Airplane Mode**: Tap this to turn on or off Airplane mode. If off, your NOOK will turn off its Wi-Fi capabilities, allowing you to read during flights.

In the top right of More Quick Settings, you have two options. You can tap the Pencil icon to adjust notification settings and tap the list icon to return to the original quick settings.

Connection Settings

You saw the Airplane mode option earlier, and the Wi-Fi options are covered in Chapter 1, "Getting Started with Your Samsung Galaxy Tab 4 NOOK." However, you also have Bluetooth connectivity options available. Bluetooth is Off by default. You can turn it on here. Tap Bluetooth to see additional options (see Figure 2.7). Here, you can scan for available devices by tapping Scan, but make sure you've tapped the check box next to your NOOK's name, which makes the NOOK visible to any Bluetooth devices around. Your NOOK looks for Bluetooth-capable devices. If it finds some, it lists them in Available Devices. Tap the device name to begin the pairing process (and each device may have its own method for completing the pairing, so reference your device's specific instructions).

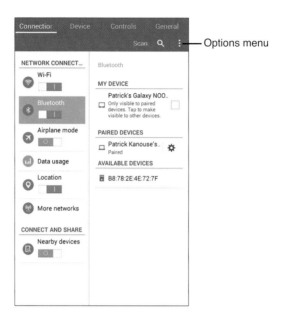

FIGURE 2.7   Bluetooth settings.

If a device has been paired, it will have a gear icon to its right. If you tap the gear icon, you can rename the paired connection or unpair the device.

In the upper right, you'll see three squares. Tap this for a few more options:

▶ **Visibility Timeout**: You can choose between 2 minutes, 5 minutes, 1 hour, and never. Essentially, you are setting the length of time that the NOOK remains visible to Bluetooth devices. If you stop using the Bluetooth device (with earbuds, for example) and power it off, your NOOK continues to look for Bluetooth connections to make for as long as the Visibility Timeout is set. Setting this timeout to the lowest possible value will conserve your power.

▶ **Received Files**: Tap this to see any files you transferred using Bluetooth (**see** the section "Adding Files to Your NOOK" in Chapter 7, "Playing Music, Audiobooks, and Podcasts," for more information about transferring files to your NOOK).

▶ **Rename Device**: If you want to rename your device, you can tap this to do so.

▶ **Help**: Tap this to get some help with Bluetooth.

NOTE: To connect a Bluetooth device, make sure you have your NOOK's Bluetooth setting turned to On. Follow the instructions that came with your Bluetooth device about pairing it with another device. When you have paired the Bluetooth device to your NOOK, you will see it in the list of Available Devices, and you can tap it to make the connection.

Tap Data Usage to get some statistics on how much data your NOOK and specific apps are using. This is particularly helpful if you are using a Wi-Fi hotspot for which you have data limits.

Location settings give you a bit more control over how the Location functions work. When you tap Location, you see a number of options (see Figure 2.8).

FIGURE 2.8 Location settings.

Tap Mode to adjust how accurate your NOOK is in locating you. Tap My Places to save your locations, which various apps can use. Tap the plus button to add a new location.

The More Networks option allows you to set up a printer or VPN if those are available. If you have a wireless printer, you can add it here so that you can print directly from your tablet. Tap the plus button, which launches the Google Play Store with print service apps. Find yours and install.

Device Settings

Here is where you can make all sorts of customizations to the sound, display, and usability of the device.

Sound

Control sound volume, notifications, and so on here (see Figure 2.9).

- ▶ **Volume**: Tap this to adjust the volume. The great thing about the setting here is that you can be very fine-tuned with it, for you can set the volume on media differently from that of notifications and the overall system.

- ▶ **Notifications**: By default, notifications come through with the Whistle sound. You can adjust that here by tapping Notifications and then tapping the sound. (A preview plays when you tap it.)

- ▶ **Feedback**: Feedback sounds are the sounds your NOOK makes when you tap the screen or when you lock and unlock the device. You can turn them on or off here.

- ▶ **Samsung Applications**: You can adjust the sounds for specific Samsung applications.

- ▶ **Samsung Keyboard**: This is a bit like the Feedback sounds, but it is specifically about the keyboard. As you type, you can hear sounds for when you tap each key. Turn on or off the feature from here.

- ▶ **More Settings**: Adapt Sound lets you set a sound that is best suited for you while you play music or watch a video.

Display

How bright do you want the display? Do you want to ensure it stays on longer? Use these options (see Figure 2.10).

- ▶ **Brightness**: Tap this to adjust the brightness level.

- ▶ **Screen Timeout**: Tap this to adjust how long the screen stays on before powering off. You can set if for 15 or 30 seconds or 1, 2, 5, 10, or 30 minutes. Remember to set it long enough for you to read a page. Also, if you have Smart Stay on and the conditions are right, this setting will be ignored.

- ▶ **Daydream**: This is a screensaver for when your NOOK is plugged in. Tap it to turn it on and tap again to select the screensaver. When you are selecting the screensaver, tap Preview to get a good idea of what it will look like. Tap the three-squares button to set when Daydream will turn on.

- ▶ **Show Battery Percentage**: If you don't want to see the battery percentage, tap this to turn it off.

FIGURE 2.9   Sound settings.

FIGURE 2.10   Display settings.

Multi Window

You can turn on or off Multi Window here, and you can set Multi Window to start automatically if you open an email attachment from within an email or open files using My Files.

Lock Screen

Control how the Lock screen functions here, including adding security (see Figure 2.11).

FIGURE 2.11   Lock screen settings.

▶ **Screen Lock**: Tap this to set the level of security required to unlock your NOOK. By default, the NOOK is set at Swipe (that is, no security). Depending on the type of security you select, the Lock screen settings adjust.

If you tap Pattern, trace a pattern from dot to dot (see Figure 2.12). If you use this, you will be presented the same dot pattern on the unlock screen for you to trace. You are asked to confirm the pattern and then enter a backup PIN should you forget the pattern and then confirm the PIN.

Tap PIN to a series of numbers up to 16 digits. The more digits, the more secure. You are asked to confirm the PIN.

Tap Password to enter a password. You are asked to confirm the password.

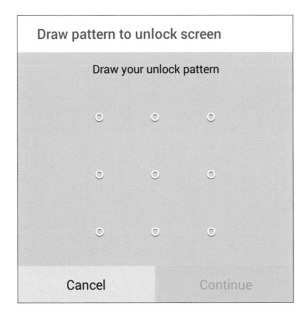

FIGURE 2.12 Define a Lock screen pattern.

Tap None to remove even the swipe screen. This also removes all other Lock screen settings.

▶ **Clock Widget Options**: No matter the screen security setting, tap this to adjust the appearance of the clock. Its size can be Small, Normal, or Large. You can also turn off showing the date.

▶ **Make Pattern Visible**: When screen security setting is at Pattern, when you swipe the pattern on the Lock screen, the pattern itself is not made visible.

▶ **Lock Automatically**: When screen security setting is at Pattern, PIN, or Password, you can adjust how quickly the lock takes effect. By default, it is set at 15 seconds when the screen turns off. Tap this setting to adjust from Immediately to 30 minutes.

▶ **Lock Instantly with Power Off**: When screen security setting is at Pattern, PIN, or Password, when your NOOK powers off, it instantly locks. When this setting is off, the timing of the lock is based on the Lock Automatically setting.

▶ **Shortcuts**: When screen security setting is at Swipe, you can set up shortcuts on your Lock screen for ready access. Tap Shortcuts on and then tap again. You see a series of icons. Tap an icon to change it or tap the plus to add an additional one. When you use the swipe gesture to unlock the screen,

you can tap the icon and swipe it. When the NOOK unlocks, it opens immediately to the app you selected.

▶ **Personal Message**: When the screen security setting is at Swipe, on the
Lock screen you can include a personal message. Perhaps you want to ask
someone if they find it to return it. Tap Personal Message to turn it on, and
then tap it again to see an option for Edit Personal Message. Tap that and
you see a preview of the Lock screen. You have a number of options to control. First, type your message. Then adjust the font and the background.
Tap Save.

▶ **Owner Information**: No matter the screen security setting, if your NOOK
goes missing, you can leave some contact information that's visible on the
Lock screen without someone having to unlock it. You can include an email
address or phone number or any other pertinent information. Tap Owner
Information to get a pop-up screen where you can enter what you want. Tap
OK when complete.

▶ **Unlock Effect**: When you have Swipe as your screen security, when you
unlock your NOOK, it can give a flourish of style by making a ripple effect
or popping colors. Tap Unlock Effect and choose between None, Blind,
Popping Colors, Watercolor, and Ripple.

▶ **Help**: When you have Swipe as your screen security, if you have Help text
enabled, it displays on the Lock screen the text "Swipe to unlock."

Wallpaper

From here, you can adjust your wallpaper. **See** "Choosing a Wallpaper" earlier in this
chapter for how to use this feature.

Font

Here, you can adjust the fonts the tablet uses (but not for when reading NOOK
Books, magazines, or newspapers).

▶ **Font Style**: Tap to choose from some predefined fonts. If you tap
Download, you are taken to the Samsung store, from which you can buy
additional fonts.

▶ **Font Size**: Tap this to adjust the size of the font.

Notification Panel

Here, you can adjust items related to the Notifications pane:

▶ **Brightness and Volume**: If in the Notifications pane you don't want to use
the space for controlling brightness or volume, you can turn that off here.

▶ **Recommended Apps**: Your NOOK can show different notifications based on the context. A simple example is, when you plug in earphones, some apps will now send notifications where they would not have before. You can simply turn these off or you can add or subtract from them. Tap the switch to turn it off. To adjust which apps can do this, tap the text beside the switch. You'll see a screen that appears. By default, these are the apps that will send notifications when your earphones are plugged in. Tap the pencil icon to adjust this. You can designate a maximum of five apps. Select or deselect the check marks as appropriate for any app installed on your NOOK.

▶ **Set Quick Setting Buttons**: When you open the Notifications pane, you have the Quick Settings and More Quick Settings options at the top. You can change the order of the icons. Tap Reset to restore the buttons to the original factory defaults.

Accessibility Panel

Your NOOK offers a variety of options to make the device more usable for special needs. The options are numerous, including general accessibility settings along with those for vision, hearing, dexterity, and recognition.

Blocking Mode

Blocking mode allows you to control when notifications end up in the Notification pane. When Blocking mode is on, you can turn off *just* notifications, *just* the alarm, or both. You can also set the time. Tap Always so that the check mark disappears and then adjust the time you want to ensure you are not disturbed.

Controls Settings

Controls settings allow you to adjust the language options, the palm motion gesture, and smart screen behavior.

Voice and Input

▶ **Samsung Keyboard**: Tap the gear icon to access a set of options for using the keyboard (see Figure 2.13). Here you can adjust smart typing actions like turning off predictive text. (While typing **typ**, predictive text displays *type*, *typing*, and such. If you tap the space key, the word highlighted in blue is spelled out without any other typing.) You can also adjust auto replacement, capitalization, spacing, and punctuation.

In the Keyboard Swipe section, you can adjust how text is entered via the keyboard. By default, it is set to None, which means that you tap a key to enter that letter or number. If you tap Continuous Input, you then enter text by tapping the keyboard and, without lifting your finger, you slide your finger over the keyboard to the next letter or number you want to enter—no up and down motions.

I know when I type, I often make mistakes. By default, you can press on the text where the error is and the text cursor will appear there, allowing you to correct the mistake. However, you can, by tapping on Cursor Control, use the mouse keyboard to control the location of the text cursor.

If you like sounds when you tap keys on the keyboard, you can turn that on or off here. In addition, you can tap a key on the keyboard and a bubble or magnification of that key displays if you tap Character Preview.

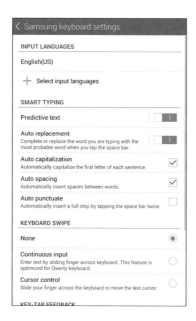

FIGURE 2.13 The Samsung Keyboard settings.

▶ **Google Voice Typing**: By default, Google Voice Typing is off, which means you cannot start talking and have your NOOK type for you. You can turn it on and then make adjustments to that by tapping the gear icon next to Google Voice Typing.

▶ **Voice Search**: This feature allows you to say what you want to search on and browsers like Chrome will conduct a web search. Tap this option to adjust its settings.

▶ **Text-to-Speech Options**: Your NOOK can use text-to-speech options for onscreen information—for example, reading out loud messages. Tap this to adjust its options.

▶ **Pointer Speed**: If you have a Bluetooth connected mouse or trackpad, tap this to adjust the pointer speed.

Palm Motion and Smart Screen

▶ **Capture Screen**: If you take the edge of your hand and swipe from the right edge to left edge of the screen, you can take screen shots. You can turn this feature on or off here.

▶ **Mute/Pause**: If a video is playing, you can cover the screen with your palm to mute the sound or pause the music. You can turn this feature on or off here.

▶ **Smart Screen**: You can turn on or off Smart Stay here.

General Settings

A large number of options exist here. So let's take them in order.

Accounts

You can add accounts here. Tap Add Account to do so. This displays a list of options from which you can choose. Tap what you want and then enter the required credentials.

Note that these accounts are *not* linked to your BN.com account, which means if you add accounts here, they will not let you share reading progress and on your NOOK. See "NOOK Settings" later in this chapter for information about that.

Cloud

You've heard of the cloud (that is, your files are stored on a remote server someplace that you can always access), right? Your NOOK can be automatically backed up if you have a Samsung account. Under Personal Data, you can see what account is linked to this device for backup, how much storage space is being used on the cloud, and what is synced to the cloud. If you tap Backup, you can enable auto backup so that if you have to restore your device, all your data can be restored quickly and easily. Tap Restore to restore your NOOK back to the latest back up made.

Finally, here you can see some information related to your Dropbox account, if you have one.

Backup and Reset

Here are some additional Backup options. The Automatic Restore is if you ever delete an app (to make space, for example); if you reinstall it, the information and data will also be restored.

Tap Factory Data Reset to restore your NOOK back to its factory settings, removing all personal information and files.

Date and Time

You can adjust the date and time settings here. Tap Set Date or Set Time to manually set the time. Tap Select Time Zone to change the time zone. Tap the Use 24-Hour Format check box if you want to adjust to using 13:00 for 1:00 p.m., and so on. Tap Select Date Format to switch the appearance of the day, month, and year.

Accessories

You have two options here: Dock Sound and Audio Output Mode. By default, anytime you plug in or remove the plug from the NOOK, the device makes a sound. You can turn that off here. Also, if you have external speakers attached to a dock (you can get one from BN.com in NOOK accessories), if Audio Output Mode is set to on, those speakers will provide sound instead of the NOOK's internal speakers.

Applications

The Applications settings give you a number of options for storing, removing, and otherwise dealing with the applications installed on your NOOK. When you tap Applications, you see a list of applications you have downloaded to your NOOK (see Figure 2.14). You can scroll at the top through apps on the microSD card, running apps, and all apps. Just tap the setting you want to see. Note that running and all apps is generally less useful because you will see a bunch of apps the NOOK has running in the background that you don't normally interact with. At the bottom of the screen, you are also provided a handy diagram of how much of the NOOK's memory is used and free.

Swipe here to
see more options.

FIGURE 2.14   Downloaded applications.

If you tap an application, you see the App Info screen for that application (see
Figure 2.15).

FIGURE 2.15   Detailed information about the app.

From here, you can uninstall the application by tapping Uninstall. If the application is running but causing you difficulties (like any other program on a computer, sometimes they encounter issues), you can force stop the application from running by tapping Force Stop. In addition, you can control if this app provides notifications in the Notification pane by tapping Show Notifications.

The Storage section gives you some data about how much space is used by the app, which can help if you begin to run short of memory and need to remove larger apps to make space.

If you have a microSD card installed (**see** the section later in this chapter, "Adding and Using a microSD Card," for more information about installing one), you can move the application to the microSD card by tapping Move to SD Card. This can help save space on your NOOK proper. If you do move an app to the microSD card, it may run a tad bit slower than if it were directly in the NOOK's internal memory.

> NOTE: Not all apps can be moved to the microSD card.

If the app stores password or other information, you can tap Clear Data, which removes all data associated with that app and returns it to its originally downloaded version. Tap Clear Cache to remove any recent data. This is particularly relevant to apps that store data temporarily, like a history of website visits, and so on.

You may have noticed that when you tap some items, for example, hyperlinks, you are given a choice, as shown in Figure 2.16.

FIGURE 2.16   Choose which app to use.

What this means is that you have not selected a default app to deal with hyperlinks or whatnot. (And that's OK; you are not obliged to.) However, if you tap an app and then tap Always, you are setting that app to be the default app for that type of activity or file. If an app has such defaults, the Clear Defaults button is active, and you can tap it to remove the default action; thus, you would again see the option available in Figure 2.17.

If you scroll a bit further down, you can also see what permissions the application has for such things as accessing the Photo Gallery, recording audio, and more.

Default Applications

These settings (see Figure 2.17) provide a listing of which apps have default settings. You can tap Clear next to the app to remove any defaults.

FIGURE 2.17 The default applications for certain actions.

Users

From here, you can begin to control Profiles for this NOOK. **See** Chapter 10, "Creating and Using Profiles on Your Samsung Galaxy Tab 4 NOOK," for more information about using Profiles.

Battery

Tapping Battery gives you some insight into how your NOOK's battery is performing. You can turn off the percentage of battery left in the status bar by tapping the check box at the top. You can see in the Battery settings the percentage of power left and if the battery is charging right now. An estimate is provided for battery life based on what apps are running, which appears below and their "stake" in how much they are using the battery. You can tap each app for more information about how much of the CPU time it is taking, force stopping the app, and so on.

Power Saving Mode

If you find you are running through your battery power fast, you might try the Power Saving Mode. Tap the switch to turn on this feature. After you do so, you have two options:

▶ **CPU Performance**: Your NOOK can ensure that the CPU is not running at *full* capacity, which will save the battery. However, you may see a slight dip in performance.

▶ **Screen Output**: By having this option on, your NOOK will adjust the brightness of the screen based on the surrounding conditions and also lower the rate at which the screen refreshes. You might see a bit of dip in perfor-mance if you play high-resolution games with the lower screen refresh rate.

Storage

Tapping Storage provides information about your memory space on the NOOK. The screen shows you what is minimally necessary to run the device efficiently, how much is used, and so on. If you tap Cached Data, you can clear the cache for *all* apps.

In the section titled SD Card, you can see how much space is available on the microSD card, presuming one is installed. In addition, you can tap Unmount SD Card so that you can remove it without damaging the data on the microSD card.

CAUTION: Do not remove a microSD card without unmounting it first. You could damage the data on the card.

If you have a microSD card in the device and want to clear out its data and format it, tap Format SD Card.

See the section later in this chapter, "Adding and Using a microSD Card," for more information about installing a microSD card.

Security

You have a variety of options for Security settings on this screen (see Figure 2.18).

FIGURE 2.18   Security settings.

▶ **Encryption**: For maximum security, your device can be encrypted. This means that even if a thief makes off with your NOOK and breaks the PIN or password that locks the device, he will still have to decrypt the device to access passwords and so on used by apps. To begin the process, tap Encrypt Device.

You can also encrypt the microSD card if one is installed. If you have apps running from the microSD card, you can protect their passwords by encrypting the microSD card. Tap Encrypt External SD Card to begin the process.

▶ **Find My Mobile**: The Remote Controls option allows you to lock and erase your NOOK's data remotely. For this to work, you need a Samsung account and have to use a Google location service. If you want to use this feature, tap Remote Controls, enter your Samsung account information, and tap OK.

Lost your NOOK and you want to know where it is? If you have a Samsung account, you can use its Find My Mobile feature. If your device is lost, go to http://findmymobile.samsung.com, sign in with your Samsung account information, and click Locate My Device (see Figure 2.19). Samsung will provide a location based on the GPS locator in your NOOK. At that site, you can see options as well to lock and wipe your NOOK of data.

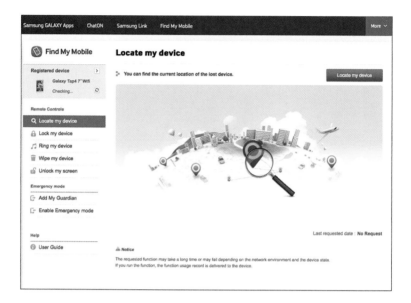

FIGURE 2.19   Find your NOOK with your Samsung account.

▶ **Passwords**: As you enter passwords, the last letter is shown briefly before changing to an asterisk. This helpful for ensuring you are typing your passwords accurately; though it is not completely secure from someone looking over your shoulder. Turn on or off this feature here.

▶ **Device Administration**: These settings are a bit more technical but potentially important. Device Administrators are applications and settings that control your device. Many companies install such managers to ensure corporate security policies are followed. You can see here, by tapping Device Administrators, what administrator settings are on your NOOK.

Although the Google Play Store offers more than a million apps, other sites and sources offer apps as well. If you use those sites or services, tap Unknown Sources so that those apps work on your NOOK.

Your NOOK can warn you if you are installing apps that may cause harm. Turn that off here.

▶ **Security Update Service**: If your company has specific security policies, you can ensure they are working here and update accordingly.

▸ **Credential Storage**: Certification Authorities (CA) are companies that offer digital certificates (CA certificates) that help ensure security on apps and websites. Trusted Credentials are CA certificates that have been accepted as valid and trustworthy by your NOOK. If you have a CA certificate, you can install it, making it a trusted one as well. Tap Install from Device Storage, browse to the location, and tap Install.

About Device

These settings allow you to update the NOOK software, see what version of software it is running, and so on (see Figure 2.20).

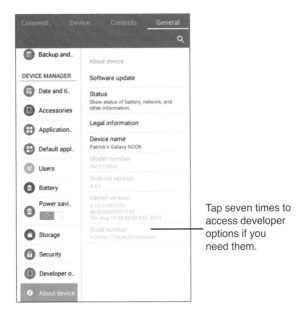

FIGURE 2.20   The About Device settings on your NOOK.

Tap Software Update to get two options: Update Now and Auto Update. Tap Update Now to have your NOOK determine if a software update is available. (The most recent check is shown.) By default, your NOOK checks for updates automatically. You can turn this off by tapping the check box next to Auto Update.

Tap Status to get information regarding the battery charging, IP address, serial number, and so on.

NOTE: Forgot your passcode? The good news is that you can get your NOOK back. The bad news is that you have to reset your NOOK to factory settings, which means you lose all content you placed on your device.

To reset your NOOK to factory settings, do the following:

1. With the NOOK powered off, press and hold the Home key, Power button, and the Volume Up button.

2. When the Samsung Galaxy Tab 4 log appears, release the keys. The Android mascot appears in what looks like a terminal screen. The top reads "Android system recovery."

3. Press the Volume Down button until Wipe Data/Factory Reset is highlighted. Press the Power button.

4. Press the Volume Down button until Yes – Delete All User Data is highlighted. Press the Power button.

5. Your NOOK erases the data. A new menu appears with Reboot System Now highlighted.

6. Press the Power button. Your NOOK reboots, reset to its factory settings.

NOOK Settings

The NOOK Settings are specific to the NOOK reading, library, and store apps. To access these, tap the Apps Drawer and then tap NOOK Settings. The NOOK Settings appear (see Figure 2.21).

Tap My Account to see the Owner, Account and Profile name.

Tap NOOK Library Widget to see options for what the NOOK Library displays (see Figure 2.22). The modifications you make here affect the widget on the Home page only. The NOOK Library itself is unaffected.

First, you can control what you want to see in the NOOK Library widget displays. Don't want to see catalogs, tap the check box next to Catalogs to turn off visibility. For Magazines, TV Shows, Newspapers, and Catalogs, you can adjust how many you see as well. Tap the Quantity icon to the right, and tap the number of most recent items for each you want to see. By default, you will see only one most recent item.

You can also hide specific content. Tap Hide Selected Content and either select the whole category or tap the upward pointing arrow on the far right and select individual items. Tap Save.

NOTE: At the time of writing, the Hide Selected Content feature is not working.

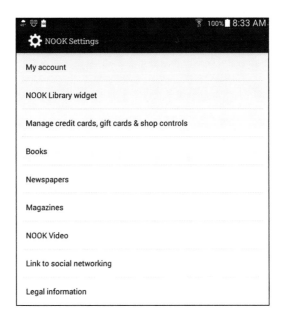

FIGURE 2.21 The NOOK Settings screen.

FIGURE 2.22 The NOOK Library Widget settings screen.

Tap Manage Credit Cards, Gift Cards, and Shop Controls to see the options shown in Figure 2.23.

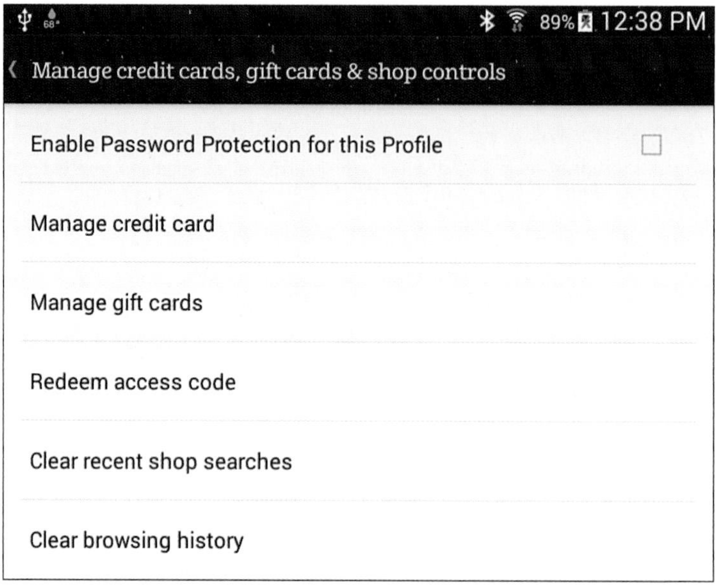

FIGURE 2.23   These settings control how the NOOK Shop works.

▶ **Password Protect Purchases for Profiles**: You can require a password to be entered prior to making a purchase. If you tap this to turn it on, a dialog appears and asks you to enter your BN account password. Enter it and tap OK. To turn it off, tap Password Protect Purchases for Adult Profiles, enter your BN account password, and tap OK.

▶ **Manage Credit Card**: Tap this to change your default credit card. If you have an expired credit card you need to change, use this feature as well. Tap Change, enter the information, and then tap Next. The information is verified, and it now becomes your default credit card.

▶ **Manage Gift Cards**: Tap this to enter a gift card (which is used first when making purchases). Tap Add Gift Card and enter the necessary information. Tap Submit and the Gift Card is added to your account.

▶ **Redeem Access Code**: Tap this to enter an access code for content. The code is 13 characters. To redeem one, enter the code and tap Add Now.

▶ **Clear Recent Shop Searches**: This setting enables you to clear the shop searches. Whenever you search the NOOK Store on the NOOK, it saves the recent searches. The searches are saved to make it easier to conduct searches. For example, you can search for ebooks related to Sherlock Holmes but decide not to purchase now. When you go back to the NOOK Store on your NOOK, you can type **Sher**, and Sherlock Holmes appears below the search text. You can then tap Sherlock Holmes, and the search is performed.

▶ **Clear Browsing History**: As you browse items, look at their details; those items are captured and kept in a recently viewed list. If you want to clear those and start fresh, tap Clear Recently View List, and tap OK.

Book Settings

These options (see Figure 2.24) relate to the Reader app, which is where you read NOOK Books:

▶ **EPUB Page Turn Effect:** How do you want pages to turn? Curl? Slide? Or no effect at all? Choose what you want here.

▶ **Enable 2-Page PDF Display Mode in Landscape**: When reading PDFs, when you switch to landscape mode, you can either see two pages of the PDF or a single page of the PDF. Here is where you control that. If this option has a check mark, when you move to landscape mode, you see two pages of the PDF.

FIGURE 2.24 The Reader settings screen.

▶ **Show Status Bar**: By default, this feature is off, which means you do not see the status bar while reading. However, if you want to see any notification icons, battery power, and so on, tap this to turn on the status bar while reading.

▶ **Adobe DRM Settings**: Adobe DRM provides DRM protection, which is used by libraries and other companies. You can read Adobe DRM protected titles in your NOOK Reader. Tap Adobe DRM Settings and enter your Adobe ID. If you don't have an Adobe ID, go to http://www.adobe.com/solutions/ebook/digital-editions.html and click Sign In.

▶ **Dictionary**: Here, you can see which dictionary is installed (so that when you look up words, you get a definition). You can download others by tapping the Download icon (the cloud with a green arrow).

Newspaper, Magazine, Comics, and Catalogs Settings

The only option available when you tap Newspapers is a list of available and installed dictionaries.

When you tap Magazines, you see the options in see Figure 2.25, which relate to reading magazines, comics, and catalogs in the NOOK Reader app:

▶ **Page Turn Effect:** How do you want pages to turn? Curl? Slide? Choose what you want here.

▶ **Enable Zoom View Letterboxing in Comics**: When reading comics, you can use B&N's Zoom View, which focuses in on individual panels in order. Having this one does not require you to use it, but it does make it available. It is on by default. For more details about that, **see** Chapter 3, "Reading on Your Samsung Galaxy Tab 4 NOOK and Beyond."

▶ **Enable Hotspots**: Catalogs often have hotspots, which you can tap and launch a webpage with more information about that car or box of chocolates or pears. By default this is on.

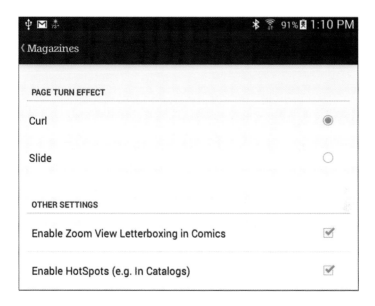

FIGURE 2.25 The Magazines settings screen.

NOOK Video Settings

The options here (see Figure 2.26) revolve around viewing your NOOK Video.

▶ **Manage NOOK Video on Your Devices:** Tap this to control which devices you can view NOOK Video on. All your applicable devices (including iPhones, iPads, and Android phones) will be listed. Tap the X to deauthorize a device from viewing NOOK Videos. You can reauthorize a device by logging into NOOK Video there.

▶ **UltraViolet Account**: UltraViolet is a system that, when you purchase some Blu-ray items, gives you a free digital copy of that item. You can also buy digital versions directly that are supported by UltraViolet. For example, if you buy *The Maltese Falcon*, it comes with an UltraViolet copy of the movie, which you can access with a code provided in the package. To use UltraViolet, you must set up a separate account at www.uvvu.com. You can use the UltraViolet option in Account Settings to link your UltraViolet account to watch your movies on your NOOK. Just tap UltraViolet and enter your UltraViolet account information to view UltraViolet films on your NOOK.

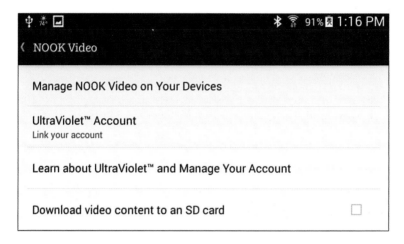

FIGURE 2.26   The NOOK Video settings screen.

> NOTE: Not *all* UltraViolet movies are supported as yet by NOOK (or other devices). To be sure you can watch an UltraViolet movie on your NOOK, double-check BN.com to see if the UltraViolet logo appears.

▶ **Learn About UltraViolet and Manage Your Account**: Tapping this launches the UltraViolet website where you can log in to your account, sign up, or just learn more about it.

▶ **Download Video Content to an SD Card**: Video can take up a lot of space, and you have only 8GB or 16GB on your internal memory. You can install up to a 32GB microSD card. To save space on your internal NOOK memory, you can choose to have video content downloaded to the microSD card instead.

Link to Social Networking

This setting allows you to link your Twitter and Facebook accounts (assuming you have them) to your NOOK device, allowing you to post-reading statuses, recommend books, and so on (see Figure 2.27).

▶ **Facebook**: This enables you to link your Facebook account to your NOOK. If you have already linked your Facebook account, you can unlink it. To link it, tap Link Your Account. Then enter the required information and tap Log In. The NOOK by Barnes & Noble screen appears. If you tap the friends image, you can choose with whom you share posts. Tap the group you want to see the posts. Tap Install and then tap Allow. Then determine if you want to allow access and actions by your NOOK. Tap the check box to uncheck the item. When you are ready, tap Allow All or Allow Some. For more information about Facebook with your NOOK, **see** Chapter 11, "Using the Social Features of Your Samsung Galaxy Tab 4 NOOK."

► **Twitter**: This enables you to link your Twitter account to your NOOK. If you have already linked your Twitter account, you can unlink it. To link it, tap Link Your Account. Then enter the required information and tap Authorize App. For more information about Twitter with your NOOK, **see** Chapter 11.

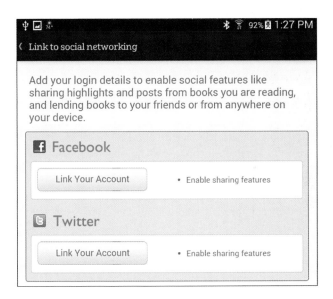

FIGURE 2.27   Link your Facebook and Twitter accounts to share and recommend books with friends.

Tap Add Facebook Friends as NOOK Friends. If any of your Facebook friends are also NOOK friends, you'll start seeing their updates in the NOOK Friends online, covered more in Chapter 25, "Using My NOOK Library."

Adding and Using a microSD Card

Your NOOK has approximately 8GB or 16GB of built-in memory. This is a lot of memory for books, but music and videos can begin to eat that space up. Therefore, your NOOK's memory is expandable by up to another 32GB using a microSD card.

> TIP: A microSD card is not the same as an SD memory card like the kind typically used in digital cameras. A microSD card is approximately the size of your fingernail.

> NOTE: You will see both microSD and microSDHC. Your NOOK can use either format—they are the same for all intents and purposes. The HC is used for microSD cards greater than 2GB in size.

Installing a microSD card in your NOOK is easy—you don't even need to turn off your NOOK:

1. Flip your NOOK so that you are looking at the screen. On the right side toward the bottom, you see a little plastic flap. Pull that flap out to expose the microSD slot.

2. The microSD slot is the small opening. With the metal connectors of the microSD card facing the back of the NOOK, slide the microSD card in, and push until it locks into place. The NOOK automatically recognizes the card. Close the flap.

3. If the microSD card has not yet been formatted, go to Settings, Storage and tap Format SD Card.

> NOTE: My fingers are too large, so I have to use the edge of a letter opener to get the microSD card to lock or unlock. Just be careful if you have to do this.

In the Storage settings, you can unmount the SD card (which you should do before removing it) by tapping Unmount SD Card.

To remove a microSD card, follow these steps:

1. From the SD Card screen, tap Unmount SD Card.

2. Flip your NOOK so that you are looking at the screen. On the right side toward the bottom, you can see a little plastic flap. Pull that flap out to expose the microSD slot.

3. The microSD slot is the small opening. Push the card until it unlocks. Pull out the card.

4. Close the flap.

Now that you have a microSD card installed, how do you access those files? From Apps, tap My Files. This opens the My Files app (see Figure 2.28). You can use this to navigate and access the files.

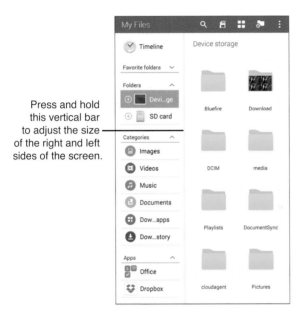

FIGURE 2.28   The My Files app.

If you want to move them so that your NOOK Library can see them, follow these steps:

1. Open the My Files app. Ensure that your microSD card has a folder called NOOK with the subfolders Books, Magazines, Newspapers, and My Files.

2. Navigate to the files you want to appear in the NOOK Library. Tap the three square icon in the upper-right and tap Select. The files now have a little square in the upper-right corner of the thumbnail. Tap the files you want to move.

3. Tap the Move icon.

4. Navigate to the folder you want the files to appear, and then tap Move Here. The files are moved.

CHAPTER 3

Reading on Your Samsung Galaxy Tab 4 NOOK and Beyond

Although your NOOK has many unique features and capabilities, its primary purpose is for reading ebooks and other content. One of the benefits of owning a NOOK is that you can carry a complete library with you everywhere you go. If you don't have your NOOK with you, you can also read your ebooks on your PC, Mac, iPhone, iPad, iPod touch, Android phone, or Android tablet.

Various forms of content are available to read on your NOOK—NOOK Books and other EPUB files, along with PDFs; Microsoft Word, Excel, and PowerPoint files; and plain text files. Appendix A, "Understanding ebook Formats," explains more about the details of ebook formats. You are probably already familiar with Microsoft documents; although, you can use either the DOC or DOCX formats (and the corresponding XLS or XLSX and PPT or PPTX formats) used in all versions of Word.

Browsing Your Library

The Library

The Library contains all the content you've purchased from B&N and the content you have sideloaded (see Figure 3.1). This includes not only ebooks you've purchased, but also magazine and newspaper subscriptions, sample books, videos, music, Microsoft documents, PDFs, ebooks purchased from other sources, and free books downloaded from B&N and other sites.

From the NOOK Library widget, you can tap the cover to immediately open that book or resume watching that movie. To go to the full Library, tap the Library icon in the upper-right corner of the NOOK Library widget. When at the Library, you see a list of large categories. Next to each category is a small arrow. Tap it to show the covers, which you can scroll through by sliding across them left or right. To see only your Books or Magazines, tap Books or Magazines (or whatever):

FIGURE 3.1   The Library where all your books and content are stored.

- ▶ **Books**: Tapping this displays the full list of ebooks on your NOOK, whether from B&N or other sources.

- ▶ **Magazines**: Tapping this displays the full list of magazines on your NOOK, whether from B&N or other sources.

- ▶ **Movies and TV**: Tapping this displays the full list of movies and TV shows on your NOOK or available for streaming, whether from B&N or other sources.

- ▶ **Kids**: Tapping this displays the apps and books categorized for kids.

- ▶ **Catalogs**: Tapping this displays the catalogs on your NOOK.

- ▶ **Newspapers**: Tapping this displays the full list of newspapers on your NOOK, whether from B&N or other sources.

- ▶ **My Shelves**: Tapping this displays the full list you've created. You can tap the shelf to browse what you've filed there.

- ▶ **My Files**: Tapping this gives you access to the files you have added to your NOOK that don't fit neatly into one of the existing categories or are downloaded via the browser, Dropbox, and so on.

NOTE: For more information on using My NOOK Library on bn.com, **see** Chapter 25, "Using My NOOK Library."

If you purchase a book using the Shop on your NOOK, that book is automatically downloaded to your NOOK within a few minutes. If you purchase an ebook from B&N using your computer, the ebook is added to My NOOK Library on bn.com, but it isn't downloaded to your NOOK automatically—although the cover appears. You can tell it was *not* downloaded because a white cloud with a green down-pointing arrow icon appears on the upper left of the cover. Tap the cover to download the NOOK Book.

CAUTION: If you plan to be away from Wi-Fi hotspots, you should make sure that the items that appear in My NOOK Library have actually been downloaded to your NOOK.

At the top of the screen, you have a few options buttons.

Tapping the Search allows you to enter text for a search. As you type, your NOOK searches through its library and displays results, which you can tap to access. If you finish typing your search terms and then tap the magnifying glass on the keyboard (where Return or Enter usually is), then a screen appears showing you the results.

Tap the Profile icon to manage content on any profiles. When you tap it, you see the screen in Figure 3.2.

Tap Manage Your Own Content to receive a screen that looks like the library (see Figure 3.3).

You can tap entire categories or tap the arrow on the far right to display specific items, which you can then check or uncheck. Tap Save when done.

If you want to manage content for another profile, tap Manage Content and select the items you want or don't want to appear. Tap Save when done.

Tap Delete to delete a profile. **See** Chapter 10, "Creating and Using Profiles on Your Samsung Galaxy Tab 4 NOOK," for more information regarding profiles.

Tap the NOOK Store button to open the NOOK Store app.

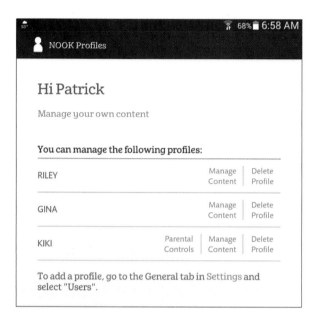

FIGURE 3.2   Managing content on profiles.

FIGURE 3.3   Select the content you want for this profile.

Tapping Options gives you five choices:

▶ **Create New Shelf**: Tapping this lets you create a shelf. **See** the "My Shelves" section later for more details.

▶ **Remove Items from Device**: Tapping this lets you select content to remove from your NOOK. When you tap this, you can select whole categories or individual items. Tap Remove from Device when complete. Note, this does not *delete* the content or even archive it. Rather, it simply removes the item from the library, forcing you to download it again.

▶ **View Archive**: Tapping this displays the full list of archived materials. To remove something from the archive, simply tap the cover to download it.

▶ **Reorder**: Tapping this lets you reorder the list you see in this Library screen. Tap it to display a screen that lists Books, Magazines, and so on. Press and hold one of the items, and drag it to the new location you want. Tap Save.

▶ **Refresh**: Tapping this updates the content appearing here.

Books

Note that all files placed in the microSD card's NOOK\Books folder are shown here along with all NOOK Books and documents in the NOOK's My Files\Books folder or NOOK's Digital Editions folder.

At the top of the screen, you have the Search, Profile, and NOOK Store buttons, which function as they normally do. Tapping Options gives you five choices:

▶ **View As**: Tapping this lets you adjust how the books are viewed. You can choose between Grid or List. List view (see Figure 3.4) shows smaller covers with the text to the right.

▶ **Sort By**: Tapping this lets you adjust how the books are sorted. You can choose between Most Recent, Title, or Author Name.

▶ **Remove Items from Device**: Tapping this lets you select content to remove from your NOOK. When you tap this, you can select whole categories or individual items. Tap Remove from Device when complete. Note, this does not *delete* the content or even archive it. Rather, it simply removes the item from the library, forcing you to download it again.

▶ **View Archive**: Tapping this displays the full list of archived materials. To remove something from the archive, simply tap the cover to download it.

▶ **Refresh**: Tapping this updates the content appearing here.

FIGURE 3.4   Your library in List view.

From the Books part of the Library, you can interact with your ebooks in two ways. First, you can just tap the cover to open the ebook. Second, if you tap and hold the cover, a pop-up menu appears (see Figure 3.5) with several options:

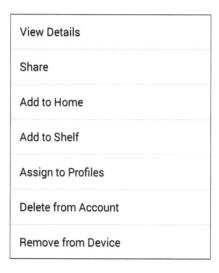

FIGURE 3.5   The pop-up menu that appears after pressing and holding a cover.

▶ **View Details**: Tapping this option opens a screen with many options (see Figure 3.6). **See** "The View Details Screen" section for more about this screen and its options.

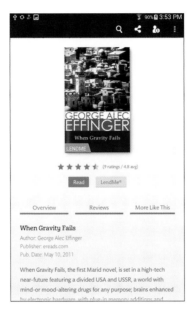

FIGURE 3.6 The View Details screen.

TIP: To access the View Details screen, you can also double-tap the cover.

▶ **Full Version Available**: This option appears for NOOK Book samples. Tapping it takes you to the View Details screen.

▶ **Share**: This enables you to recommend, rate and review, like on Facebook, or lend. For more about recommending and liking, **see** Chapter 11, "Using the Social Features of Your Samsung Galaxy Tab 4 NOOK." For more about lending, **see** Chapter 6, "Lending and Borrowing Books with LendMe on Your Samsung Galaxy Tab 4 NOOK."

▶ **Add to Home**: This option lets you add it to the Home screen so that the title is available there.

▶ **Assign to Profiles**: This option lets you quickly assign a book to a particular profile.

▶ **Add to Shelf**: This option lets you add it to a shelf. A Select Shelf screen appears. You can tap an existing shelf to add that ebook to that shelf. Alternatively, you can tap Add to a New Shelf. The Create New Shelf screen appears. Type in the shelf name and tap Save. The shelf is created and that ebook is added to that shelf. You can add ebooks to multiple shelves.

▶ **Remove from Shelf**: This option lets you remove the ebook from a shelf. If you tap Remove from Shelf, the Select Self screen appears and displays all the shelves this ebook is in. Tap the shelf you want to remove this ebook from.

▶ **Delete from Account**: This option enables you to delete items. If it is B&N content (for example, a NOOK Book), the content will be deleted from your NOOK Library—meaning you *cannot* redownload it or read it on other devices. If the content is additional content that you added (for example, a Project Gutenberg ebook), the content is deleted from the device—you can put it back on later. In short, be careful with this option. When you tap Delete, you are asked to confirm that you do indeed want to delete it.

▶ **Remove from Device**: This option removes the content from the device (but not to the archive). You can redownload it by tapping the cover.

Books, magazines, and newspapers purchased from B&N often have notices on the cover regarding them:

▶ **New**: This is a recent NOOK Book you have purchased and not yet downloaded.

▶ **LendMe**: This NOOK Book can be lent to a friend.

▶ *x* **Days**: You have borrowed this NOOK Book from a friend. Instead of the *x*, you see the number of days.

▶ **Lent**: You have lent this NOOK Book to a friend. The number of days left (out of 14) is in a small, gray circle at the bottom right of the cover.

▶ **Sample**: This is only a portion of the NOOK Book to give you a chance to review before you buy.

The View Details Screen

The View Details screen for B&N content has a number of options. If it is a NOOK Book, you see the star rating from B&N. Tapping the Read button opens the ebook for reading. (Alternatively, if you have not downloaded the NOOK Book yet, you can tap Download to download the NOOK Book.)

Tap LendMe to see the LendMe screen. For more information on the LendMe feature, **see** Chapter 6.

Tap Share (the thought bubble icon) to see options for Recommend, Rate and Review, Like on Facebook, and LendMe (if available for that particular title). For more information on the Recommend, Rate and Review, and Like on Facebook features, **see** Chapter 11. For more information on the LendMe feature, **see** Chapter 6.

Tap Profiles (the person's head icon) to manage which profiles on this NOOK have access to that content. **See** Chapter 10 for more information about profiles. The number beside the head (if one appears) indicates how many profiles on this NOOK can see this content.

Overview provides a description of the ebook. Tap More Like This to see other available B&N content by other customers who have purchased the same item, by the same author, or in the same series (see Figure 3.7). Tap a cover or icon to go to a View Details screen for that item (including an option to purchase or sample the content).

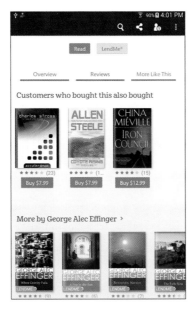

FIGURE 3.7 The View Details screen showing what other customers have purchased.

If the NOOK Book is a sample or borrowed (for more information related to shopping and sampling NOOK Books, **see** Chapter 12, "Shopping and Visiting B&N on Your Samsung Galaxy Tab 4 NOOK"), you can tap Read Sample (or just Read for borrowed NOOK Books) to read the sample or tap the Price button and then tap Confirm to purchase the NOOK Book.

Tap Reviews to see what reviewers have written or what other customers have posted about the NOOK Book (see Figure 3.8). You can sort the comments by tapping the drop-down list and choosing from among the options. If you find any of the reviews helpful (or not), you can tap Yes or No for that review. If you think the review is off base for any number of reasons (see Figure 3.9), tap Report This Review, tap the reason, and then tap Send to report the review to B&N, who may remove the review.

Tap Editorial from that drop-down list to see what professional reviewers say (for example, excerpts from *The New York Times Book Review* or *Kirkus Reviews*).

FIGURE 3.8   The Customer Reviews tab.

Magazines

This is where B&N places all your magazines (as opposed to newspapers) that you purchase from B&N (see Figure 3.10). Also, if you placed any files in either the NOOK's Magazines folder or in the microSD card's My Files\Magazines folder, those documents are shown here as well. You have the same options here as you do with the Books section.

Why do you want to flag this review?	
Plot Spoiler	○
Inappropriate or abusive language	○
Off-topic content	○
Spam, private or commercial solicitation	○
Suspected underage user	○
Terms of use violation	○
Cancel	Send

FIGURE 3.9   The options when you flag a review as problematic.

FIGURE 3.10   The Magazines screen.

For magazine subscriptions, you probably have multiple issues here. (More than one cover is stacked on top of the other.) To open and read an issue, tap the cover, which opens a screen and shows all available issues. Tap the cover of the issue you want to open and read.

Movies and TV

This is where B&N places all the videos that you purchase or rent from B&N (see Figure 3.11). Also, if you have placed any files in either the NOOK's Videos folder or in the microSD card's My Files\Videos folder, those videos are shown here as well. **See** Chapter 8, "Watching Videos on Your Samsung Galaxy Tab 4 NOOK," for more information on videos. In the options menus, you have the ability to add your UltraViolet account if you have not linked it already.

FIGURE 3.11   The Videos screen.

Note that if you have rented a movie, a banner indicates the amount of time left to watch.

Kids

This is where B&N places all your content (apps, books, whatever) that you purchase from B&N (see Figure 3.12) related to kids. **See** Chapter 5, "Reading and Using NOOK Books for Kids Features," for more information about NOOK Books for kids.

FIGURE 3.12 The Kids screen.

Catalogs

This is where B&N places all your catalogs that you purchase from or subscribe to at B&N (see Figure 3.13). You have the same options here as you do with the Books section.

Newspapers

This is where B&N places all your NOOK Newspapers™ (as opposed to magazines) that you purchase from B&N (see Figure 3.14). Also, if you have placed any files in either the NOOK's Newspapers folder or in the microSD card's My Files\Newspapers folder, those documents are shown here as well. You have the same options here as you do with the Books section.

FIGURE 3.13   The Catalogs screen.

FIGURE 3.14   The Newspapers screen.

For newspaper subscriptions, you probably have multiple issues here. (More than one cover is stacked one on top of the other.) To open and read an issue, tap the cover, which opens a screen and shows all available issues. Tap the cover of the issue you want to open and read.

My Shelves

The NOOK enables you to organize your ebooks into categories (or shelves) that you can name (see Figure 3.15). If you have a lot of ebooks and you want to categorize them beyond just author name, title, and most recent, this is how you can do it.

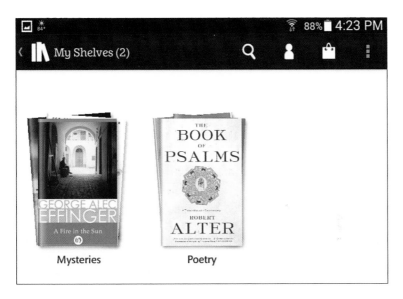

FIGURE 3.15   The My Shelves screen.

My Shelves shows you any existing shelves. You can use the View option at the top right to show your shelves as a grid or list and to sort by either shelf name or most recently created.

To add a shelf, from the top-right Options menu, tap Create New Shelf. The Create New Shelf screen appears. Type the name of the shelf and tap Save.

You can also edit existing shelves by pressing and holding a shelf's covers. When you lift your finger, you get three options. Tap Manage Content in Shelf to see the Library options. Expand each category by tapping the small arrow to the right of the content type (see Figure 3.16). Here you can do several things. A listing of titles appears. To add titles to this shelf, tap the check box next to the title so that a check mark appears. Removing check marks remove that title from that shelf. Tap Save to make the changes.

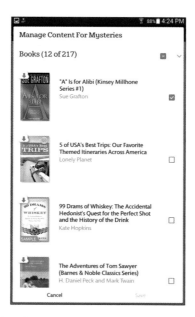

FIGURE 3.16   Edit existing shelves.

To rename a shelf, press and hold the shelf's covers. Choose Rename Shelf from the resulting pop-up menu. Enter the new name and tap Rename.

To delete a shelf, press and hold the shelf's covers. Choose Remove Shelf from the resulting pop-up menu. Your NOOK asks you to confirm. Tap Remove to delete the shelf.

> NOTE: When you delete a shelf, you are not deleting the content in the shelf.

My Files

My Files enables you to access files on the NOOK internal memory or on the microSD card so long as they are part of the NOOK\My Files folder.

> NOTE: Adobe Digital Editions (ADE) ebooks also appear in the Books section of the Library. For more information about ADE ebooks, **see** Appendix A.

Tap the folder icon to go into there. You can drill down to documents you have downloaded or other items to open them directly.

Reading NOOK Books on Your NOOK

If you open a NOOK Book or sideloaded EPUB file for the first time, after you select it, you are taken to the starting point that the publisher has chosen for that item. This might or might not be the first page. For example, some ebooks open on the first page of Chapter 1. Other ebooks open on the cover or title page. The publisher of the book decides which page is visible when you first open an ebook.

If you open a NOOK Book that you have read on the NOOK before in any of the NOOK Apps, NOOK Study™, or NOOK device, you are taken to the last location you were reading. If you open a sideloaded EPUB file you have read on the NOOK before, it opens to the last page you were on in the NOOK. In other words, non-B&N content does not sync across applications.

As you're reading, swipe right across the page to go to the previous page, or swipe left across the page to go to the next page.

Of course, there's more to reading books than just reading, right? Figure 3.17 shows the reading screen and the Reading Tools available. To see the Reading Tools, quickly tap the reading screen.

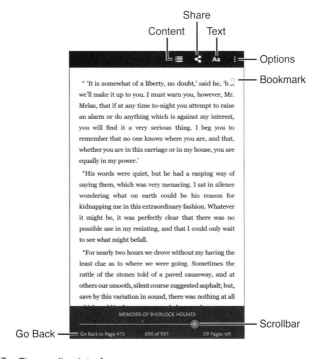

FIGURE 3.17   The reading interface.

Following are features of the Reading Tools:

▶ **Bookmark**: Tap this to add a bookmark. Chapter 4, "Using Highlights, Bookmarks, and Annotations," covers using bookmarks in detail.

▶ **Scroll Bar**: Drag this to quickly slide through the book.

▶ **Go Back to Page**: When you use the Jump to Page option or if you tap a footnote, after you have advanced to that page, you can tap Go Back to Page to take you back to the location where you just were—kind of like flipping back and forth between two channels on your TV remote.

▶ **Reading Tools Bar**: This bar has four options: Content, Share, Text, and Options. You see each of these options in action in the following sections.

To exit the Reading Tools, tap anywhere on the reading screen where those tools do not appear.

While reading, you can press and hold on a word. You will see a definition appear if one is found and the Text Selection toolbar appears (see Figure 3.18). If you want to select more than that single word, drag the selection highlight to the end of the block of text you want to select. For the Highlight, Notes, and Look Up buttons, **see** Chapter 5. For the Share button, **see** Chapter 11. Looking up and finding words is discussed in the "Looking Up Words" section of this chapter.

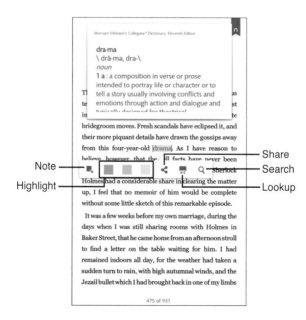

FIGURE 3.18   The Text Selection toolbar.

Finally, you can get to the status bar if it is hidden by swiping quickly at the top edge of your NOOK. The status bar appears, which you can then swipe again to get to the Notification pane.

Fixing Reading Orientation

With your NOOK, you can read in either portrait or landscape mode. The NOOK switches between these two modes depending on how you hold the NOOK—flip it sideways to have it shift to landscape, or flip it upright to display in portrait mode. However, if you want to fix the mode so that even if you flip the NOOK on its side or upright it remains in the same mode, from the Notification pane, tap Screen Rotation off (so that it is gray in color). To unlock, from the Notification pane, tap Screen Rotation on.

Changing the Text Font and Text Size

Your NOOK enables you to easily change the text font and text size while reading. To change the font or the text size, tap the reading screen, and then tap Text on the Reading Tools bar (see Figure 3.19).

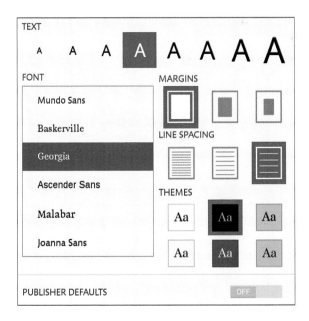

FIGURE 3.19 Use this screen to adjust the font size among other things.

Your NOOK supports eight text sizes, represented by the A. The current text size A is boxed in blue. Tap the A for the size you want. You can see the text size adjust behind the text menu. Adjust the text size to whichever size you want.

The current font selected is boxed in blue. To change the text font, tap the font you want. The text adjusts to the new font behind the text menu. You have six fonts to choose from, and you can see a representation of them in the font selection.

▶ You cannot change the text font if the publisher created the content with a specific font embedded in it.

▶ You cannot change the text font for PDF files. If the creator of the PDF file embedded a particular font, your NOOK uses that font. Otherwise, it uses the default font.

▶ Some ebooks consist of pages scanned as images, usually as PDF files. You cannot change the text font for these ebooks.

NOTE: Tapping Publisher Defaults to On changes all settings on this screen to the options chosen by the Publisher for all content that you read. You can toggle that back to Off at anytime.

Changing the Theme, Line Spacing, Margins, and Brightness

Your NOOK enables you to change the color scheme, space between lines, and margins while reading. To change these, tap the reading screen, and then tap Text on the Reading Tools bar. The current theme selected is highlighted in blue.

Tap the Theme box to change the color settings for the background and text. You have six options, top row from left to right first:

▶ Bright white page with black text

▶ Black background with light gray text

▶ Gray background with black text

▶ Cream background with black text (this reader's favorite)

▶ Brown background with white text

▶ Light brown background with black text

Tap your choice. The reading screen changes to reflect what you chose.

The Line Spacing options are similar to using single-space, single-and-a-half-space, or double-space. The current selection is highlighted by a blue box, and you have three options. Tap the option you want. The reading screen adjusts.

The Margin options determine the amount of white space on the right and left sides of the text. The current selection is highlighted by a blue box, and you have three options. Tap the option you want. The reading screen adjusts.

> TIP: To adjust the brightness of the screen while reading, use the Brightness setting in the Notification pane.

Looking Up Words

One of the most convenient features of your NOOK is to quickly look up the definitions of words you don't know. If you're reading a book and encounter a word you don't know or are curious about, press and hold on that word until the Text Selection toolbar appears. You get the definition on the screen. However, if you want more or a definition is not found, tap Look Up from the Text Selection toolbar. A window appears with a dictionary entry (see Figure 3.20). You can also tap Wikipedia or Google. Tapping takes you to the browser, opens up the corresponding website, and enters that word as the search criteria. (Use the Recent Drawer to return to reading your book.) If you want, you can look up another word by tapping in the Edit Your Search box and editing the word and tapping Search.

> NOTE: Looking up words is not supported for certain types of ebooks:
> ▶ Magazines (Although magazines that "function" more like newspapers or books enable you to look up words.)
> ▶ NOOK Comics
> ▶ NOOK Books for Kids

You can search your ebook for a specific word or phrase. You can tap Find from the Text Selection toolbar or tap Options and then tap Find in Book from the Reading Tools. If you use the Find option from the Text Selection toolbar, the word (or words) you have selected is automatically entered as your search term and results are found. You can also tap in the search box and enter a new term.

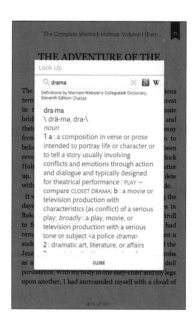

FIGURE 3.20   Your dictionary goes wherever your NOOK goes.

If you tap Options and then tap Find in Book, enter the term or words you want to find and tap the magnifying glass on the keyboard and then type the text you want to search.

In either case, your NOOK displays the locations of that word in a scrollable window (see Figure 3.21). The scrollable window provides a bit of context. Tap the location of the word you want to go to. You are taken to that location, the word is highlighted, and the scrollable window disappears, but you still see the search text box. You can tap the button immediately to the right of search box to redisplay the scrollable window, or you can tap the left or right keys next to the search word to go to and highlight the next appearance of that word. Tap the X or tap the reading screen to exit search mode. If you want to search for a different word or phrase, tap in the box that contains your original search term, type in the new word, and tap Search.

TIP: Need to type a lot of uppercase letters? Tap the Shift key twice. This enables you to enter only uppercase letters. Tap the Shift key again to release the caps lock.

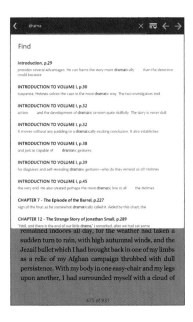

FIGURE 3.21 A scrollable list of search results.

Using the Options Menu

On the Reading Tools bar, you can tap Options, which has three other selections beyond Find in Book:

- ▶ **Jump to Page**: Tap this to enter a specific page number to go directly to that page.

- ▶ **View Details**: Opens the View Details screen for the book you are reading. (**See** "The View Details Screen" earlier in this chapter for more information.)

- ▶ **Settings**: Tap this to go to the Book settings for the NOOK. (**See** "Book Settings" in Chapter 2, "Customizing and Configuring Your Samsung Galaxy Tab 4 NOOK," for more information.)

Reading Enhanced NOOK Books

Enhanced NOOK Books feature video and audio directly within the ebook. When shopping for these ebooks at BN.com, look for the NOOK Book enhanced™ designation. The cover of the NOOK Book also shows Enhanced Edition at the bottom of the cover.

When reading one of these enhanced NOOK Books, you will encounter the enhanced material, as shown in Figure 3.22.

FIGURE 3.22   Here's a page with enhanced content.

Tap the Play button on the content. When you do, the screen adjusts to offer more control (see Figure 3.23). Tap the Pause button to pause the video, and tap the Play button to restart the video. Use the scrollbar to scroll to a specific location. Tap the Expand button (four arrows pointing away from each other) to make the video full screen; then you can switch between portrait and landscape mode for viewing if you want.

NOTE: You cannot sample enhanced NOOK Books from B&N.

NOTE: Enhanced NOOK Books at this time work only on your Samsung Galaxy Tab 4 NOOK, NOOK HD, and NOOK HD+. If you own a NOOK Simple Touch, you can see it listed in the Everything Else list, but you cannot download it. On the NOOK App for iPad, you can see it as a title, but when you try to download it, you are informed that it is not yet supported on the iPad.

The Fort

Interview: Researching *The Fort*

More Videos:
Documentary Short: Bernard Cornwell Tours the
Battlefield
Interview: The Letter "F"
Interview: Why This Battle
Interview: Paul Revere's Ride
Interview: History
Interview: The Musical
Interview: Ghost of the Drummer Boy

351 of 435

FIGURE 3.23   Enhanced content playing in your ebook.

Reading Magazines and Comics on Your NOOK

In addition to books, B&N provides magazine subscriptions and comics for your NOOK. B&N automatically delivers subscription content to your NOOK if a Wi-Fi connection is available. (For now, you purchase comics individually.) For more information on subscribing to content on your NOOK, **see** Chapter 13, "Using the Google Play Store and Google Apps."

B&N recognizes that many magazines and comics are more image-intensive than ebooks, and the NOOK takes full advantage of that to display a rich reading environment for magazines. Often, magazines are read in landscape mode; although portrait mode works as well.

> NOTE: Some magazines function more like newspapers (for example, *The New York Review of Books* or *Analog Science Fiction and Fact*), so if you encounter a magazine like that, use the "Reading Newspapers on Your NOOK" section for more appropriate instructions.

Because magazines differ, you might encounter a range of reading interfaces. The "standard" interface described here for *National Geographic* is quite common. However, many magazines feature enhanced content such as videos, interactive graphics, and so on. These activities (see Figure 3.24) use standard gestures to interact with, but the "standard" magazine reading options may not be available. Fortunately, many emagazines that differ from the standard magazine reading experience offer instructions in the first page or so.

FIGURE 3.24   A magazine with enhanced content.

When you open a magazine or comic, you can use pinch and zoom techniques to narrow in on pages. If you tap the page, you see the Thumbnail view at the bottom of the page (see Figure 3.25). This is a thumbnail of each page that you can scroll through. Tap the thumbnail to go to that page.

Pinching and zooming and dragging can be tedious for reading articles, and this is where the Article View is handy. When you see that button, tap Article View, and a secondary reading window opens on top of the magazine (see Figure 3.26). This is the text of the article (with an opening image) that you can scroll through to read more easily. Tap the Page View to close Article View. The good news is that your NOOK remembers where you were in the article, so if you tap Article View again for that article, it takes you to where you last stopped reading. You can also swipe left and right to navigate from article to article. You can also tap the corner plus icon on a page to insert a bookmark.

FIGURE 3.25   Scroll through a magazine's pages in Thumbnail view.

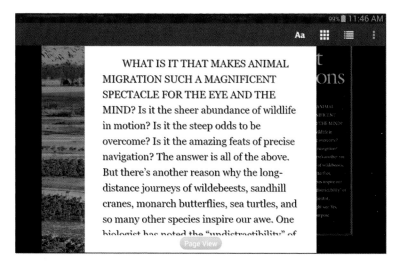

FIGURE 3.26   Reading in Article View.

> NOTE: Reading comics is best in portrait mode.

While in Article View, if you tap the screen in the article, a Reading Tools bar appears (refer to Figure 3.26). This functions the same as in a book.

> NOTE: Comics do not have an Article View.

The Content option provides a table of contents for the magazine with brief descriptions of each article (see Figure 3.27). The Text options are identical, excepting the Publisher Default option, as the Text options for ebooks.

FIGURE 3.27   The contents of a magazine.

With magazines, you have a Grid view that is available in the Reading Tools bar. Tap it, and all the pages appear in a scrollable grid in the reading screen with the page you are currently on highlighted in blue (see Figure 3.28). Tap the Grid view icon to exit this view, or tap the page you want to go to, which takes you to that page and exits Grid View.

FIGURE 3.28   A magazine in Grid View.

From the Reading tools, if you tap the Options button, you can go to the View Details screen for that magazine or go to the Magazine settings by tapping Settings.

NOOK Comics come with ZoomView. You can choose to not use ZoomView, and if so, the previous description for reading a magazine applies equally well to NOOK Comics. But those with ZoomView have a bit more you can do. As you can see in Figure 3.29, you have a Zoom View button at the bottom of the screen. When you tap this, the screen zooms in to the first panel of that page. You can then use normal page turning gestures to move from panel to panel on the page in the order specified by the publisher. This is a nice feature so that you do not need to pinch and zoom on your own. To turn off ZoomView, just tap Comic View.

FIGURE 3.29   Reading a page in a comic.

Reading Newspapers on Your NOOK

In addition to books, B&N provides newspaper subscriptions for your NOOK. B&N automatically delivers subscription content to your NOOK if a Wi-Fi connection is available.

For more information on subscribing to content on your NOOK, **see** Chapter 12.

Unlike books, newspaper content isn't presented in a linear format. Content is often presented in major sections with article headlines and possibly followed by a small synopsis of each article (see Figure 3.30). To read the specific article, tap the headline for that article. After an article is open, use swipe left and right gestures to navigate between pages just as you do when reading a book.

Tapping the screen displays the Reading Tools, which are almost the same as the ebook Reading Tools (see Figure 3.31).

To add a bookmark, tap the plus sign at the corner of the page instead of the stylized N bookmark in books. In addition, if you tap the arrow next to the section title, you are taken back.

To navigate back to the list of sections and their articles, tap the left-pointing arrow button on the top right.

FIGURE 3.30   Reading a newspaper.

FIGURE 3.31   The Reading Tools bar is nearly identical for ebooks and newspapers.

For more information on subscription content, including when your NOOK automatically deletes subscription content, **see** Chapter 12.

Reading Catalogs on Your NOOK

Catalogs are image-intensive, and the point is to find something to buy. The NOOK takes full advantage of the visual richness of catalogs and a connection with the Internet to make digital catalogs a fun experience.

When you open a catalog, it has a lot of familiarity to the magazine reading experience. You can use pinch and zoom techniques to narrow in on pages. If you tap the page, you see the Thumbnail view at the bottom of the page (see Figure 3.32). This is a thumbnail of each page that you can scroll through. Tap the thumbnail to go to that page.

FIGURE 3.32   Scroll through a catalog's pages in Thumbnail view.

Catalogs feature hotspots, which you can tap (see Figure 3.33). When you do so, you see an expanded version of that product (see Figure 3.34). If you tap Shop Online, your browser launches and displays the web page for that product, which you can then purchase. Tap Contact Catalog for information about how to call and purchase this item.

You can also add a page to a scrapbook by tapping the Add to Scrapbook button on the Reading Tools bar.

Hotspots

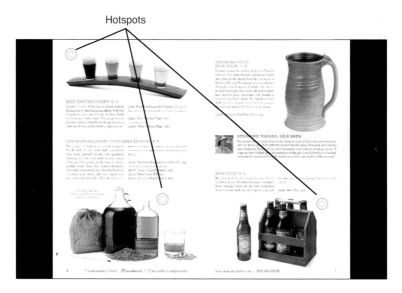

FIGURE 3.33   Hotspots on a catalog page.

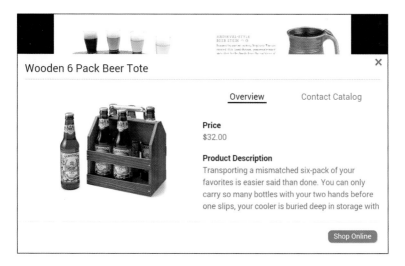

FIGURE 3.34   More information about a product.

With catalogs, you have a Grid view available on the Reading Tools bar. Tap it and all the pages appear in a scrollable grid in the reading screen. Tap the Grid view icon to exit this view, or tap the page you want to go to, which takes you to that page and exits Grid View.

To add a bookmark, tap either the top-right corner or top-left corner to fold over the bookmark.

Reading Microsoft Office and Other Documents on Your NOOK

Beyond the NOOK Books, magazines, ebooks from other sources, and newspapers you can read, on your NOOK you can also read Microsoft Office documents, HTML files, and PDFs.

Reading Microsoft Office Files

Your NOOK has Hancom Office installed, which is an application running on your NOOK that can open, read, and even edit Microsoft Office Word (see Figure 3.35), Excel, and PowerPoint files.

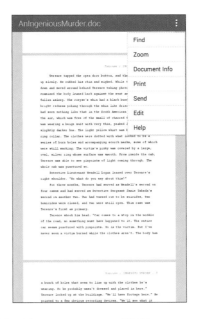

FIGURE 3.35   Reading Word documents on your NOOK.

You can access files by tapping Open and navigating to the appropriate location on the device or tap Cloud to view your Dropbox site. The bottom buttons allow you to add a folder, refresh to see if new documents have been added, adjust the sort order, view large thumbnails, or select files or folders. Tap the file you want to open.

TIP: You can read RTF and TXT documents as well.

The features for these apps are full featured and are beyond the scope of this book. Suffice it to say, if you are familiar with how to work with documents in Word, spreadsheets in Excel, or slides in PowerPoint, the features of Hancom Office will be familiar as well.

Reading HTML Files

After you tap to open an HTML file, the HTML file is opened in the web browser. For more information about using the web browser, **see** Chapter 9, "Using NOOK Apps and Surfing the Web," for more information.

Reading PDFs

This section is specifically about PDFs outside of Adobe Digital Editions PDFs (ADE PDFs). ADE PDFs operate like regular ebooks.

On the NOOK, you can save PDFs in the NOOK\Books folder and open them up just like a book. When you use Reader to read PDF documents, it mirrors reading NOOK Magazines™ and NOOK Books.

If you tap the page, you display the Reading Tools (see Figure 3.36):

- ▶ **Thumbnails**: You can scroll through the PDF like you can a magazine. Tap the thumbnail of the page you want to go to.

- ▶ **Bookmark**: Tap to mark your page.

- ▶ **Scroll Bar**: Drag this to quickly slide through the PDF.

- ▶ **Go Back**: After you have advanced to a page using the thumbnails or the Jump to Page option, you can tap Go Back to take you back to the location where you just were—kind of like flipping back and forth between two channels on your TV remote.

- ▶ **Contents**: Tap this to see Contents. More likely for most PDFs, you can access any Highlights or Notes, Bookmarks, and Lookups you marked or made.

- ▶ **Options**: Tap this to see the Jump to Page, Find in Book, and Settings options. Tap Jump to Page and enter a number to go directly to that page. Tap Find in Book to conduct a search. Tap Settings to open the settings for reading books.

FIGURE 3.36   Reading a PDF document with Reader.

While reading PDF documents, you can use pinch and zoom to zoom in and out of the document. Finally, while reading, you can press and hold on a word. The Text Selection Toolbar appears (see Figure 3.37). If you want to select more than that single word, drag the selection highlight to the end of the block of text you want to select. For the Highlight, Notes, and Look Up buttons, **see** Chapter 6. The "Looking Up Words" section of this chapter discusses looking up and finding words.

The options function just like the corresponding functions in the NOOK Books. In addition, you can freeze the orientation of a PDF just like a NOOK Book.

Reading PagePerfect Books

When you download the latest thriller, normally, the presentation of the text on the page is not all that important. But some ebooks require that the presentation in ebook format not shift based on the size of the text the reader wants, where images fall, and so on. Thus, PagePerfect books preserve exactly how the book is supposed to appear. These books function in many ways like the PDFs read with the Reader in the previous section.

You open a PagePerfect book like any other. If you double-tap the screen, it zooms into that portion of the book. Double-tap again to zoom out to the original size. If you tap once, you see the Reading Tools along with a thumbnail of the pages like a magazine (see Figure 3.38).

FIGURE 3.37   Highlight text in a PDF.

FIGURE 3.38   Reading a PagePerfect book.

All other functions of a PagePerfect book mirror reading a PDF in Reader. The only additional feature is the Share button next to the Contents button. **See** Chapter 11 for more about the social features of your NOOK.

CHAPTER 4

Using Highlights, Bookmarks, and Annotations

Take a look at one of your favorite books, and you can likely find notes in the margins and perhaps dog-eared pages. Jotting down notes about passages that impact you or marking pages you want to come back to visit later is how you make books a personalized possession. Fortunately, you don't have to forgo these things when it comes to ebooks because your NOOK lets you easily highlight passages and add bookmarks and notes to pages.

Using Highlights, Notes, and Bookmarks on Your NOOK

When you think of highlighting something in a book, you typically think of using a yellow highlighter marker to draw attention to portions of the text. Highlighting on your NOOK is similar to that…but with a highlighter that has multiple colors all in one.

> TIP: Highlighting and notes are not supported for magazine content. You can add only highlights and notes in ebooks that support them. Caveat: Magazines that are more like newspapers (for example, *The New York Review of Books*) do support highlighting and notes.

A note in an ebook is simply a highlighted area with a message attached. Therefore, the steps necessary to add, view, edit, and delete notes are the same as the steps for using highlights.

Adding a Highlight or a Note

To highlight text or add a note in an ebook, follow these steps:

1. Press and hold a word. The word appears in a bubble, and that is your signal to raise your finger. The word is highlighted, and the Text Selection toolbar appears.

2. If you want to highlight only that word, move to step 3. If you want to highlight a block of text, notice the highlighted word is bounded by two blue bars. Press, hold, and drag one of the blue bars to the location you want to end the highlight (see Figure 4.1).

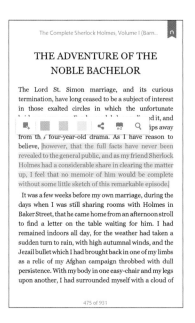

FIGURE 4.1   Highlight the text you want to add a note to.

3. Tap one of the highlight colors to just add a highlight. Tap Note if you want to add a note. If you chose the former, the text is highlighted. If you chose the latter, the Add Note screen appears (see Figure 4.2).

4. Type your note and tap Save.

5. The highlight is added, and a Note icon appears next in the margin (see Figure 4.3).

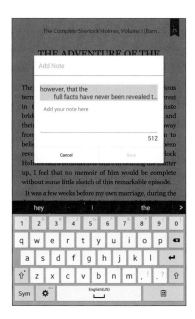

FIGURE 4.2 Enter your note.

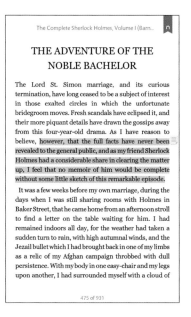

FIGURE 4.3 Your note is added.

Viewing, Editing, and Deleting Highlights and Notes

The simplest way to edit a note is to tap the highlighted text. A modified version of the Text Selection toolbar appears (see Figure 4.4), giving you several options:

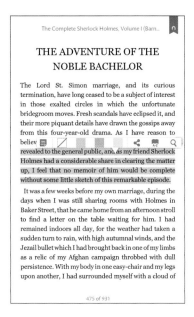

FIGURE 4.4   Your options after you have added a highlight and note.

▶ **Note**: Tap this to add, edit, or remove a note.

▶ **Remove Highlight**: Tap this to remove the highlight and the note.

▶ **Highlight Colors**: Tap a different color to change the highlight color.

> TIP: You can view the note text by tapping the Note icon on the page. From there, you can then tap Edit to edit the text of the note.

To navigate or jump to notes throughout an ebook, from the Reading Tools toolbar (tap the screen), tap Content. Then tap Highlights and Notes. You see a listing of the notes in the ebook (scroll if you need to see more), as shown in Figure 4.5. You see the text that was highlighted, the page number of the note, and the date and time it was last edited. Tap the particular note you want to jump to. The contents screen disappears, and you are taken to the page with the highlight or note you tapped.

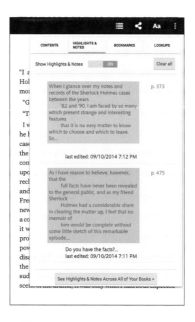

FIGURE 4.5   Jump to a specific note.

Three other options exist on the screen shown in Figure 4.5: Clear All, Show Notes & Highlights, and See Highlights and Notes Across All of Your Books. If you tap Clear All, you delete all notes and highlights in the ebook. If you turn Show Notes & Highlights to Off, you turn off the visibility of the highlights; although, the Note icon stays in the margin. You can turn Show Notes & Highlights back to On to have the highlights reappear.

If you tap See Highlights and Notes Across All of Your Books, the NOOK Highlights and Notes app opens, which is covered in the following section.

Using NOOK Highlights and Notes App

If you make a lot of highlights and notes in books, magazines, and newspapers, you may not remember where you took a particular note or just want to see what notes were made. If that's you, then the NOOK Highlights and Notes app is for you (see Figure 4.6).

FIGURE 4.6   The opening screen of the NOOK Highlights and Notes app.

Here you can see quickly every book, magazine, or newspaper you've made a note in or highlighted any text in. If you tap the top-right button, you can sort by either book title (on by default) or by date. To the right of each book's cover, you see a count of the number of highlights and notes you've made in that book. Tap the book to see more details (see Figure 4.7).

Each note or highlight is provided. The text you highlighted is in bold and to the left of the page number. If you made a note, the note itself appears immediately below the highlighted text. For each highlight, you can tap a menu of options in the bottom left. From here, you can add a note if it's just a highlight, edit the note, delete it, delete just the highlight, and even open the book to the page where the note or highlight appears. To perform any of these actions, the book, magazine, or newspaper must be downloaded to the NOOK. Good news: You can download the book from right here by tapping the cover.

Using Bookmarks

Bookmarks enable you to easily return to a particular page. Unlike notes, bookmarks do not have any text associated with them. Bookmarks work in all your ebooks, magazines, and newspapers.

FIGURE 4.7   Detailed view of the notes and highlights in a book.

For ebooks, to add a bookmark on the page you're reading, tap the reading screen, and then tap the icon that looks like a bookmark in the top-right corner. It drops down a bit and changes to blue. Tap it again to remove the bookmark. Alternatively, you can tap the upper-right corner of the screen to place a bookmark or tap the bookmark to remove it.

For magazines, comics, catalogs, scrapbooks, and newspapers, to add a bookmark on the page you're reading, tap the reading screen and then tap the + icon in the top-right or top-left corner (see Figure 4.8). It folds down. (Think of flipping the corner of a page in a book.) Tap it again to remove the bookmark.

To return to a bookmark, from the Reading Tools toolbar, tap Content and then tap Bookmarks. A list of pages containing bookmarks appears (see Figure 4.9). Tap the bookmark you want to go to; your NOOK immediately takes you to that page.

To remove a bookmark, tap Clear All to remove all bookmarks in that ebook, magazine, or newspaper. If you are on that particular page, you can also tap the bookmark to remove it.

— Tap to add bookmark.

FIGURE 4.8   Bookmarks in newspapers.

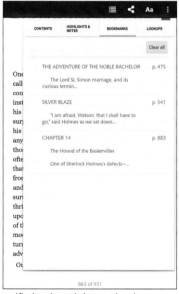

FIGURE 4.9   Jump to a specific bookmark in an ebook.

PagePerfect Books

PagePerfect books function identically to regular ebooks. You can select text and receive the same Text Selection options. To make selecting text easier, double-tap to zoom into the section you want, and then press and select the text.

CHAPTER 5

Reading and Using NOOK Books for Kids Features

The NOOK has several features geared specifically to kids, and the device takes full advantage of the landscape reading mode and touch technology to offer an immersive and entertaining experience for kids.

Some kids' books have prerecorded readings (those labeled Read to Me), and others have interactive features (those labeled Read and Play). The NOOK also has a microphone that enables you to record your own reading of the story.

Reading NOOK Books for Kids on Your NOOK

One of the exciting things about the NOOK is the NOOK Books for Kids; many of them (and growing) feature Read to Me or Read and Play. In addition, the NOOK enables you to record your own reading of children's books; a feature called Read and Record for NOOK Books for Kids. When you shop for NOOK Books for kids, you see four formats for children's books:

▶ **NOOK Kids™ Read to Me**: The books have the enhanced Read to Me experience.

▶ **NOOK Kids (eBook)**: The regular NOOK Kids book lacks the Read to Me or Read and Play features; although, it functions in every other way as a NOOK Book for Kids. If you have a NOOK, you can use the Read and Record feature.

▶ **NOOK Kids Read and Play**: These books feature not only the Read to Me feature but also interactive activities. (For example, the narrator asks the child to tap the pig that is running; the child does so, and the running pig, well, runs.) These books have the most options of all the NOOK Books for Kids.

▶ **NOOK Kids Interactive**: These are Read and Play books but with a different designation.

NOOK Books for Kids function differently than other content you read (or listen to) on the NOOK. The books open in landscape mode. The first page you are presented with has at least Read by Myself buttons, although it can also have a Read to Me or Read and Play buttons (see Figure 5.1). In addition, it has the Read and Record button.

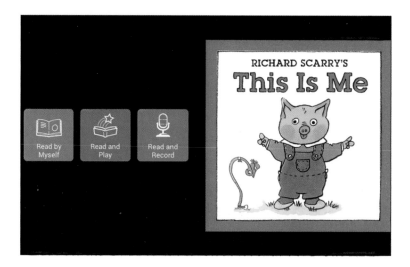

FIGURE 5.1   Tap Read and Play to have your NOOK read to you.

Read to Me and Read and Play open the next page of the book, and you hear a voice reading the title (and not a mechanical voice). Each time you swipe to the next page, the voice reads the text on that page.

Read by Myself opens the next page of the book, but no voice begins reading. Instead, you can choose to have segments of the text read to you while you're reading if you want.

If you have already made a Read and Record book, you can tap the recording you want to listen to. (You can have more than one.) The book functions like a Read and Play or Read to Me book.

Picking any of the choices does not limit you to that choice again when you next open the book or return to the cover page. Also, Read and Play books do not have a specific choice to activate that option. When you open the book in either Read to Me or Read by Myself mode, the Read and Play activities are available.

NOOK Books for Kids features a Thumbnail view much like magazines (see Figure 5.2). Tap the upward pointing arrow to display the thumbnails. You can then scroll through these and tap the thumbnail you want to advance directly to that page. If you chose Read to Me, after that page opens, the reading begins. Tap the page to hide the thumbnails.

FIGURE 5.2 NOOK Book for Kids' Thumbnail view.

If you double-tap a block of text, the text displays in a whitish balloon for easier reading (see Figure 5.3). In addition, you see a right-pointing red arrow. Tapping that arrow reads to you that particular bit of text in that balloon. This works whether you chose Read to Me or Read by Myself earlier and does not alter what happens on the next page. In other words, if you chose Read by Myself, choosing to have a balloon of text read to you does not then activate Read to Me for the rest of the NOOK Book for Kids.

If you are reading a Read and Play NOOK Book, tap the Star button at the top of the page to begin the activities for that page. Just follow the instructions.

Tapping the Home button takes you back to the Home screen.

NOTE: NOOK Books for Kids are only available to read on the Samsung Galaxy Tab 4 NOOK, NOOK HD, NOOK HD+, NOOK Tablet, NOOK Color, or NOOK Kids for iPad™ app.

FIGURE 5.3   Reading only a specific bit of text.

Using Read and Record

When you tap the Read and Record button, the book advances to the title page with the controls onscreen, as shown in Figure 5.4. You can record page by page, and don't worry about keeping up; the NOOK has made it easy to record that page.

FIGURE 5.4   The Record button.

NOTE: All NOOK Books for Kids have the option to Read and Record.

Follow these instructions to record your narration:

1. Tap Record.

NOTE: If you don't like the location of the controls, press and hold the Move button, and drag the Record button out of your way.

2. Read the text.

3. Tap Stop. The options in Figure 5.5 appear.

FIGURE 5.5 The options after you have recorded.

4. Tap Play to hear the recording.

5. If you are unhappy with the recording, tap Re-Record and repeat the process. If you are happy with the recording for that page, swipe advance to the next page, and repeat the process. Do not press Done until you are completely done recording for that book.

> NOTE: You do not need to record the entire narration in one sitting. You can save the recording (described in the following text) and return to continue the recording later.

6. When you finish recording for the book, tap Done.

7. Choose a picture to associate with that recording (see Figure 5.6).

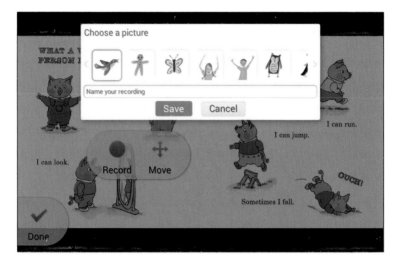

FIGURE 5.6   Choose the image you want to associate with this recording.

8. Type a name for the recording (see Figure 5.6). If you type nothing there, the default recording name is My Recording.

9. Tap Save.

Now when you open a NOOK Book for Kids, your recording appears as an option (refer to Figure 5.1). Just tap the icon for your recording rather than the Read to Me or Read and Play buttons. The NOOK Book for Kids functions identically as it did without your recording, with the added bonus that it is your recording.

If you need to edit an existing recording, tap Edit and then tap the Edit button on the icon of the particular recording you want to modify to see your editing options (see Figure 5.7). If you choose Edit Recording, you perform the same steps as previously described (rerecording or recording for the first time). You can also change the name and picture associated with that recording or delete it outright. Tap Done to save your changes.

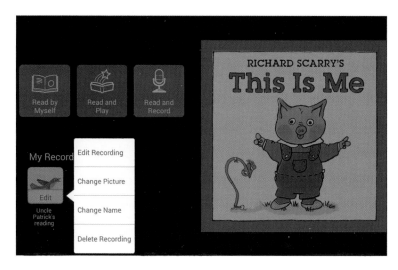

FIGURE 5.7   You can edit your recording.

CHAPTER 6

Lending and Borrowing Books with LendMe on Your Samsung Galaxy Tab 4 NOOK

To keep readers from sharing ebooks with all their friends, publishers usually protect ebooks with digital rights management (DRM), which ties an ebook to an individual, and unless that individual can prove that he is an authorized reader, the ebook will not open.

DRM is one of the reasons some people don't like ebooks. After all, when readers find a good read, they like to pass it on to friends and family. The number of people with whom you can share a physical book is fairly limited, but because ebooks are digital copies of a book, they can be shared with millions of people quite easily via email, Facebook, and any number of other methods.

One of the unique features that B&N added to your NOOK is the ability to lend some NOOK Books to other readers using the LendMe feature. Although there are some restrictions when lending and borrowing books, the LendMe feature is a step in the right direction.

> TIP: If you receive a LendMe offer, the LendMe logo appears in the notification area of the NOOK. You can tap the logo and then tap the You Have a New LendMe Item link. From here, you can cancel the item (that is, make a decision later), decline the offer, or accept the offer.

Lending Books with LendMe

To lend a book to someone, the book must support LendMe. Not all books do. If a book does support lending, you see the LendMe logo on the book's page in My

NOOK Library on bn.com, as shown in Figure 6.1. You also see the LendMe logo banner on the top-right corner of the cover on the NOOK.

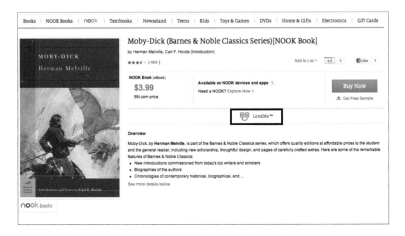

FIGURE 6.1   The LendMe logo appears on a book's page at bn.com if the book is lendable.

The NOOK has many methods for lending books to your friends.

Lending from Your Library

If you are at the Home screen or in your library:

1. Press and hold the cover, and then tap View Details. The details screen appears.

2. Tap LendMe. The LendMe screen appears.

3. Tap With Contacts to see the Lend to a Contact screen (see Figure 6.2).

4. Type a message to send with the lend invitation.

5. Tap Post.

Your NOOK sends the offer and lets you know when it is successfully sent. The cover banner LendMe changes to Lent.

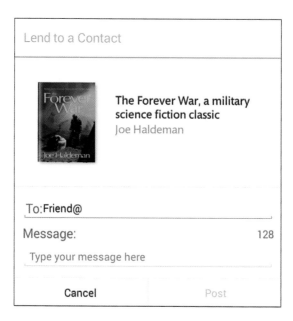

FIGURE 6.2   Enter a friend's email address.

Rules for Lending

Choose carefully when lending a book because after you lend a NOOK Book, you
can never lend that particular NOOK Book to anyone again. However, a NOOK Book
is considered to be on loan only if your friend accepts the LendMe offer. If your
friend rejects the offer or if she allows the offer to expire without accepting it, you
can lend the NOOK Book again after it's returned to your library.

**I Want to Lend a NOOK Book to One of My Friends. Does My Friend Have
to Own a NOOK for Me to Lend Her a NOOK Book?**

No. Your friend can read a NOOK Book you've lent to her using the NOOK Apps,
NOOK Color, NOOK Simple Touch, or original NOOK. However, your friend cannot
read the book unless the email address you used to send the LendMe offer is
associated with her B&N account.

The person to whom you've loaned the NOOK Book has 7 days to accept the loan
offer. If she doesn't accept within 7 days, the book is returned to your library. The
loan offer can also be rejected, in which case the book is returned to your library
immediately.

A NOOK Book is loaned for 14 days, and while it is on loan, Lent appears on the cover, and you cannot read the book. When you loan a book, you also loan your DRM rights to the book. Only one person can possess the DRM rights to a book at any one time, so you need to wait until the book is returned to your library before you can read the book again.

> CAUTION: You cannot cancel a LendMe offer.

Borrowing Books

When a friend lends you a book, you receive a notification of the offer (see Figure 6.3). You have 7 days to either accept the offer or reject it. You can accept or reject the loan offer from your NOOK device or any of the NOOK Apps.

FIGURE 6.3   Versions of the LendMe offers on different NOOK devices: NOOK for Mac™ app, My NOOK Library, Samsung Galaxy Tab 4 NOOK, and NOOK Simple Touch.

If you accept a loan offer from your NOOK, that book is also available for the loan period in NOOK Apps or NOOK device, and vice versa.

CHAPTER 7

Playing Music, Audiobooks, and Podcasts

For those of you who love to read, almost nothing stirs up as much nostalgia as the thought of listening to some nice music while reading a good book and maybe sipping a nice glass of wine. Your NOOK can't make wine, but it can provide the other two ingredients to this nostalgic scene.

NOTE: You can also listen to music via the online music service, Rhapsody. To learn more about using Rhapsody, **see** Chapter 9, "Using NOOK Apps and Surfing the Web."

Adding Files to Your NOOK

If you buy music from the Google Play store, you will see it here. **See** Chapter 13, "Using the Google Play Store and Google Apps," for more about the Google Play store.

The Music folder on your NOOK is used specifically for audio files (whether on the NOOK or on the microSD card). When you add audio files to this folder, your NOOK recognizes the files and enables you to play the audio using its built-in audio player.

NOTE: Your NOOK supports the following audio file types: MP4, MP3, M4A, AAC, WAV, FLAC, OGG, 3GP, and AMR. The best options are MP3 and AAC given their ubiquitous presence.

You have several options for getting files onto your NOOK (and this applies to music, book, photos, and so on). One way is to upload items to Dropbox, find those items in Dropbox, and export to your NOOK. Samsung also offers its own software called Kies, which you can find here at http://www.samsung.com/in/support/usefulsoftware/KIES/. Full discussion of this software is out of scope of this book, but you can use it to place music, photos, or video onto your NOOK. However, you *cannot* use Kies to place books from non-BN sources onto your NOOK to read in the NOOK Reader app.

The easiest way to transfer files, in my opinion, is to use Bluetooth. Pair your Bluetooth-enabled computer to your NOOK. Then use the Send File to the Device to send the file to your NOOK. You can then use the My Files app to move the files to where you want.

> TIP: If you haven't done so already, first load your music into a music player on your desktop or laptop (iTunes, Media Player, and so on). Doing so enables you to set the album and artist name, and so on, which affects how easy it is to navigate your music in the Music Player on your NOOK.

Using Google's Play Music App

The Google Play Music app on your NOOK is a basic music player for playing music and for listening to audiobooks and podcasts.

To launch the music player, from the Home screen, tap Google, and then tap Play Music. The music player opens with several ways to browse your music. Tap My Library to see the screen in Figure 7.1.

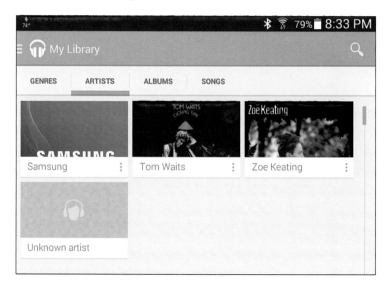

FIGURE 7.1   Browsing albums in the Music Player.

The following browser options are available:

- **Genres**: Displays your music according to genre. Tap a genre to see the songs associated with it. Tap a song to play it.

- **Artists**: Displays your music according to artist. Tapping the artist name shows the albums associated with that artist. Tapping the album takes you to a song list of tracks in that album. Tap a track to begin playing.

- **Albums**: Displays your music by albums in alphabetical order (by the name of the album). You can scroll through this list. Tapping the album takes you to a song list of tracks in that album. Tap a track to begin playing.

- **Songs**: Displays your music in alphabetical order (by the name of the song). You can scroll through this list. If you scroll to the top and try to scroll beyond, a small, blue icon appears with up and down arrows. If you press and hold that, you can drag between the songs faster, jumping from A to B to Z (based on the song title) faster. Tap a song to play it.

If you have playlists, tap Google Play Music in the top left and tap Playlists from the menu.

Tap the three dots to see particular options for that view. For example, if you are viewing by Album and tap the three dots, you will see the following options (see Figure 7.2):

- **Start Instant Mix**: Tapping this starts an Instant Mix, which means that Google Play Music will play a mix of music based on the artist or song.

- **Shuffle**: Tapping Shuffle starts playing the album on shuffle.

- **Play Next**: Tapping Play Next makes this album next up to be played, overriding any options you make in the queue.

- **Add to Queue**: Tapping Add to Queue adds an album or song to the end of the current playback queue—basically, you can set up what you want to hear next.

- **Add to Playlist**: Tapping Add to Playlist displays the Add to Playlist popup. You can tap an existing playlist to add that album to that list or tap New Playlist to create a new playlist. Type in the playlist name and tap Save.

- **Go to Artist**: Tapping Go to Artist pulls up all music on your device by the same artist.

▶ **Shop This Artist**: Tapping Shop for Artist opens the Google Play store, where you can buy more music if you'd like. **See** Chapter 13 for more information.

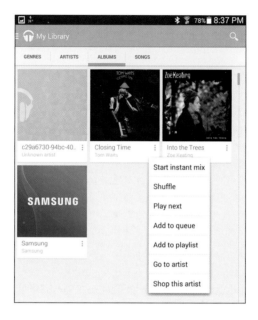

FIGURE 7.2   Your options when pressing an album in the list.

If you are looking at songs, you have an option to tap Delete to delete the song from your NOOK. If you purchased it from Google Play, you are deleting *only* the song from the device, not the Google cloud.

To search your music, tap the magnifying glass in the top right and begin typing. Album, artist, and other results appear.

When you tap a song or album to play, the screen changes to the player. The initial view is a list of all the tracks in that album. If you tap the album cover at the bottom of the screen, you get your typical music player controls (see Figure 7.3):

▶ **Location in Track**: Informational items only. The time listed on the left shows the time location within the track.

▶ **Play/Pause**: If the Music Player is playing audio, tapping this button pauses the audio. Otherwise, it resumes playing the audio.

▶ **Previous/Next Track**: Tapping this button takes you either to the previous or next track.

FIGURE 7.3   Now Playing view in the Play Music app.

▶ **Scrubber**: The scrubber enables you to change the position in the current audio file quickly. Drag your finger on the scrubber to change the position. When you lift your finger from the touchscreen, the track plays from that location.

▶ **Shuffle**: Toggles shuffle mode on or off. Each time shuffle is toggled on, a new random order is created for the currently playing tracks.

▶ **Repeat**: Tapping once repeats that playlist, album, or set of songs you see in the player. Tap Repeat again. A 1 appears. This song is now set to repeat until you turn off repeat by tapping the Repeat button again.

▶ **Back**: Tapping this takes you back to browsing your music. However, you see the currently playing track displayed at the bottom. Tap the play button to go back to the player.

If at the top you tap the three lines next to the music symbol, you see a list of all the tracks. If you press and hold a track, you can drag the track to a different location. Tap the three lines next to the music symbol to go back to the full album image view.

While playing audio, exit the Play Music app by pressing the Home button. Your audio continues playing, but you can interact with other items on your NOOK. To stop the audio from playing, you can navigate back by starting the Play Music app in Apps or tapping the music controls in the Notification pane. You'll see an item there describing the current album playing (see Figure 7.4). Tap the album cover to go back to the Play Music app. You can also pause and play music directly from the Notification pane.

FIGURE 7.4   You can control the music player from the Notification pane.

Playing Podcasts and Audiobooks on Your NOOK

In addition to listening to music, you can also use the audio player on your NOOK to play podcasts and audiobooks.

Podcasts

Podcasts are audio programs released on a regular schedule. You can subscribe to a podcast using any number of software applications, and when a new episode is released, it's automatically downloaded to your computer.

Podcasts are available that cover just about every topic of interest that you can think of. For example, podcasts can help you use your computer or help you take better pictures. Some podcasts deliver the news daily or weekly, and some podcasts cover entertainment gossip. Other podcasts enable you to listen to your favorite radio shows on demand whenever you want.

If you own an iPhone, iPad, or iPod, you almost certainly already have iTunes on your computer. iTunes lets you easily subscribe to podcasts. You can search or browse for podcasts in the iTunes store. If you don't already have an application that you can use to subscribe to podcasts, you can download Juice, a free podcast receiver that makes finding and subscribing to podcasts easy. Juice is available from http://juicereceiver.sourceforge.net.

When you subscribe to a podcast, each time you launch your podcast application (whether that's iTunes, OneCast, Juice, or some other application), it checks for new episodes. If it finds a new episode, it downloads it automatically to your computer. You can then copy that episode to your NOOK. You need to check the documentation and options for the software you use to determine where it stores podcasts it downloads.

TIP: Be sure that you subscribe to podcasts in a NOOK-compatible format. (Most podcasts are in MP3 format.) Some podcasts offer an MP3 version and versions in other formats.

Podcasts should be copied to the Music folder on your NOOK. The podcast will be available when you start the Music Player on your NOOK.

However, you can also download a podcast playing app from the Google Play Store. **See** Chapter 13 for more about using Google Play Store.

Audiobooks

Audiobooks are recordings of someone reading a book out loud. They are the digital version of books on tape. The most popular source of audiobooks is Audible.com, and you can install that app from the Google Play Store. However, you can enjoy other sources of MP3 audiobooks on your NOOK.

Following are sources of MP3 audiobooks you can use on your NOOK:

- ▶ **Audiobooks.org**: Free audiobook versions of some classic books. There aren't many books here, but the ones it offers are of good quality.

▶ **Podiobooks.com**: Free serialized audiobooks. This site is run by volunteers and features a large number of indie authors. Podiobooks are free to listen to; though you can donate to an individual audiobook and 75% of that donation goes to the author or creator. You can download episodes via iTunes and move them to your NOOK.

▶ **Simply Audiobooks (www.simplyaudiobooks.com/downloads)**: For a few dollars per month, you can download as many audiobooks as you want. Simply Audiobooks offers both MP3 and WMA audiobooks, so be sure you choose the MP3 versions for your NOOK.

▶ **B&N Audiobooks (www.barnesandnoble.com/subjects/audio)**: B&N offers a wide assortment of audiobooks. If you're a B&N member, you can get some great deals for your NOOK.

▶ **Google Product Search**: Google Product Search (www.google.com/prdhp) is an excellent way to locate MP3 audiobooks. Simply search for **mp3 audiobook**, and you can find a vast assortment from many merchants.

After you download an audiobook, copy it to the Music folder on your NOOK. You can then play it by selecting the file from the Play music app.

TIP: You can listen to most MP3 tracks on your music player. Check out the Teaching Company's (www.teach12.com) courses, many of which are available as audio downloads. As noted, always choose files that are compatible with your NOOK or even use The Great Courses app for listening or watching its courses.

CHAPTER 8

Watching Videos on Your Samsung Galaxy Tab 4 NOOK

Just as ebooks are changing the way you interact with books, streaming video is changing the way you consume TV shows and movies. Your NOOK offers you multiple ways to view video content.

B&N Video Content

B&N offers movies and TV shows via the NOOK Store. You can buy videos in either Standard Definition (SD) or High Definition (HD). Usually, SD is cheaper. Many movies are also available as rentals, which means when you buy the rental, you have up to 30 days to begin watching it and, after you have begun watching it, you have 24 hours to finish watching the video. You can watch it as many times as you want within that 24-hour period. When either time period ends, the video is removed from your NOOK.

Regardless whether you rent or buy a video, the functionality works the same. To access your videos, from the Home screen, tap Library and then tap Movies & TV (see Figure 8.1). If the video has not been downloaded to your NOOK, you see the typical download option. In addition, if the movie is a rental, you see the number of days left you have to start watching the video. Alternatively, if you have begun watching the rental, you see the amount of time left in the 24-hour period.

Tap the cover image to open the Details screen for the movie or TV show (see Figure 8.2). For movies, if you have not downloaded the video, you have two options: Stream and Download. If you have downloaded the video, you have the single option, Watch. For a TV show, the screen is a tad different, though largely the same function. At the top, if you haven't purchased the entire season, you can tap the drop-down to buy either the HD or SD. Scroll down the screen, and you see individual episodes. For episodes you have purchased, you can tap Stream or Download. Just like with movies, if you have already downloaded the episode, you have the single Watch option. In addition, you can buy individual episodes here if you have not bought them already. Tap Show Details to get information about an individual episode.

NOTE: If you move a video to the archive by tapping Remove from Device, the video is removed from the NOOK, and the options when you tap Details become Stream and Download.

FIGURE 8.1   Your videos in the library.

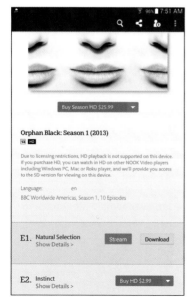

FIGURE 8.2   A TV show's Details screen.

If you have an active Wi-Fi connection and don't want to download a video to your NOOK, tap Stream to start watching (see Figure 8.3). Tap Download if you want to download the video to your NOOK. When the video is downloaded, tap Watch to begin watching the video. If you stop watching a video and come back to it later, the NOOK offers to let you resume playing from where you stopped or to start over.

The video player controls are standard controls: pause, play, fast forward, rewind, and volume control. To see the controls (if you do not see them), tap the screen. To hide the controls (if you do see them), tap the screen. At the bottom left of the screen, you see an i in a circle. Tap this and you are taken back to the Details screen for that video. Similarly, if you tap Close in the upper right, you are taken back to the Details screen.

FIGURE 8.3   Watching a NOOK Video.

Netflix Versus Hulu Plus

Netflix and Hulu Plus are two of the most popular streaming video services available, but how do they compare? What are the differences? First and foremost, neither Netflix nor Hulu Plus have all the movies and TV shows you may want to watch via streaming, so you are likely to want to watch a show that is not available. Still, both have impressive libraries.

Both Netflix and Hulu Plus cost $7.99 per month to access their content; although, Hulu does offer free content in the form of clips or a few episodes of a show (typically the three to five most recent). Those subscriptions enable you to watch unlimited video on your NOOK, iPhone, iPad, Android tablets, and any Hulu Plus or Netflix-enabled device (for example, TiVos, many Blu-ray players, Xbox, Roku boxes, and Internet-ready TVs).

> NOTE: Some content may be prevented from appearing on mobile devices because of rights-related issues—that is, the broadcaster or distributor may not allow it.

The main difference between the two is that Hulu Plus is devoted to TV shows and Netflix is devoted to both TVs and movies. Netflix has a substantially higher quantity of movies than Hulu Plus, whereas Hulu Plus has many TV shows available a few days after their original broadcast. (You'll have to wait months or more for Netflix to make TV shows available.)

One other difference is that Netflix is ad-free, whereas Hulu Plus videos start with an ad and have ads interspersed throughout the video.

Both services stream video to your device at the highest quality possible, although Hulu Plus lets you designate a lower level if you want when you start the video. What this means is that the Netflix and Hulu Plus apps "sense" how fast your network connection is operating while it plays the video. If the network is heavily used and going a bit slowly, the quality of the video will be adjusted downward to keep the video running. So, seeing fluctuations in the quality of the video as it's playing is not unusual. In general, the quality of both is excellent.

If you are debating between the two, try the free trials to see what you think. Browse around a bit to see what's available and what matches most with your interests.

Streaming Netflix and Hulu Plus Videos to Your NOOK

Both the Netflix and Hulu Plus apps start out almost the same. You need to sign in with a username and password. If you don't have one, you can request one from the Start screen. If this is the first time using Netflix or Hulu Plus, you can sign up for a free trial. With Netflix, the opening screen provides a link to Netflix.com to sign up for an account. The Hulu Plus app enables you to set up an account within the app. After you enter your username and password, the two apps—while offering streaming content—do operate differently, so now take a look at each.

NOTE: To use Netflix on your NOOK, you need to install the Netflix app from BN.com.

Using Netflix

Using the Netflix app is a straightforward thing. When you sign in, you see a screen divided into rows a bit like the NOOK Library shelves (see Figure 8.4). If you have started watching any video, it appears near the top under Continue Watching. Just tap the play arrow to start watching where you left off. The video player has the standard pause, play, fast forward, and rewind options. In the top right of the player, you may see a little talk bubble. Tap it to get options for subtitles and language options (if available). Tap the return arrow next to the title of movie or TV series to go back to the main Netflix app.

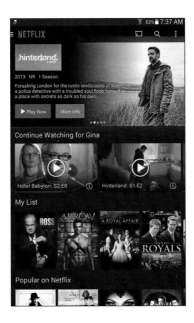

FIGURE 8.4   The opening Netflix screen after you sign in.

If you tap a cover without the play button or the i button, you see an informational screen (see Figure 8.5). Here, you can tap a star rating on how much you liked (or didn't like) the video. You can tap to +My List or –My List to do just that. Finally, you can also choose a season (if a TV series) and a specific episode to play.

FIGURE 8.5   View a TV show's details.

> NOTE: My List is a place for you to place videos that you want to watch later, sort of a wishlist for videos.

Netflix likes to recommend videos based on what you've liked or disliked in the past and shows you these recommendations in the Top 10 list. Tapping a title brings up a screen that lets you add the series or movie to your My List. You can also tap the red play button in that screen to start playing the show or movie.

The My List shelf consists of shows or movies that you have added to that queue. Swipe left and right to view it. Tap the title to see the now familiar informational screen.

The shelves below the My List offer a variety based on subjects or themes (for example, Mysteries, Dark Science Fiction, and Crime TV Dramas). You can scroll through them to see if there's anything of interest.

Alternatively, you can tap Search in the upper right and search for a specific title, series, actor, or director. What is found displays below the Search box. Tap the item to see more information, add to the queue, and so on.

Finally, you can browse by tapping Browse in the upper left. Tap the category that interests you. (Home always takes you to the initial Netflix screen after you have signed in.) You are presented with a series of shelves, further categorized to browse.

Using Hulu Plus

After you sign into Hulu Plus, your opening screen presents you with many options (see Figure 8.6). The top presents some featured content and just below that any trending videos are available. After that a number of categories of video are available that provide you quick access to videos.

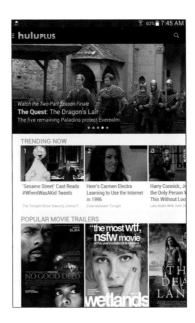

FIGURE 8.6   Hulu Plus's opening screen.

Tap the Hulu Plus logo to see a series of options for browsing content. Tap Queue to go to your queue. Tap TV or any of its divisions (Popular, Recently Added, and so on) to browse TV. The same applies with the other topics in this list. You can tap Search, which opens a search screen.

In addition, you see lots of featured clips and shows, recommendations, and other lists.

Hulu Plus TV and Movies Screens

Tapping any of these options on the startup screen takes you to a common interface used for both the TV and movies screens. However, if you tap TV, you land on the TV tab. Tap Movies, and you land on the Movies tab, and so on. TV shows, movies, and trailers screens are divided up into even more categories. Eventually, you get down to actual shows or movies (refer to Figure 8.6). Tap Details if you want to get more information about the show in general. You can also add or remove the show as a favorite there.

For TV shows, you can see individual episodes, clips, and similar shows. If you tap an individual show, you see a screen like that in Figure 8.7. You can add this to your queue (**see** the later section, "Hulu Plus Queue" for more information), play the video, and even share it with friends. When you play a video, you have the standard video player controls. Movies lack the Favorites feature that TV shows have.

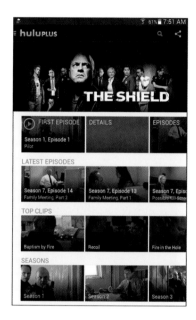

FIGURE 8.7   An individual episode's screen.

Hulu Plus Queue

Tap Queue and you are taken to the Queue screen (see Figure 8.8). These are the items that you have added to your Queue, so you can minimize searching and save them for later. You can view this by the order you have placed them in the queue (tap By Show and then tap By Position) or By Show (tap By Position and then tap By Show). In addition, you can view all videos as individual episodes or show grouped together by show.

Tap the episode cover and then tap Play Video to watch the video.

FIGURE 8.8   The Queue screen.

Watching Hulu Plus Videos

When you play a Hulu Plus video, an ad plays (and others play occasionally during the video). You may be asked to pick a quality level; if so, choose whichever quality level you want. After the video begins playing, you can tap the Back button to go back to the Hulu Plus app location you were just at. Tap More to learn more about the product advertised. From there, the video controls are the familiar controls.

CHAPTER 9

Using NOOK Apps and Surfing the Web

The NOOK includes the Chrome web browser and several pre-installed NOOK Apps as well as any NOOK Apps you've purchased from the B&N store, which include the music player you learned about in Chapter 7, "Playing Music, Audiobooks, and Podcasts," the Hulu Plus app you learned about in Chapter 8, "Watching Videos on Your Samsung Galaxy Tab 4 NOOK," and more.

Using NOOK Search

If you have an iPhone, iPad, or Android phone, you are familiar with these download-able programs you can add to those devices. NOOK Apps come in two forms: apps such as NOOK Shop, NOOK Search, and so on that are part of the NOOK and apps you purchased from B&N.

For the most part, the rest of Part I, "Samsung Galaxy Tab 4 NOOK," covers the use of NOOK Settings, NOOK Shop, NOOK Today, NOOK Highlights and Notes, NOOK Library, and NOOK Reader. One additional app is the NOOK Search app. When you open this, you see the screen shown in Figure 9.1. Here you can see *all* searches you have conducted in any NOOK App. You can tap on it to see results or enter a new search, which returns results (see Figure 9.2).

From the results, you can purchase content, redownload content, or even open it and start reading. The real power of this feature is that is gives you a central search loca-tion for all B&N content; thus, you don't have to open a particular app for a search.

FIGURE 9.1   The NOOK Search app.

FIGURE 9.2   Search results.

Using NOOK B&N Apps

If you purchased apps from B&N, you can access those apps with the NOOK Apps app (see Figure 9.3).

FIGURE 9.3   NOOK Apps purchased directly from B&N.

You can install them by tapping them. You can use them just like any other app. Even wallpapers become an option when you change wallpapers (**see** Chapter 2, "Customizing and Configuring Your Samsung Galaxy Tab 4 NOOK"). If you tap Options, you'll have features for sorting and viewing like you do for other NOOK Apps. Tap Check for Updates to see if any apps have updates.

If you purchase more apps from B&N, they will end up here as well.

Browsing the Web with Your NOOK

The NOOK comes with a full-featured web browser called Chrome (see Figure 9.4). This browser, like many mobile-based browsers, does not support Flash content.

> NOTE: To access web pages, you must be connected to a Wi-Fi hotspot.

FIGURE 9.4   The NOOK's web browser.

An Overview of Browsing on Your NOOK

Browsing the web on your NOOK is easy. From the Home screen, tap Web to open the browser. The browser opens to the homepage or last page you were on.

At the top, you see a typical-looking web browser interface:

- ▶ **Back button**: Tap to go back to the previous web page.

- ▶ **Forward button**: Tap to go to the web page you were on prior to clicking the Back button.

- ▶ **Stop button/Refresh page**: Tap the X button to stop the current page loading. When the page is loaded, it changes to a circular arrow. Tap that to refresh the page.

- ▶ **Address bar**: Tap to enter a new web address or search the web. Tapping gives you the keyboard, and you can either enter a specific web address, or you can type a search term. As you type, a series of tappable links appears below the bar. This displays previously searched terms and websites. You can continue typing and tap Enter, which performs a Google search.

▶ **Make Bookmark button (star)**: Tap to make a bookmark to this page. A screen appears that lets you name the bookmark as you want and pick a location for the bookmarks. Tap Save when you are ready to save the bookmark.

▶ **Talk**: Tap activate the voice recognition software and say a Google search or website address you want to go to.

▶ **Options (three squares)**: Tap to see more options:

  ▶ **New Tab**: Tap to open another tab.

TIP: To open a new tab, you can also tap the small rectangle to the right of the last tab.

  ▶ **New Incognito Tab**: Tap to open what Google calls an incognito tab—basically, a tab that does not store any information on the NOOK or in the cloud about where you have been. This gives you privacy while surfing the web. Note that if you go to websites that require a username and password, you have to enter them every time in an incognito tab.

  ▶ **Bookmarks**: Tap to access bookmarks and most visited sites. For more information about the Bookmarks options, **see** "Using the Bookmarks Screen."

  ▶ **Recent Tabs**: Tap to see a list of the most recent tabs you have opened. If you have used Chrome on other browsers using your Google account, you will see tabs you have opened there as well. You can tap any of them to open that website.

  ▶ **History**: Tap to see a history of websites you have visited. Tap a site to return to it. If you want to clear your browser's history, tap Clear Browsing Data at the bottom of the screen. The Clear Browsing Data dialog appears. Tap the items you want to clear and tap Clear.

  ▶ **Share**: Tap to share the website via email or other apps (for example, Twitter, Google+, Evernote, and so on).

  ▶ **Print**: Tap to print the website to any Wi-Fi connected printers or as a PDF.

  ▶ **Find in Page**: Tap to search for text on the visible page.

▶ **Add to Homescreen**: Tap to add the website to the Home screen, allowing you to quickly access the site without opening Chrome first.

▶ **Request Desktop Site**: This appears if the website has a special mobile site. Tap Request Desktop Site to load the desktop version of the site.

▶ **Settings**: Tap to access Chrome's settings.

▶ **Help**: Tap to load Google's Chrome for Mobile web page.

> NOTE: You can view web pages in either portrait or landscape mode.

When you are at a web page, zoom in and out. If you have zoomed in, you can press and hold and then drag to maneuver the page. If you have zoomed in on a page, to zoom back out, tap twice on an area of the screen.

> NOTE: To use a lot of the functions in the web browser, you must wait for the page to load completely.

Tap a link to go to that link if it is a regular hyperlink (for example, going to another web page). Some links download items to your NOOK. For example, if you press and hold on an image, you can get a menu to save or view the image (see Figure 9.5). However, if you are at Project Gutenberg, go to the download section for a specific book, and tap the EPUB link; the file downloads to your NOOK and opens in the chosen application—choose Chrome (see Figure 9.6). These downloads go to the My Files\Downloads folder.

If you press and hold a hyperlink (see Figure 9.7), a menu appears with these options:

▶ **Open**: Opens the link. This is the same as tapping the link.

▶ **Open in New Tab**: Opens the link in a new tab, thus leaving your existing tab in place.

▶ **Save Link**: Adds a bookmark to the link you are pressing.

▶ **Copy Link URL**: Copies the link to the Clipboard.

▶ **Select Text**: Selects the hypertext's text.

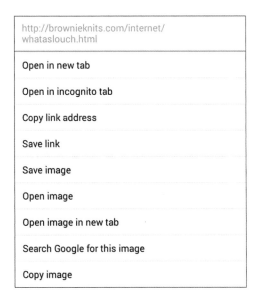

FIGURE 9.5   Some links offer you an opportunity to save or view the file.

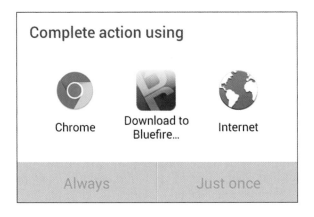

FIGURE 9.6   Some links download the file to your NOOK.

NOTE: In the browser, copying text or links is allowed in a couple places. However, I have yet to find a place where I can paste the said text.

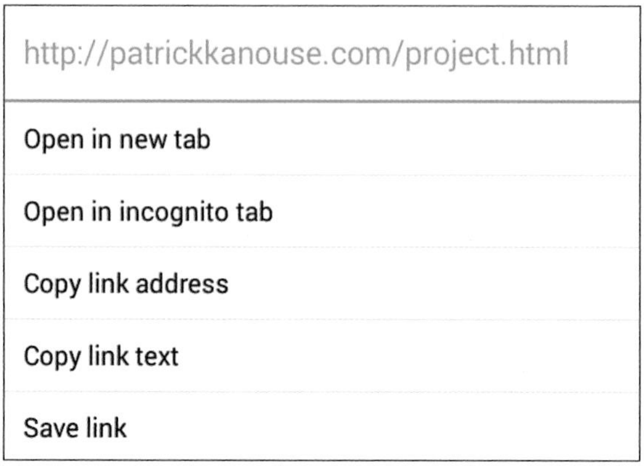
http://patrickkanouse.com/project.html
Open in new tab
Open in incognito tab
Copy link address
Copy link text
Save link

FIGURE 9.7 Your options after you press and hold a hyperlink.

If you press and hold in a nonlink area of the web page, the text you select appears similar to an ebook, and a series of options appears at the top of the screen (see Figure 9.8):

2:06 PM
DONE
SELECT ALL
COPY
SHARE
WEB SEARCH
patrickkanouse.com/work.html
THE SHATTERED BULL
patrick kanouse
Poetry.
Gary Weir In Nuvo
JL Kato On IndyBookings

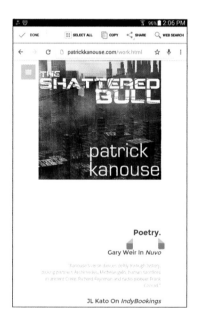

FIGURE 9.8 Your options after you press and hold a nonhyperlink area on a web page.

- **Select All**: Selects all text on that web page.
- **Copy**: Copies the selected text.

▶ **Share**: Lets you share the text via email or other compatible apps.

▶ **Web Search**: Tap this to open a new tab, in which the selected text is used to perform a Google search for the selected text.

Using the Bookmarks Screen

The Bookmarks screen, shown in Figure 9.9, enables you to add bookmarks, modify existing ones, and perform other options. The screen opens with three tabs: Bookmarks, History, and Saved Pages.

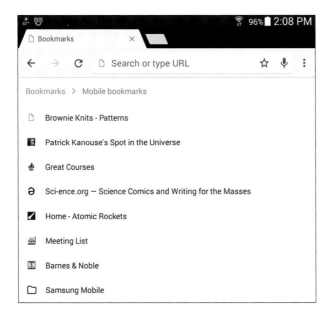

FIGURE 9.9   The Bookmarks screen.

To get to the Bookmarks screen, tap Options and then tap Bookmarks. The Bookmarks screen opens. The bookmarks are generic thumbnails of the web pages with the title of the website.

The other thumbnails are your bookmarks. Tap the thumbnail to open that web page. If you press and hold the thumbnail, a pop-up menu provides these options (see Figure 9.10):

▶ **Open in New tab**: Opens the link in a new tab, thus leaving your existing tab in place.

▶ **Open in Incognito tab**: Opens the link in an incognito tab.

▶ **Edit Bookmark**: Opens the Edit Bookmark window. Here you can adjust the name and location (that is, the hyperlink address) of the bookmark.

▶ **Delete Bookmark**: Deletes the Edit Bookmark window.

Open in new tab
Open in incognito tab
Edit bookmark
Delete bookmark

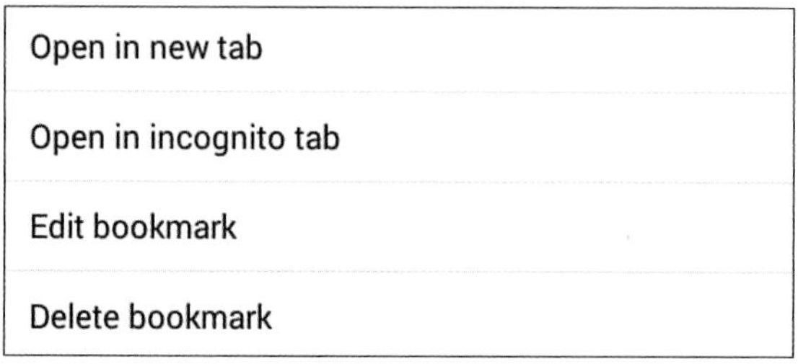

FIGURE 9.10   Additional options on the Bookmarks screen.

Using Gallery

The Gallery is a listing of all your images. You can access it by tapping Gallery from the Apps screen. You have several things you can do with your images in the Gallery (see Figure 9.11):

▶ If you tap Display, if any connected devices (other computers, Chromecast, and so on) are connected, you can "throw" the image there to display.

▶ Tap the Share button to send the image via email or to an app (including Twitter if you have it installed).

▶ Tap the Camera to open the camera app.

▶ If you are looking at images *not* on the NOOK (for example, in Dropbox), tap Download to download the image to your NOOK.

▶ If you tap Options and then tap Slideshow, the images in that folder automatically cycle through each image. Tap the screen to stop the slideshow.

▶ Tap Options and then tap Set As to set the image as wallpaper or a contact image.

▶ Tap Delete to delete the image.

▶ You can cycle through the images by swiping left or right.

FIGURE 9.11 Looking at an image.

CHAPTER 10

Creating and Using Profiles on Your Samsung Galaxy Tab 4 NOOK

With profiles, more than one person can use your NOOK and customize it for when they are using it. In addition, you can control what B&N content is available to profiles. What this all means is that you can control what content a specific profile has access to, all on the same device. This chapter explores how to make and manage profiles.

Understanding Profiles

Three types of profiles exist on the NOOK:

▶ **Primary**: This is the profile to which the NOOK is registered. This profile has access to all content and can create and modify profiles. If something is bought on this NOOK, this profile's credit card is charged.

▶ **Adult**: This profile has only slightly fewer options than the primary. It can control what content it sees, it can make purchases, and it can alter child profile settings.

▶ **Child**: This profile is more severely restricted. Unless otherwise altered, a child's profile can see only what has been assigned to that profile. A child's profile cannot override parental controls or alter or add any profiles.

Your NOOK can support a maximum of six profiles (including the primary).

Creating a Profile

Although the process for creating an Adult and a Child profile are similar, a couple of key differences exist, so let's explore creating each in turn. Regardless, they both start with creating a NOOK device profile. Then you modify that content specifically for B&N content.

Creating an Adult Profile

To create a device profile, follow these steps:

1. Tap the status bar and then tap Settings.

2. Tap General and then tap Users.

3. Tap the Add Profile button. You are presented with two options: User and Restricted Profile. The user profile is just like yours. The restricted profile allows you to control access to apps and content that are outside the B&N content (that is, Google Play Store apps and so on). To set up an adult profile, tap Users. You see a screen like that in Figure 10.1.

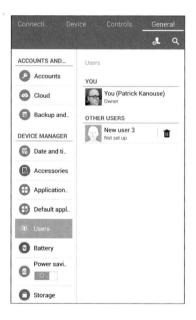

FIGURE 10.1   A new profile has been created.

4. A dialog appears asking you to set up the user now. You can tap Now and come back later and tap the image of the profile user or tap Set Up Now. When you tap Set Up Now, the screen changes to the default Lock screen with profile images in the top right (see Figure 10.2). The new one is already selected. Unlock the screen.

5. You are then taken through the set up process outlined in Chapter 1, "Getting Started with Your Samsung Galaxy Tab 4 NOOK." Tap Next to move from the Welcome screen.

FIGURE 10.2 The Lock screen with two profiles.

6. Tap that you agree to the EULA and tap Yes or No Thanks for the Diagnostic Data and then tap Next.

7. If this new profile user has a Google account, you can tap Yes and enter those Google account credentials. This means that this person's Google account is attached to this profile, doing some automated work in linking email and such when she uses the NOOK. Otherwise, tap No.

8. Tap what you want to share regarding your location on the Google and Your Location screen and tap Next.

9. Enter a name for this profile and tap Done.

10. You can then sign in to a Samsung account, create a new Samsung account, or skip it. Tap Sign In and enter the appropriate credentials. Tap Create Account and enter the required information. Or tap Skip.

11. You can then sign in to a Dropbox account, create a new Dropbox account, or skip it. Tap Sign In and enter the appropriate credentials. Tap Create Account and enter the required information. Or tap Skip.

12. Give the "device" a name so that this profile is recognizable to you and other devices. Tap Finish.

13. You then are asked to sign in to your NOOK account. Tap Sign In. The Sign In to Your NOOK Account screen appears.

14. You should use the same account you used or created in Chapter 1. In fact, you are provided the email address automatically and cannot change it. Tap Sign In. You see the Choose a Profile screen (see Figure 10.3).

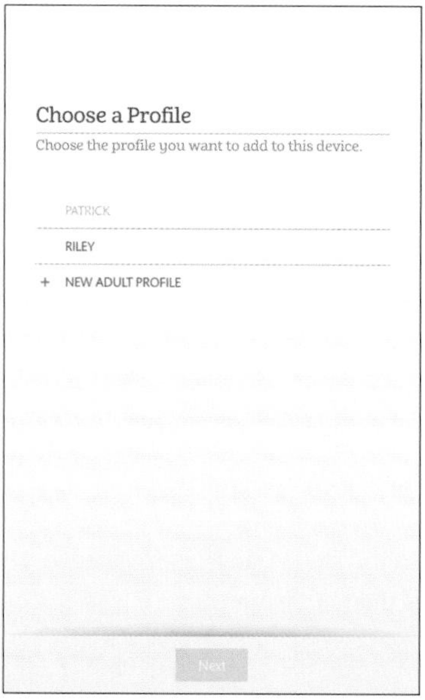

Choose a Profile

Choose the profile you want to add to this device.

PATRICK

RILEY

+ NEW ADULT PROFILE

Next

FIGURE 10.3 Choose a NOOK Profile™.

Any existing profiles appear here that have not been added to this device. You can tap the name and then tap Next.

To create a new adult profile, tap New Adult Profile and then tap Next. The screen in Figure 10.4 appears.

15. Provide a name. Also, if you want to allow this account access to all B&N content you've purchased, downloaded, and so on, then tap the check box. If you have a lot of content, you can do this and then *remove* access to specific content. If you leave this unchecked, you need to specifically add any content you want this profile to have access to. Tap Next.

See the later section "Managing Content Visible to a Profile" to determine what this profile can or cannot see.

FIGURE 10.4 Name this NOOK Profile.

Creating a Child Profile

To create a device profile for a child, follow these steps:

1. Tap the status bar and then tap Settings.

2. Tap General and then tap Users.

3. Tap the Add Profile button. You are presented with two options: User and Restricted Profile. The user profile is just like yours. The restricted profile allows you to control access to apps and content that are outside the B&N content (that is, Google Play Store apps and so on). To set up an adult profile, tap Restricted Profile. If you have not set up the primary user's Lock screen to use at least a PIN for security, you'll be prompted to do so now. After you have a PIN and have selected Restricted Profile, you see a screen like that in Figure 10.5.

4. You now have to determine what applications the restricted profile has (see Figure 10.6). In the list of applications, scroll through and mark with the check box which applications you want this profile to have. Note that you will not see the NOOK Apps listed. That's fine. You see that a bit later.

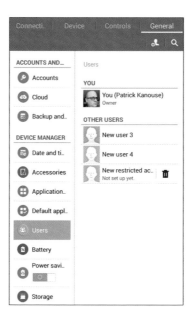

FIGURE 10.5 A new profile has been created.

FIGURE 10.6 What this profile can access on the device.

5. Go to the Lock screen now and tap the profile for the new restricted profile user.

6. Unlock the device. You see a blank screen like that in Figure 10.7.

FIGURE 10.7   The Home screen after setting up a Child device profile.

7. Tap the Continue Reading button, which starts up the NOOK sign-in process. Tap Sign In.

8. You should use the same account you used or created in Chapter 1. In fact, you are provided the email address automatically and cannot change it. Tap Sign In. You see the Choose a Profile screen. The name of the child screen appears.

9. Tap First Name and enter a name.

10. Tap Age, and enter a month and year when the child was born. B&N uses this to help define age-appropriate material. Tap Done after you enter the month and year.

11. Tap Child to indicate if this is a girl, boy, or child. Tap Next. The Parental Controls screen then appears (see Figure 10.8).

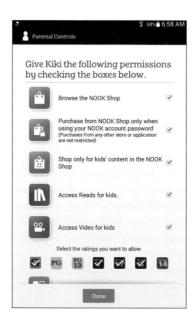

FIGURE 10.8   Setting up parental controls for the Child account.

12. On this screen, you can identify what kind of NOOK Store access they have along with if they are allowed to access NOOK Books, videos, apps, and games designated for kids by B&N. For the videos, you can set the rating level by tapping icons corresponding to G, PG, PG 13, and so on. Note that you can change these settings and allow access to specific content not included here at a later time. Tap Done.

> NOTE: On the Parental Controls screen, what you select for apps and games apply *only* to NOOK Store apps and games. This does not restrict access to the Google Play store apps and games you download. You can control that in the Settings>General>Users screen by tapping the Restricted Account (refer to Figure 10.6).

The child profile is now set up. After you complete creating a child's profile, B&N sends an email to the primary profile's email to alert him or her of its creation.

See the following section, "Managing Content Visible to a Profile," to determine what this profile can or cannot see.

Managing Content Visible to a Profile

One of the reasons to use profiles is to control the content visible to individual profiles. You have two primary ways to do this.

1. Open the NOOK Library and tap your profile image at the top of the screen, which shows the NOOK Profiles screen (see Figure 10.9).

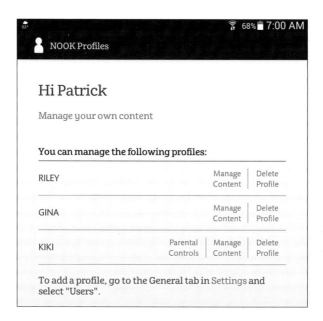

FIGURE 10.9   Edit profiles from this screen.

2. To update the Parental Controls (only available on child profiles), tap Parental Controls and adjust your selections.

   To modify the content that is visible to the profile, tap Manage Content to see the Manage Content for that profile screen (see Figure 10.10).

   You can tap entire categories or tap the arrow on the far right to display specific items, which you can then check or uncheck. Tap Save when done.

That's all there is to managing a profile.

Tap Delete to delete a profile.

FIGURE 10.10   Select the content you want for this profile.

The other location you can manage content for profiles is on the View Details screen. Tap the Profiles to see which profiles have this title assigned to it (see Figure 10.11). Tap the profile images to select or deselect it. Tap Save.

The final location you can control visibility is from the cover pop-up menu. Press and hold a cover, tap Assign to Profiles, and tap the profile you want to assign this content to. Tap Save when done.

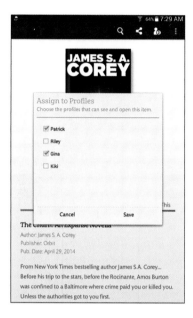

FIGURE 10.11   Seeing a specific title's profile assignments.

CHAPTER 11

Using the Social Features of Your Samsung Galaxy Tab 4 NOOK

As you probably know, Facebook and Twitter are big deals these days—everyone is sharing everything. The NOOK makes this sharing even easier. You can share your reading status, share quotes, and rate and recommend books. You can share with specific contacts on BN.com, Facebook, and Twitter. Because many of these options overlap and at the same time are scattered across the interface, this chapter focuses on Facebook sharing and the NOOK Friends™ app.

Although the locations for the sharing features are scattered, they make sense in their location. Basically, B&N provides many locations for the sharing features to make it easy to share.

> NOTE: For LendMe coverage, **see** Chapter 6, "Lending and Borrowing Books with LendMe on Your Samsung Galaxy Tab 4 NOOK."

Using Facebook and Twitter features requires that you link your Facebook and Twitter accounts to your NOOK. **See** Chapter 2, "Customizing and Configuring Your Samsung Galaxy Tab 4 NOOK," for linking your accounts.

You can access the Facebook social features by

- ▶ Pressing and holding a cover image and tapping Share
- ▶ Pressing and holding a cover image, tapping View Details, and tapping Share
- ▶ Tapping Share from the Reading Tools toolbar
- ▶ Tapping Share Quote from the Text Selection toolbar

Now look at these contexts in turn.

Using Recommend from the Cover Menu or View Details Screen

Pressing and holding a cover in the Library displays a menu. Tap Share and then tap Recommend to see your recommend options (see Figure 11.1). Tap To My Facebook Wall to see the Facebook Recommendation screen (see Figure 11.2)—if you are not currently connected to a Wi-Fi hotspot, the Network Setting screen appears for you to connect to one.

FIGURE 11.1   Where do you want to recommend this NOOK Book?

FIGURE 11.2   Use this screen to post a recommendation to your wall.

To post to your Facebook wall

1. Press and hold a cover. From the pop-up menu, tap Share, tap Recommend, and then tap To My Facebook Wall. From the View Details screen, tap the Share button, and tap Recommend. Tap To My Facebook Wall.

2. Type your message that will appear. As you type, you see the number of available characters (max of 420) go down, giving you an indication of how much space you have left.

3. Tap Post. Your NOOK sends the recommendation to your wall.

You can recommend a title to a specific contact or via Twitter. The methods are essentially the same.

Using Social Features from the View Details Screen

Pressing and holding a cover in the Library displays a menu. If you tap View Details, you see the View Details screen, which contains many options. To access the social features, tap Share, which displays a menu with several options (see Figure 11.3).

FIGURE 11.3   The Share menu.

From here, you can recommend a book, rate and review the book on BN.com, and like the book on Facebook. (If you have previously liked this on Facebook, the final menu option is Unlike on Facebook.)

If you tap Recommend, the steps are exactly the same as in the preceding section.

If you tap Rate and Review, the Rate and Review screen displays (see Figure 11.4). The main purpose of this screen is to post your feedback on this title to BN.com. You can give it an overall star rating by tapping the star you want to give it. (For example, tap the middle star to give it a three-star rating.) Type in a brief headline for the review (for example, **Awesome history**). You can then type in your full review, for which you have plenty of space to do (3500 characters). At the bottom, you have two options: Post on Facebook and Twitter. You can choose both, one, or neither. If you choose to send it to either Facebook or Twitter, a link to your review is posted to Facebook or Twitter. This alerts your friends and followers that you have posted a review on BN.com for the book. Tap Post to post the review to BN.com.

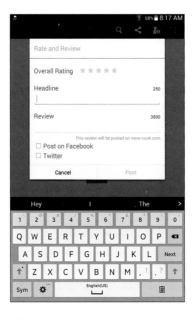

FIGURE 11.4   The Rate and Review screen.

TIP: After you tap Like on Facebook, this option changes to Unlike on Facebook.

To like the book on Facebook, from the Share menu, tap Like on Facebook. This happens immediately.

If you press and hold a cover and choose Share from the pop-up menu, you have the Recommend, Rate and Review, and Like on Facebook options as well.

Using Share from the Reading Tools Toolbar

While reading a NOOK Book or newspaper, you can tap the Share button on the Reading Tools toolbar. You have four options (see Figure 11.5):

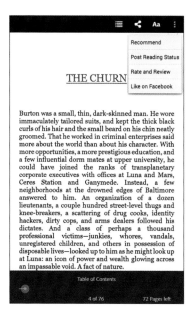

FIGURE 11.5   Tap the Share button to access the social features for NOOK Books.

- ▶ **Recommend**: This functions exactly as in the earlier section, "Using Recommend from the Cover Menu or View Details Screen."

- ▶ **Post Reading Status**: This option enables you to post how far along you are in reading this NOOK Book to Facebook and Twitter. You can find a brief headline indicating how far you are into the NOOK Book, and its title is followed by the synopsis of the NOOK Book on BN.com (see Figure 11.6). You can choose to post your status to Facebook or Twitter or both.

  After tapping Share and tapping Post Reading Status, tap the check box for Facebook or Twitter (or both) and then tap Post. The update is sent.

FIGURE 11.6   Sharing the reading status posts how far you are into that NOOK Book on Facebook and Twitter.

▶ **Rate and Review**: Tapping this allows you to rate and review the book on BN.com, which appears on the B&N book's specific web page. You must provide both a rating and either a headline or review before you can post. After you tap Post, the information is sent to BN.com.

▶ **Like on Facebook**: This option enables you to post to your Facebook wall that you like this book. Tap this link, and your NOOK posts on Facebook that you like the book. (If you have previously liked this book on Facebook, the option changes to Unlike on Facebook.)

Using Share from the Text Selection Toolbar

Use this share function when you have a quote you want others to see:

1. Press and hold the word you want to start the quote.

2. When the Text Selection toolbar appears, finish highlighting the quote by dragging the ending blue bar to where you want.

3. Tap Share Quote (see Figure 11.7).

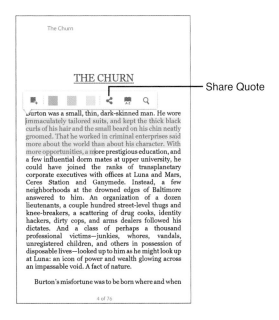

FIGURE 11.7 Highlight a quote and tap Share Quote.

4. Tap To My Facebook Wall.

5. Type your message. Tap Post.

The appropriate wall or walls are updated (see Figure 11.8).

Table 11.1 quickly shows you where you can find which social action.

TABLE 11.1 Quick Chart of Where You Can Find Social Actions

	Library/Home Page Details Screen	Store Details Screen	Cover Pop-Up Menu	Reading Tools Toolbar	Text Selection Toolbar
Recommend	YES	YES	YES	YES	NO
Rate and Review	YES	YES	YES	YES	NO
Like on Facebook	YES	YES	YES	YES	NO
Post Reading Status	NO	NO	NO	YES	NO
Share Quote	NO	NO	NO	NO	YES

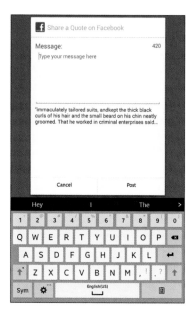

FIGURE 11.8   Sharing a quote.

So What About Twitter and Contacts?

NOOK's support for Twitter and Contacts functions identically to Facebook, except that you share with specific contacts via email or your Twitter feed. Twitter has a more limited character count, however, than do wall posts on Facebook (140 character, to be exact). To share to Twitter, in the Library, press and hold the cover. When the menu appears, tap Share, tap Recommend, and then tap Via Twitter. Alternatively, if you are reading the book, tap Recommend from the Reading Tools and tap Via Twitter.

CHAPTER 12

Shopping and Visiting B&N on Your Samsung Galaxy Tab 4 NOOK

One of the greatest features of your NOOK is the capability to sample and buy content from B&N directly from the device. As long as you have a Wi-Fi connection, you can get new content for your NOOK no matter where you are. However, you can also use the B&N website to sample and purchase content for your NOOK.

> NOTE: Only customers with billing addresses in the United States, Canada, a U.S. territory, or UK can order content from the B&N eBookstore. Citizens of U.S. territories cannot preorder items.

Shopping on Your NOOK

To shop on your NOOK, from the Home screen, tap NOOK Shop. Your NOOK displays the NOOK Store Home screen (see Figure 12.1).

Navigating the NOOK Store

The NOOK Store is divided into three parts. The top right features several categories of items: Books, Magazines, Movies & TV, Kids, Apps, Newspapers, and Catalogs. To browse that category, tap the category's name.

The top left highlights features such as bestselling magazines, new NOOK videos, best reading lists, and so on.

The bottom half contains Channels, which are lists of titles related to your interests (remember selecting those in creating your profile) and purchasing habits. Channels are descriptive and—I have found—useful ways of categorizing titles. Instead of just a big collection of history books, you have Space Opera, History by Plot, Notorious

American History, and History Buff. The Channels descriptions are themselves evocative of the types of content you will find. In addition, Channels allow for titles from
multiple genres to appear (Science-Fiction Science-Fact is a good example).

FIGURE 12.1   The opening of the NOOK Store.

The bottom status bar has three options: Search, Profiles, and Options. The Options
menu has Browse History, Wishlist, and Shop Settings choices.

The Browse History option opens up a screen that shows items you've recently looked
at in the NOOK Store. The Options button in the top right lets you adjust how you are
viewing the items (Grid or List) as well as the Wishlist and Shop Settings options.

The Wishlist option shows your wishlist of items added from your specific NOOK
device. While your Samsung Galaxy Tab 4 NOOK, the NOOK HD, and the
NOOK HD+ share a wishlist, it is not the same as your BN.com wishlist or any
other NOOK Simple Touch or NOOK GlowLight.

TIP: Myself? I dislike managing multiple wishlists, so I use the NOOK's
browser to add to my B&N wishlist via the BN.com website. I use the Shop feature on my NOOK for its ease of use.

The Shop Settings option opens up the NOOK Settings for the NOOK Shop.

Type into the search box keywords, authors, titles—what have you. Tap the search button. A set of results appears. You can tap the cover to see the Details screen and tap the price to purchase the ebook (followed by a Confirm button). You can sort the list by a variety of options by tapping the Options button (see Figure 12.2).

FIGURE 12.2   Sort your search results.

Browsing the NOOK Store

Tap any of the categories from the NOOK Store to stroll through the available content in that category (see Figure 12.3). From here, you can narrow down even further on the category you want to browse, see all the books, or select a title or list from the options at the bottom of the screen.

As you work your way through the lists, the items are listed in Channels. You can scroll through the Channel's list of titles. In addition, tap the cover to see the Details screen. To go backward, tap the Back key. To return to the NOOK Store front, tap the shopping bag in the top left.

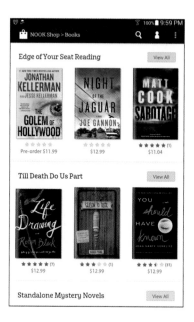

FIGURE 12.3   Browsing the NOOK Store.

Sampling and Buying Content

After you locate and select an item you're interested in, if you tap the cover to get to the Details screen (see Figure 12.4), you see an overview page that describes the item and shows the rating of the item from other B&N readers. In addition, you see the following options:

- ▶ **Play Trailer**: For some movies, you see a play button on the cover. Tap it to watch the trailer.

- ▶ **Add to Wishlist**: Adds the item to your NOOK's wishlist. Tap it and the heart's plus turns to a minus. Tap it again to remove it from your wishlist.

- ▶ **Share**: Gives you the opportunity to recommend the title, like it on Facebook, or rate and review it. **See** Chapter 11, "Using the Social Features of Your Samsung Galaxy Tab 4 NOOK," for more information.

- ▶ **Profiles**: Tap this and a menu appears with all your profiles so that you can assign this product to whichever profiles you want presuming you purchase it.

- ▶ **Price**: Tap this button to purchase the book. You are asked to confirm your purchase. For movies and TV shows, you have an option to buy or rent the

HD or SD version. Tap the arrow next to the price, and tap the one you want (if it is different than the default HD pricing). If rentals are available, you can rent the HD or SD version. Tap the arrow next to the price and tap the one you want.

FIGURE 12.4   The Details screen in the NOOK Store.

▶ **Free Sample**: Tap this to download a free sample from the book.

▶ **Previous/Next**: If you got to the Details screen because of a search that returned multiple titles or via browsing, these buttons let you go forward and backward in the list.

▶ **Overview**: The default view displays when you select an item. This includes screen shots for apps. Scroll down to see the full listing.

▶ **Reviews**: Displays reviews from other B&N customers. The number of reviews presented is likely to be smaller than the number of ratings. In addition, you can access the Rate and Review and Like on Facebook social features from this screen. Tap Most Helpful to sort the customer reviews. If a number of reviews are available, you might need to scroll down to see more.

NOTE: On the Reviews screen, you also can provide feedback to the reviewers. Tap Yes or No depending on how helpful you felt the review is. In addition,
if you find a review is problematic (for example, it spoils the plot or uses abu-
sive language), tap Report This Review. You are asked to cite a reason, after
which you can tap Send. The review is reported to B&N, which may take steps
to correct the review.

▶ **More Like This**: Displays similar titles that you might be interested in.
   Usually these are sorted by what other B&N customers who purchased the
   book you are looking at have purchased, more titles by the author, and other
   titles in the series. Tap the cover to jump to that ebook's Details screen. If
   you like what you see, you can download a sample to your NOOK by tapping Free Sample. (Sampling is valid only with NOOK Books.) Samples
   typically consist of the first chapter of an ebook. However, it's up to the
   publisher to decide what to provide as a sample. In some cases, samples
   might contain just a few pages. In other cases, samples consist primarily of
   front matter, such as the title page, table of contents, dedication, and so on.

NOTE: Samples never expire. You can keep a sample for as long as you
like. If you send a sample to the NOOK Cloud, you have an opportunity to
redownload it.

If you decide to buy a book after reading the sample, simply go to the Details screen
by tapping the cover (you can do this in the NOOK Store or in the Library) or tapping
Buy Now in the reading screen of the sample. Because samples and full NOOK
Books are completely separate products, a purchased book will not open at the point
where the sample ended. You need to manually navigate to the point where you
stopped reading the sample.

NOTE: If a B&N gift card is associated with your account, the cost for items
purchased from the B&N NOOK Store are applied against that gift card. If there
is not enough credit left on the card, B&N charges the remaining balance to
your credit card on file.

If you want to remove a sample from your NOOK, press and hold the cover, and tap
Delete from Account from the pop-up menu if you want to remove it from your
library entirely. If you delete a sample unintentionally, you can download it again.

For more information on using My NOOK Library, **see** Chapter 25, "Using My NOOK Library."

Is It Possible to Accidentally Purchase a Book You Have Already Purchased from B&N's eBookstore?

Your NOOK will not present the option to purchase a book you already own. If you select a book in the NOOK Store that you already own, you are shown an option to download or read the book, depending upon whether the book is already on your NOOK. However, you will not be shown an option to buy the book. It will read Purchased.

Some classic titles are released by multiple publishers. Two books of the same title from two different publishers are not considered the same title, so in these cases, you can purchase the same book twice.

Subscription content also enables sampling prior to purchasing, but it works a bit differently than it does with NOOK Books. When you subscribe to a newspaper or magazine, you are given a 14-day free trial (see Figure 12.5). If you cancel your subscription within that 14-day period, you will not be charged. If you cancel after the 14-day trial period, you will be refunded a prorated amount based on when you cancel.

FIGURE 12.5   The trial period for a magazine.

> NOTE: You can buy the current issue by tapping Buy Current Issue without subscribing.

You can use a trial subscription only once for any particular item. For example, if you subscribe to *The New York Review of Books,* cancel your subscription within the 14-day trial period, and then later resubscribe again, you will be charged beginning immediately because you have already taken advantage of a trial subscription.

> NOTE: Subscriptions can be canceled only using My NOOK Library at bn.com. You cannot cancel a subscription using your NOOK.

Your NOOK automatically downloads subscription content when it's available. In addition to seeing the new content in your library and Active Shelf, you'll also receive notifications in the status bar for any new subscription content your NOOK downloads.

> NOTE: You cannot sample NOOK Books for Kids that have Read to Me or Read and Play functionality.

Shopping on Your Computer

Although B&N has made it easy to shop for content directly from the NOOK, sometimes it is easier and more convenient to shop for ebooks from your computer. Any books you purchase on your computer are added to the NOOK Library and are available for reading on your NOOK.

To shop for NOOK Books, magazines, and newspapers on your computer, browse to bn.com/ebooks. You can get samples of ebooks, subscribe to periodicals, and purchase books and apps from the NOOK Store.

When you purchase, subscribe to a periodical, or choose to sample a NOOK Book from the online NOOK Bookstore™, the content is automatically added to your My NOOK Library. You can read the item on your NOOK by connecting to Wi-Fi or Fast and Free Wireless. You can also tap the Sync button in the Library to force your NOOK to connect with B&N and download any new content.

One of the great features of using the B&N website for browsing NOOK Books is that you can see which other formats are available. For example, if an MP3 audio-book is available for a title you're browsing, a link to the audiobook is there, so you can download it if you want.

When shopping for NOOK Books for Kids, look for the "NOOK Kids Read to Me" statement in Format section. These NOOK Books have the Read to Me feature enabled. If the format for a NOOK Book for Kids is simply NOOK Book, you will not have the Read to Me option for that NOOK Book for Kids. You can learn more about this feature in Chapter 5, "Reading and Using NOOK Books for Kids Features."

Whether you choose to shop from your NOOK or your computer, B&N provides plenty of great content for your NOOK at the NOOK Bookstore. However, there are also many other sources for great ebooks for your NOOK. Some of those sources you can find in Appendix B, "Sources for ebooks Other than B&N," which you can then sideload to your NOOK.

Using Your NOOK in a B&N Store

As mentioned earlier, B&N stores have a Wi-Fi hotspot, so your NOOK can access free Wi-Fi while you are in the store (see Figure 12.6). Your NOOK automatically connects to a B&N hotspot when you are in the store so long as Wi-Fi is turned on. (It's on by default.)

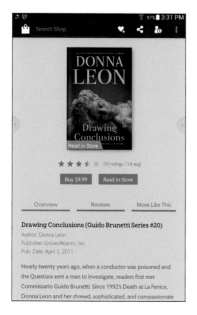

FIGURE 12.6   Tap the Read in Store button to enjoy something to read on your NOOK while drinking a coffee.

After your NOOK connects to the B&N hotspot, from the Home screen, tap NOOK Store.

When you're connected to a B&N hotspot in a B&N store, you have the ability to read nearly any NOOK Book in the B&N store for up to 1 hour. Find a NOOK Book you'd like to read, tap the cover, and the Details screen opens (refer to Figure 12.6). Tap the Read in Store button, which opens a Read In-Store confirmation screen explaining the program and asking you to proceed. Tap Read to continue (see Figure 12.7). At this point, you can read for up to 1 hour.

> NOTE: Bookmarks, annotations, and highlights are not supported for Read in Store content.

> NOTE: You cannot read magazines, newspapers, comics, or NOOK Books for Kids on your NOOK for free in a B&N store.

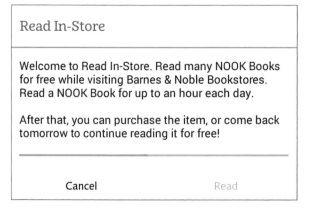

FIGURE 12.7   The details for reading this book in store.

If you read a bit of a book in the store, exit out of the book you were reading, get up for a cup of coffee, and decide you want to keep reading, at the top of the NOOK Store, tap Recently Viewed. Tap the cover to see the Details screen.

If you want to see what is available for reading in the store, go back to the main NOOK Store page, and swipe left in the top half until you get to the Read in Store page. Tap Browse Read in Store eBooks.

There's no doubt that B&N has a unique opportunity because of its brick-and-mortar presence. No other ebook reader has the capability of being paired with a retail outlet.

> NOTE: If you had the original NOOK, you know that you could show it to get a free cookie, coffee, smoothie, percentage off something, and more in the store. Currently, you can't get freebies or discounts with the NOOK.

Using NOOK Today

NOOK Today is an app that B&N has to offer you content based on your interests. To see what they think, tap NOOK Today from the Home screen (see Figure 12.8).

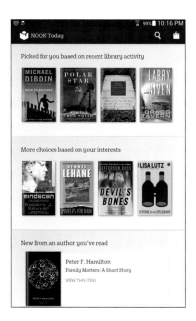

FIGURE 12.8 Your NOOK Today.

The three sections feature items for sale at B&N based on library activity, interests, and so on. Tap the covers to go to the View Details screen.

CHAPTER 13

Using the Google Play Store and Google Apps

Until May 2013, all apps purchased for older NOOKs were done via B&N's NOOK Store. Since then, the Google Play Store is open to you with many more apps now available.

In addition, a few Google apps are now available by default:

- ▶ Maps

- ▶ Hangouts

- ▶ Google+

- ▶ Play Music

- ▶ Play Store

- ▶ YouTube

- ▶ And others

This chapter explores all these except for the Play Music app, which is covered in Chapter 7, "Playing Music, Audiobooks, and Podcasts."

Using the Google Play Store

The Google Play Store is where Google sells its apps, music, and more. You can buy apps and run them on your NOOK or you can buy music, which downloads to the Play Music app. To start the Play Store, from the Home screen, tap Play Store (see Figure 13.1). At the top of the store, you can see the various sections the store is divided into. Tap them to browse, see bestsellers. (In Apps, those are Top Paid and Top Free; in Music, those are Top Albums and Top Songs.) You can also tap the magnifying glass to search for apps.

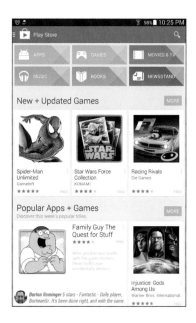

FIGURE 13.1   The opening screen of the Play Store.

For apps, when you find an app you want to buy, tap Install (see Figure 13.2). Tap Accept in the permissions screen that appears. When the app finishes installing, it appears in the Apps list of My Library. Next to the title, the bookmark adds the app to your wishlist to buy later. Farther down, you have another location for adding the title to your wishlist. In addition, you can tap the Share button, which opens up a screen (see Figure 13.3) that allows you to share the app with an application, social network, or email. You can also tap the +1 button to +1 the app on Google+.

If you want to get back to the previous page, tapping the left-pointing arrow at the top of the page takes you back, or tap the Back key. If you tap Google Play Store bag at the top, you are returned to the store home. Tap the Play Store bag and the store home opens a menu where you can access My Apps, My Wishlist, and so on.

For music, much is the same as for apps. However, instead of Install, you see the price to purchase the entire album (see Figure 13.4). You can also purchase individual tracks. (Just tap the price next to the track name.) If you want to sample the music, tap the track number to listen to a short sample. Tapping Play All lets you hear a short sample for all the tracks.

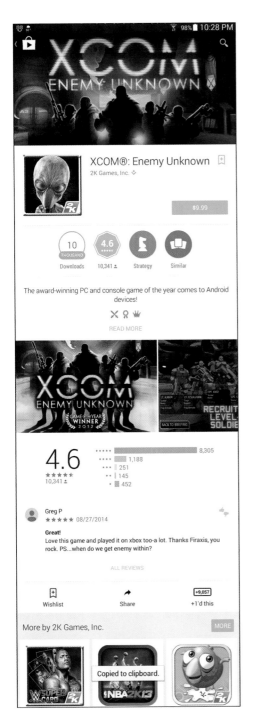

FIGURE 13.2 An app's screen.

FIGURE 13.3 Sharing an app's page.

FIGURE 13.4 Viewing an album of music.

Using Google Maps

Google Maps is what it says it is: an atlas in your NOOK. To open it, from the Home screen, tap Google. Find Maps and tap it. Maps opens to your current location with a blue dot marking your location (see Figure 13.5).

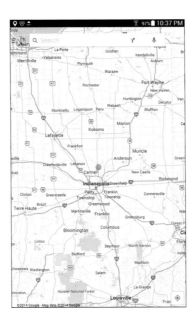

FIGURE 13.5   The opening of the Maps screen.

To scroll in or out, use pinch and zoom gestures. If you are looking for something specific, tap Search Text and enter your search criteria. You can search for specific addresses, specific businesses, or just generic terms. For example, if you type **sushi**, you see a number of results (see Figure 13.6), which appear as a set of stacked cards. Tap Results List to see all the results. The cards have specific information about the restaurants, any review, distance, and so on. You can tap a specific item to get more details (see Figure 13.7).

You can get directions by tapping the Car button wherever you see it. When you do so, you see the screen in Figure 13.8. Here, you can adjust the locations you want directions for, reverse the order, and even set whether driving by car, using mass transit, riding a bicycle, or walking. When you finish, tap Go.

Maps offers a lot of other options, so feel free to explore.

FIGURE 13.6   Search results for sushi.

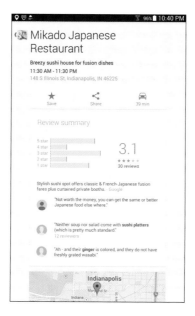

FIGURE 13.7   Exploring more detail for the search results.

FIGURE 13.8   Setting the parameters for directions.

Using Google+

Google+ is Google's social network. You can follow friends or sports teams, participate in communities, and much more. You need a Google+ account first, which you can get here after clicking Join Google+: www.google.com/+/learnmore/getstarted/guide.html.

To start the app, from the Home screen, tap Google, find Google+, and tap it. Google+ opens (see Figure 13.9). Whatever is most recent appears. You can scroll through what appears in your feed. Each one allows you to +1 it, share it on your own Google+ feed, and comment.

If you want to share something brand new, at the bottom of the Google+ app, tap the pencil icon. A new post screen appears with several options:

- ▶ **Photos**: Tap this to open a view into your gallery. You can scroll through, find the photo you want to share, and tap it. You can select multiple photos. When done, tap Select in the top right. A screen like Figure 13.10 appears.

FIGURE 13.9   The opening screen of the Google+ screen.

FIGURE 13.10   Sharing a photo.

▶ Tap the Back key to stop the process. Tap the Share arrow whenever you are ready to share the photo. You can limit who sees the image by tapping the text next to To below your name.

▶ If you want to enter text, type it in. If you tap Add Your Location, Maps opens and gives you some options to choose from. If you want to add more photos, tap the Add More button below the photo.

▶ **Add Your Location**: If you are at a great restaurant, museum, or just want to share your location, tap this option. Maps opens and provides you a number of options. Tap the one you want. The screen changes to the same as photos. In fact, you can add photos, a web page link, or a mood indicator.

▶ **Mood**: If you want to use an icon to indicate your mood, tap Mood to see a number of options. Tap the one you want. The screen changes to the same as photos.

▶ **Link**: Allows you to enter a web link you'd like to share.

Tap the Options button icon in the top right to get a drop-down list of options. Tap your image to see your profile page. If you tap the Options button in the top right, you get access to edit the information and images. From this drop-down list of options, if you tap People, Google+ offers a number of suggestions for people and pages to follow. Tap Notifications to see any notifications you may have received.

Using YouTube

You are probably familiar with YouTube. You can find any number of videos here. You can upload your own as well. When you first start the app, you see a list of videos recommended for you based on your watching habits and subscriptions you follow (see Figure 13.11).

Tap a video to watch it. A screen appears and begins playing the video. Standard pause, play, and volume controls are available. In addition, you can like or dislike the video. At the top of the video, if you tap the plus icon, you can add the video to a Watch Later list or Playlist or make it a favorite. The Share button lets you share the video via email Google+ or other apps you have installed that work with sharing. The Throw button lets you watch the video on YouTube connected devices (such as ChromeCast, TiVos, and so on).

Tap the YouTube icon to see a list of options. You can access a playlist or videos you've saved for later. Any subscriptions you have are available here as well.

Tap Search to enter a search term and see what videos are available.

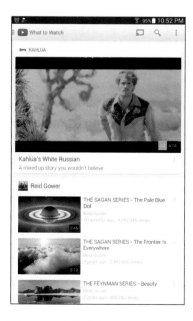

FIGURE 13.11   The opening screen of YouTube.

If you have a video to share, tap the YouTube icon and tap Uploads, which displays any videos you have uploaded. Tap the Upload icon in the top right to get a list of options to pick your video from (for example, Dropbox, Gallery, and so on).

CHAPTER 14

Using the Samsung Galaxy Tab 4 NOOK Camera and Google Hangouts

When the first NOOK Color was released, no camera was part of the device. As the NOOK Tablet and NOOK HDs followed, no camera was added. That's all changed now with the Samsung Galaxy Tab 4 NOOK. In fact, you have a front-facing and rear-facing camera. The rear-facing camera is a 3 megapixels, while the front-facing is 1.3 megapixels. Neither of these cameras will match digital SLRs, but they are decent cameras that perform well.

Using the NOOK Camera

To use the camera, turn it on by tapping Camera from the second Home screen page. The camera starts up (see Figure 14.1).

Let's get oriented to this screen:

▶ Tap Effects to see particular effects available for that mode. (**See** the section "Using Modes" later in this chapter for more information about settings.)

▶ Tap Gallery to go to the Gallery.

▶ Tap Settings to go to the Camera, Video, and General Settings. (**See** the section "Using Camera, Video, and General Settings and Features" later in this chapter for more information about settings.)

▶ Tap Camera Switch to switch between using the back-facing and front-facing cameras.

▶ Tap Gallery to go to the Gallery.

▶ Tap Features to access additional features for the camera. (**See** the section "Using Camera, Video, and General Settings and Features" later in this chapter for more information about settings.)

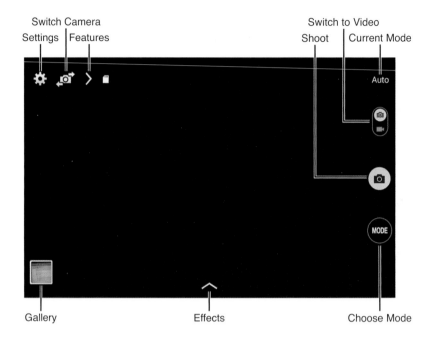

FIGURE 14.1   The camera has a number of features.

▶ Current Mode tells you what mode you have selected. (**See** the section "Using Modes" later in this chapter for more information about settings.)

▶ Tap Camera/Video to switch between taking videos and still.

▶ Tap Shoot to take the shot. For videos, it is a Record button, which you tap again to stop recording.

▶ Tap Mode to change the shooting mode. (**See** the section "Using Modes" later in this chapter for more information about settings.)

To take a photo, simply tap the Shoot button. Most likely, though, you'll want to explore the many other options with the camera that can give you panoramic shots, delay photos, and so on. The following sections get into more depth about using the camera.

You can zoom in or out by tapping the Volume buttons or pinching and zooming.

Using Modes

Modes are different configurations the camera uses to take shots, adjusting color balance, shutter speed, and so on. The intent is to give you options to capture the optimal photo and is just like many settings on dedicated digital cameras. By default, your camera starts in Auto mode. Tap Mode to see your options (see Figure 14.2).

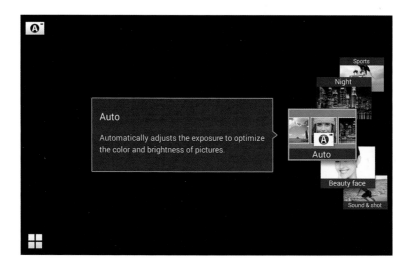

FIGURE 14.2   Selecting the Mode.

You can scroll through the modes on the right by swiping. When you pause on a mode, it gives you a brief definition of its purpose. To change to a different mode, tap the mode. If you don't tap a different mode, the currently selected one remains. You can switch back to Auto quickly by tapping the Auto icon in the top left.

Tap the bottom-left four-square icon to see the modes in the center of the screen (see Figure 14.3). Tap the bottom-left scroll icon to return to the scrolling view of modes if you want.

You have a total of six modes to choose from:

- ▶ **Auto**: This is the default mode and gives the NOOK full control over the settings for shooting.

- ▶ **Beauty Face**: This is intended for portraits, including selfies, and softens edges and highlights facial features.

- ▶ **Sound and Shot**: This uses the Auto settings but records nine seconds of sound before or after along with the picture.

- ▶ **Panorama**: This allows you to take sweeping panorama shots. You can take panorama shots either vertically or horizontally. When you tap to take the shot, move your NOOK left or right with as steady a hand as you can. Keep the blue rectangle in the larger rectangle for the best shot. Slow and steady here does win the race. When you have reached the end of your panorama, tap the Shoot button to stop.

▶ **Sports**: This adjusts the settings—usually shutter speed—to capture fast moving sports. In general, this is good for any action photography.

▶ **Night**: Your NOOK doesn't have a flash, so if you are in a low-light setting, this mode gives you the best chance at capturing the photo.

FIGURE 14.3 A different way for selecting the mode.

Using Camera, Video, and General Settings and Features

Tap the Settings icon to see the settings screen (see Figure 14.4), which is divided into three sections: Photo, Video, and General.

The Photo settings are only available if you are currently in photo mode and not video mode. You have two options in Photo settings:

▶ **Photo Size**: You can also call this resolution, and you have several options to choose from (see Figure 14.5). The number in the circle (3.2, 2.4, and so on) along with the M beside it refers to the number of megapixels—thus, corresponding to resolution and aspect sizes (that is, width:length). The W in front of the numbers help identify the 16:9 aspect ratio choices.

Simply put, the higher the resolution, the larger the file size of the final photo.

FIGURE 14.4   Camera and video settings.

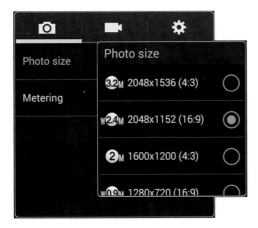

FIGURE 14.5   You have a number of photo resolution options.

▶ **Metering**: This is about how your NOOK measures the light for making adjustments to the shutter speed and so on. Center-weighted metering means putting a priority on the center of the screen and averages it out with the rest of the screen's image to give an overall light measurement. Matrix metering uses brightness and contrast to determine an overall best exposure setting for the camera. Matrix is usually recommended for beginning photographers. Spot metering uses the center of the screen and does not average the rest of the area outside the spot.

The Videos settings are only available if you are currently in photo mode and not video mode. You have a single option here: Video size. As in photos, the larger the size, the larger the file.

The General settings provide many options:

▶ **Location Tag**: Off by default, you can turn this on to have your NOOK tag each photo with your location at the time of taking.

▶ **Volume Key**: By default, the Volume Keys control the zoom, but you can change it so the Volume Keys will take the photo or start and stop the video.

▶ **Timer**: Off by default, you can adjust how long of a delay the camera waits before taking the picture after you have tapped the Shoot button.

▶ **White Balance**: Auto by default, white balance is actually a way of saying how your camera records the whiteness of the scene and adjusts the final photo to compensate. This is particularly helpful on bright days or with interior shots. Tapping it gives you several options, which adjust how your NOOK measures the light and alters the final photo.

▶ **Brightness**: You can adjust the brightness by hand. Tap this and then adjust the scrollbar. As you do, you'll see the image get brighter or darker.

▶ **Guidelines**: Off by default, you can turn this on, which displays gridlines on the screen as you take the shot. The gridlines break up the screen into nine equal segments, which can aid in composing the shot before taking it.

▶ **Contextual Filename**: You must have Location Tag turned on to use this feature. When you take a photo, it gets a filename by default. Here's an example filename: 20140919_075748. The part before the underscore is the date. The part after is a randomly assigned number. If you turn on Contextual Filename, you still get the 20140919_075748, but after the random number, the camera will assign a street name or other location detail to make identifying easier (20140919_075748_Meridian Street, for example).

▶ **Save as Flipped**: Off by default, this option is only relevant for the front-facing camera, and it happens only when you save the file. Essentially, what this does is force the mirror effect. Leaving this off is the more natural setting, but that's up to you.

▶ **Storage**: Allows you to define if you want photos to be stored on the device or an installed microSD card.

▶ **Reset**: This is a quick way for you to reset the camera to all its default settings.

▶ **Help**: Tap to get some help installed on the NOOK for using the device. The information is basic, but it can be handy if you need it.

For the Auto, Video, and Sound and Shot modes, you have additional features you can apply before you take the shot. These features are available from the upward pointing arrow at the bottom of the screen. With the camera set to Auto, tap the button, and see the four features available (see Figure 14.6).

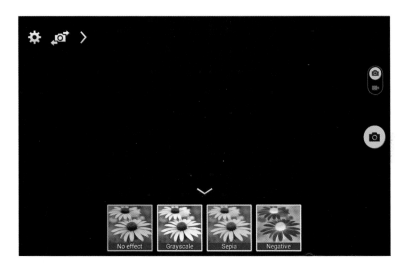

FIGURE 14.6   You can have some more fun with photos using features.

These are the features available for each mode:

▶ **Auto and Video**: No Effect, Grayscale, Sepia, Negative.

▶ **Sound and Shot**: Pre-Shot, Post-Shot. Determines when the nine seconds of audio is recorded.

You should have enough information about how to get the best use out of your NOOK camera. Now it just takes practice.

Using Google Hangouts

With the front-facing camera, you can now use your NOOK to video chat with friends and family. We'll use Google Hangouts here, but you can install Skype and use it as well.

Google Hangouts is both a video chat and message chat service available to those with a Google account. Hangouts is pre-installed on your NOOK. Just tap the Google folder on the Home screen and tap Hangouts to open it (see Figure 14.7).

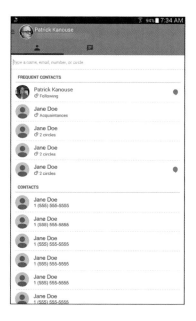

FIGURE 14.7   The opening screen of Hangouts.

The People screen shows you your contacts. You can scroll through the list and tap any of them to open the Conversations screen (see Figure 14.8).

Tap History to see a list of recent interactions. You can tap anyone of them to get to the Conversations screen.

The Conversation screen is where you can actually begin to use Hangouts to connect with people. If you want to use instant messaging, just type into the text box at the bottom of the screen. You can tap the smiley face to access a set of emoticons. Tap the Send button to send the message on its way.

Call button
Video Call button

Send an instant
message

FIGURE 14.8   The Conversations screen.

You can even send photos by instant message. Tap the paper clip icon in the bottom
right to get three options:

▶ **Take Photo**: Tap to open the camera, take a photo, and have it automatically
attached to the message. Tap the x to discard the image.

▶ **Attach Photo**: Tap to open the Gallery and select an existing image. Tap the
x to discard the image.

▶ **Location**: Tap to attach a Google Maps location of your current location.
Tap the x to discard the image.

You can call a person by video by tapping the Video Call or Call button. The button
function is essentially the same in that both initiate a video call (see Figure 14.9). The
difference is that when you tap Video Call, the camera is on already, and when you
tap Call, the video doesn't begin until the person you are calling answers.

When calling you can tap the Microphone icon to mute the line and the Camera icon
to turn off the video camera. Tap the Add Caller icon to add additional participants.

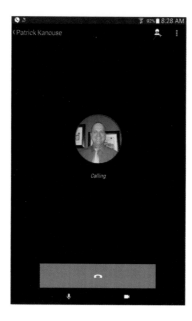

FIGURE 14.9   Initiating a call.

While in the call, you can mute the line or turn off the camera as you like. You can also reverse the camera and have it use the back-facing camera. To end a call, tap the red phone button.

That's all there is to connecting with friends and family with Hangouts.

CHAPTER 15

Getting Started with Your NOOK GlowLight

Congratulations on your new NOOK GlowLight. The NOOK GlowLight was released by B&N in November 2013. The NOOKGlowLight and the NOOK Simple Touch feature a touchscreen interface, and the NOOK GlowLight has a built-in light that distributes a soft, even light over the entire screen.

> NOTE: Barnes & Noble uses a lowercase *n* when it spells *NOOK* and for the NOOK's logo.

Before getting into the details of using your NOOK GlowLight, you need to do some things right now.

> NOTE: From here on out, I will simply refer to the NOOK rather than the long-winded NOOK GlowLight or NOOK Simple Touch.

Understanding NOOK Gestures

You control your NOOK (except the Power and Home buttons and page turn controls—these page turn controls only appear on the NOOK Simple Touch) with gestures:

- ▶ **Tap**: This is the most common gesture. Just press your finger to the screen and raise it. Usually, you use this gesture with buttons and covers.

- ▶ **Double Tap**: This is the same as the Tap gesture, but just press twice quickly.

- ▶ **Swipe Left/Swipe Right**: This gesture is mostly for turning pages. Like a tap, touch your finger on the screen and quickly drag it to the left (or right) and lift your finger up.

▶ **Scroll**: Essentially, this is the vertical version of the Swipe gesture. You can control the speed of the scroll by swiping up or down rapidly. You can slow down or stop the scroll by tapping the screen (to stop) or pressing and holding to slow the scroll.

The NOOK Buttons

The NOOK features six physical buttons:

▶ **Power**: This does what it promises: turns your NOOK on or off. If you press it briefly while your NOOK is on, the NOOK goes to sleep. If the NOOK is asleep and you press it briefly, the NOOK wakes up.

▶ **Home**: The Home button (it's the lowercase n below the screen) shows you the Quick Nav Bar and is your way to change settings, go shopping, and so on. If you want to return to a starting point, just press the Home button and tap Home.

Press and hold the Home button for two seconds to turn the GlowLight on or off.

If your NOOK is asleep, press this button to wake it up (and then drag your finger from left to right on the arrows at the bottom of the screen).

▶ **Page Turn (NOOK Simple Touch only)**: These four buttons turn the page backward or forward and are alternatives to swiping left or right to turn the page. By default, the top buttons advance you forward one page, and the bottom buttons take you backward in the book.

Registering Your NOOK

When you first turn on your NOOK, it asks you to register it to get started. The first step is to register it with Barnes & Noble (simply B&N from now on). To do that, you need an account on the B&N website. If you don't have one, you can create one in the process of setting up your new NOOK.

> NOTE:　B&N requires a default credit card with a valid billing address to be associated with your B&N account to register your NOOK.

Tap Next on the screen. You then see a screen with Terms and Conditions. Tap Agree if you agree to the terms. The next screen is the Time Zone screen. Tap the circle corresponding to your time zone, and then tap Next.

The next part is to set up your Wi-Fi connection. (Or you can go into a B&N store where it has a connection you can connect to.) Your NOOK displays the available networks. Tap your network. If it is a secure network, enter the password and tap the check mark button. (This appears in the keyboard where you would normally see an Enter button.)

Tap Continue with Setup.

On the Register Your NOOK screen, enter the email address and password you use to sign in to your account on the B&N website; then tap Sign In on the touchscreen. To move from the email field to the password field on the registration screen, tap in the Password field. If you need to create an account, tap Create Account and enter the required details.

You are then taken to the Get Started screen. You can tap Shop Now to begin shopping, tap Reader Guide to see the preloaded reader guide, or press the Home button to go to the Home screen.

> NOTE: If you live outside the United States and have trouble registering your NOOK, make sure you've upgraded to the latest firmware. As of version 1.1, B&N enables registration outside the United States.

For more information on connecting your NOOK to a Wi-Fi hotspot, **see** the next section, "Using Wi-Fi Hotspots."

Using Wi-Fi Hotspots

Your NOOK can also connect to other active Wi-Fi networks. B&N offers free Wi-Fi access in all B&N stores. If you take your NOOK to a B&N store, it automatically connects to the Wi-Fi hotspot in that store.

For more information on using your NOOK in a B&N store, **see** Chapter 21, "Shopping and Visiting B&N on Your NOOK GlowLight."

To connect your NOOK to a Wi-Fi hotspot other than one in a B&N store, follow these steps:

1. Tap the Gear icon in the top-left corner or, if that is not visible, tap the Battery icon. An initial Settings screen appears.

2. Either tap the check box to turn Wi-Fi on or tap Change if you are connected to a Wi-Fi network already. The Wireless screen appears, listing all the nearby wireless networks. (Your NOOK displays the SSID for all Wi-Fi hotspots in range.)

3. Tap the Wi-Fi hotspot you want to use.

4. Tap Connect and enter the password for your Wi-Fi hotspot. (If you want to hide the password while typing, tap the Hide Password check box.) Enter a username or login name as well, if required.

5. Tap the check mark button on the keyboard.

Your NOOK should now show that you are connected to your Wi-Fi hotspot on the reading screen. You should also see the Wi-Fi signal indicator at the top of the screen next to the battery indicator.

NOTE: On the Home screen, you can tap the Wireless icon in the top bar. (Or tap just to the left of the battery.) Follow the preceding steps 2 through 5 to complete connecting to a Wi-Fi network.

If your Wi-Fi hotspot isn't listed after you tap Wi-Fi hotspot, but you know you are in range of a specific active Wi-Fi network, tap Other hotspot. You can then enter the service set identifier (SSID), select the type of security (if the Wi-Fi is secured), and enter the password for your Wi-Fi hotspot. If you don't know this information, ask the person who set up the Wi-Fi network.

Your NOOK can connect to a Wi-Fi hotspot that requires you to browse to a web page to authenticate yourself. For example, many hotel Wi-Fi hotspots require you to enter a room number or other information to connect. First, follow the previous steps to find the wireless network you want to connect to. When you tap a network name that requires you to go to a web page, you are asked if you want to forget the network or continue to a "redirect" to enter a password or other information. Tap Continue to continue the sign-in procedure. Your screen becomes a web page and you can enter any necessary credentials.

Does My NOOK's Battery Drain Faster with Wi-Fi Connected?

I tested my NOOK's battery life with both Wi-Fi on and off. In my testing, the battery life was shorter when actively using Wi-Fi than it was when not. However, Wi-Fi affects battery life only when your NOOK is actually connected to a Wi-Fi hotspot. Simply having Wi-Fi turned on does not affect battery life.

Disconnecting from a Wi-Fi Hotspot

If you want to stop using a Wi-Fi hotspot, you need to disconnect your NOOK from the Wi-Fi hotspot. To do that, follow these steps:

1. Tap the Gear icon in the top-left corner or, if that is not visible, tap the Battery icon. An initial Settings screen appears.

2. Tap the check box to turn Wi-Fi off.

If you want to forget a wireless network entirely, tap the name of the network in the Wireless Settings screen. Tap the Forget button.

For more information on configuring the settings in your NOOK (including turning off the Wi-Fi card), **see** "Your NOOK's Settings" in Chapter 16, "Customizing and Configuring Your NOOK GlowLight."

Caring for Your NOOK's Battery

Your NOOK uses a high-tech battery called a lithium polymer battery. Unlike older rechargeable batteries, your NOOK's battery doesn't suffer from a charge "memory." Older batteries (when you recharged them over and over especially without letting them drain all the way) "remembered" the lower charge rather than the real charge capacity. That said, you should still follow some basic rules to maximize the life of your battery:

▶ Try to avoid fully discharging your battery. Recharge it when it gets down to approximately 20%. Although charging it repeatedly is not necessarily a bad thing, the battery seems to function optimally if you charge it only when it drops down toward that 20% area.

▶ To maximize battery life, turn Wi-Fi off and leave it off. Turn on Wi-Fi to download your new books and subscription content and sync your reading across devices.

▶ Avoid high heat. Reading in sunlight is fine, but avoid storing your NOOK near a heat source.

▶ If storing your NOOK for a long period (a week or more), charge the battery to approximately 50% rather than giving it a full charge.

By following these steps, your NOOK's battery should last for years.

Charging Your NOOK's Battery

You can charge your NOOK's battery either by plugging it into your computer's USB port (so long as your computer has power) or by plugging it into a wall outlet using the supplied AC adapter.

Plugging your NOOK into a wall outlet charges it more quickly.

Should I Plug My NOOK into a Surge Suppressor?

Just like any electronic device, your NOOK is susceptible to power spikes and other electrical anomalies. If you want to ensure that your NOOK is protected from electrical problems, plug it into a surge suppressor.

When You Are Not Reading

When you finish reading, let your NOOK go to sleep instead of turning it off. You may find it counter-intuitive to leave electronic devices turned on, but because your NOOK uses almost no power unless you do something that requires it to refresh the E Ink display, you can leave it turned on without draining your battery.

By leaving your NOOK on, it occasionally downloads content from B&N such as subscription content (assuming you are connected to a wireless network), and any books that you purchase from the B&N website. When you're ready to start reading again, press and release the power switch at the top of your NOOK to wake it up.

How Should I Clean My NOOK's Touchscreen?

Your NOOK's touchscreen is going to get dirty and covered in fingerprints. The best way to clean it is to use a dry, microfiber cloth like the one you would use to clean eyeglasses. If you must use a cleaning fluid, spray it lightly on the cloth and then wipe the touchscreen.

CHAPTER 16

Customizing and Configuring Your NOOK GlowLight

Your NOOK has many features that enable you to easily customize it and make it your own and many settings that control how it operates. In this chapter, you examine how to customize and configure your NOOK.

Using Custom Screensavers

You can customize your NOOK by using custom screensaver images, which it displays on the reading screen when it is sleeping. Even though your NOOK's reading screen isn't a color screen, it can display 16 levels of gray, making it ideal for displaying black-and-white versions of your favorite pictures.

Creating Screensaver Images

Before you use a picture as a screensaver on your NOOK, you need to resize it to fit the dimensions of its reading screen. Screensaver images should be 800 pixels high and 600 pixels wide.

> NOTE: You don't need to resize your images, but by doing so you can display them at their maximum size.

Should I Use a Specific File Format for Images?

Your NOOK supports JPEG (.JPG), GIF, and PNG files. For images, using either JPEG or PNG is your best option. GIF isn't a good option for photographs, but if your image is a line art or text, GIF can work fine. If you're unsure, stick with JPEG. That's what Picasa uses by default.

Copying Screensaver Images to Your NOOK

Screensavers on your NOOK consist of a series of images. Each time your NOOK sleeps, it displays the next image in the series on the reading screen. You select a specific set of images to use as a screensaver by placing them in a folder on your NOOK.

Copy screensaver images to your NOOK by following these steps:

1. Connect your NOOK to your computer with the USB cable. When you do, your device appears in your computer as a new drive called NOOK.

2. If your computer doesn't automatically display the folders on your NOOK, open it via File Explorer on Windows or the Finder on the Mac. You should see the Screensavers folder.

3. Open the Screensavers folder.

4. Create a new folder for your screensaver. The new folder's name is the name of your screensaver on your NOOK. Note that the folder name should not be two words: Vacation-Pictures is correct, but Vacation Pictures is incorrect.

5. Copy the image files for your screensaver into the folder you created in step 4.

For example, if you have a series of images of your summer vacation, you might want to create a new folder in the Screensavers folder called Vacation-Pictures and copy your images into that folder. You can then use the images in that folder as your screensaver by selecting Vacation-Pictures as your screensaver.

Now that you've copied your custom images to your NOOK, you can change its settings to use the new images as your wallpaper or screensaver.

Choosing a Custom Screensaver

Your NOOK's Settings menu enables you to change the screensaver. Here's how:

1. Tap the Gear icon.

2. Tap All Settings.

3. Tap Screen on the Settings menu.

4. To change the screensaver, tap Screensaver and select the folder name of your screensaver. The Authors and Aspiration screensaver folders are on the NOOK by default, and you cannot remove them.

Screensavers from Other Sources

You can use several online sources for NOOK screensavers. One of the best is NOOK-Look (www.NOOK-look.com). NOOK-Look provides a wide assortment of quality screensavers for your NOOK.

Another way you can locate screensavers for your NOOK is by using the image search feature on your favorite search engine. A search for "NOOK GlowLight screensavers" in Google turns up plenty of images presized for your NOOK.

The same search on Bing is less helpful, but by clicking the Images at the top of the search results screen and selecting Tall on the Layout menu, plenty of correctly sized images are available.

One Step Further—Decals

If you want to take the ultimate step to customize your NOOK, a DecalGirl skin (www.decalgirl.com) is the perfect addition. DecalGirl skins are vinyl skins with adhesive backing that you can easily apply. Many skins also include matching NOOK wallpaper that provides a truly unique look.

Your NOOK's Settings

Your NOOK offers configurable settings for controlling many of its features. Tap the Gear icon, and then tap All Settings to access the Settings menu. Your NOOK displays the following information on the Settings menu.

GlowLight

This section allows you to turn on or off the GlowLight as well as control its brightness. Tap the check box to turn it on or off. Drag the slider for how bright you want the illumination.

The good news is that you don't have to go this far into the settings to turn the GlowLight on or off or control the brightness. Pressing and holding the Home button for two seconds turns on or off the light. Tap the Gear icon and use the slider just above the All Settings button to control the brightness.

Device Info

The Device Info section displays a variety of information about your NOOK:

▶ **Battery**: Displays how charged your battery is and whether it is charging or discharging.

▶ **B&N Content Storage Available**: Shows how much free space you have on the internal memory of the NOOK for B&N content (ebooks, newspapers, and magazines you buy from B&N). Your NOOK has 4GB of storage space. B&N reserves 2.05GB of that for B&N-specific storage.

▶ **Other Storage Available**: Shows how much free space you have on the internal memory of the NOOK for content you sideload—for example, ebooks you have purchased from another site. Of the 4GB of storage on the NOOK, 508MB is available for non-B&N content.

▶ **SD Card (NOOK Simple Touch only)**: Shows whether you have a microSD card installed. **See** "Adding a microSD Card to Your NOOK Simple Touch" for more about microSD cards.

▶ **About Your NOOK**: Shows the personal information related to your NOOK: owner name, account to which this NOOK is associated, software (also called firmware) version, and such.

The Software Version displays the version of software (called *firmware*) currently installed on your NOOK. B&N releases periodic updates to the NOOK to improve performance and fix known issues. As long as your NOOK has a connection to a Wi-Fi connection, your NOOK automatically downloads any updates that B&N releases.

Not all NOOK owners receive new firmware updates at the same time. B&N rolls out new firmware over a period of about a week. If you would like to update your NOOK manually, you can visit http://www.barnesandnoble.com/u/nook-support-software-updates where B&N typically provides instructions for manually updating your NOOK to the latest firmware.

If I Don't Like Changes Made by a Firmware Update, Can I Go Back to an Older Version?

On some sites, you can download older versions of NOOK firmware (www.NOOKdevs.com), but because it automatically installs firmware updates when B&N makes one available, your NOOK always installs the latest update unless you keep Wi-Fi turned off or if you root the device and block over the air (OTA) updates.

▶ **Erase & Deregister Device**: Enables you to erase all content from and deregister the device. This action resets the NOOK to factory defaults, which is something you should consider doing if you are going to give it to someone else. B&N technical support also might ask you to reset your NOOK during troubleshooting. However, outside of those reasons, you likely won't ever need to reset it.

> CAUTION: Resetting your NOOK to factory defaults removes all content from its internal memory, although content stored on a microSD card is not removed. Before you reset it to factory defaults, make sure you have backups of any personal documents stored in your NOOK's internal memory.

▶ **Legal**: Takes you to a screen where you can choose to read the Terms and Conditions or the Open Source Licenses. Most of the time, you won't need these. (You agreed to the Terms and Conditions already when you got a BN.com account and registered your NOOK.)

Wireless

This setting enables you to turn on or off Wi-Fi access and set up connections to Wi-Fi networks. **See** the section "Using Wi-Fi Hotspots" in Chapter 15, "Getting Started with Your NOOK GlowLight," for more information about Wi-Fi hotspots.

> TIP: If you travel on a flight that offers Wi-Fi service, and you want to use the hotspot with your NOOK, turn off Wi-Fi access. When aboard and cleared to turn on electronic devices, turn on Wi-Fi access and select the airplane's network. However, check with the flight crew first to avoid any problems.

Screen

Here you can alter the screen timeout length and change screensavers.

The Screen timeout option controls the time interval after which your NOOK puts itself to sleep. This timer is set to 5 minutes by default. To change the interval, tap Screen Timeout, and then tap the wanted time interval.

> TIP: If you set the sleep timer to a time interval shorter than the amount of time it takes you to read a page on the reading screen, your NOOK goes into sleep mode while you are reading. So be sure you set the interval appropriately for your reading speed.
>
> Because your NOOK uses almost no battery power when you read, 15 minutes is likely a suitable interval for most people.

To change the screensaver, tap Screensaver, and then tap the folder of screensavers you want to use.

Time

These settings enable you to select your current local time zone and select a 12-hour or 24-hour clock format.

Reader (NOOK Simple Touch Only)

This option enables you to adjust the setup of the physical page control buttons. By default, the top buttons advance you forward in a book. But if you want the bottom buttons to advance you forward in a book, tap the Open button just above Page Forward with Bottom Buttons.

Shop, Gift Card, and Credit Card

This option enables you to set up some basic shopping features when shopping from your NOOK:

- ▶ Require Password for Purchases enables you to require a password be entered for any purchases.

- ▶ Manage Credit Card enables you to change the default credit card new book purchases are charged against. Tap Change Default Credit Card and then enter the necessary information in the Add a Credit Card screen.

- ▶ Redeem Access Code enables you to enter an access code you have been given to obtain content. You may receive a card for an ebook. The code is 13 characters. To redeem one, enter the code and tap Add Now.

- ▶ Gift Cards enables you to check a gift card balance and add any gift cards you've been given. When you purchase items from B&N, any gift cards are charged first before charging your default credit card. Tap Add Gift Card, enter the card number and PIN, and tap the check mark button to add another gift card.

- ▶ Clear Wishlist and Clear Recently Viewed Lists do just what they say they do. The wishlist on the NOOK is not connected to any other NOOK GlowLight, NOOK Simple Touch, NOOK HD, or NOOK HD+ devices or to your BN.com wishlist, so clearing the wishlist does it for this device only.

Social

This option contains several screens for configuring your NOOK's Social settings, for which you must have an active Wi-Fi connection. Basically, you can link your Facebook and Twitter accounts and Google Contacts lists to this NOOK, which enables you to share quotes and recommendations directly to your and your friends' Facebook walls and your Twitter account.

TIP: If you have earlier set up your Facebook, Twitter, and Google Contacts info (for example, you have a NOOK Color or NOOK Tablet) for this username, your NOOK automatically sets up your Facebook, Twitter, and Google Contacts information on this NOOK.

▶ **Tap Link to Facebook, Twitter, and Google to access these specific settings**: If you have already linked your Facebook account, you can unlink it. To link it, tap Link Your Account. Then enter the required information and tap the check mark button. You'll be asked to allow Facebook and your NOOK to share information. Tap Allow. For more information about Facebook with your NOOK, **see** Chapter 20, "Using the Social Features of Your NOOK GlowLight."

For Twitter, if you have already linked your Twitter account, you can unlink it. To link it, tap Link Your Account. Then enter the required information and tap the check mark button. Twitter asks you to allow this linking to occur. Tap Allow to do so. For more information about Twitter with your NOOK, **see** Chapter 20.

▶ **Google Contacts**: This enables you to link your Google Contacts list to this NOOK. If you have already linked your Google Contacts list, you can unlink it. To link it, tap Link Your Account. Then enter the required information. If you want the NOOK to remember this information should you come back to this screen, tap the Remember Me check box; then tap the check mark button. Google asks if you want to grant access to the NOOK to do this linking. Tap Grant Access to do so.

▶ **Manage My Contacts**: This enables you to add and edit your NOOK contacts list. (For example, if you don't use Google Contacts, you can just use contacts on your NOOK.) When you tap this, you see a list of your contacts. From the drop-down list, you can choose to see only your NOOK Friends or Google Contacts. The default is to see all your contacts. To see the details for your contacts, tap the contact's name. If the contact is not a NOOK Friend, you can tap the check box Invite as NOOK Friend and tap Send to invite that person. Tap View Emails to see all the email addresses. If the contact is not a Google Contact or NOOK Friend and is one you added directly to the NOOK, you can tap Modify to adjust the contact's information. Those are the only contacts you can delete as well. (Tap Modify and then tap Delete This Contact.) To update Google Contacts, log in to your Google account on your computer and update.

▶ **Manage My NOOK Friends**: This takes you to a screen to see who your NOOK Friends are, who has requested to be your friend, and who you have invited to be your friend. If you tap the plus button, you are provided a list of contacts. To invite any one of them to be a NOOK Friend, tap Invite. An invitation is immediately sent to that person. **See** Chapter 20 for more information related to NOOK Friends. To delete NOOK Friends, **see** Chapter 25, "Using My NOOK Library."

▶ **Manage Visibility of LendMe Books**: This enables you to control what books your NOOK Friends see as lendable. **See** Chapter 18, "Lending and Borrowing Books with LendMe on Your NOOK GlowLight," for more details about LendMe.

▶ **Auto-friending**: This setting automatically adds any Facebook friends as NOOK Friends. If you don't like that, just tap the check box to clear it.

Search

This option enables you to clear recent searches you have made on your NOOK. For example, if you have searched for "poetry" in your library, that appears when you go to do a new search in your library. If you want to clear those historical searches, tap Clear Recent NOOK Searches. Tap OK to confirm.

Adding a microSD Card to Your NOOK Simple Touch

Your NOOK Simple Touch has approximately 1GB of built-in usable memory. That's enough memory for an enormous library of books; however, it might not be enough memory if you add pictures and even more books to your NOOK Simple Touch. Therefore, your NOOK Simple Touch's memory is expandable using a microSD card.

> TIP: A microSD card is not the same as an SD memory card like the kind typically used in digital cameras. A microSD card is approximately the size of your pinky's fingernail.

To install a microSD card, you need to open the flap on the top right of your NOOK
Simple Touch:

1. The microSD slot is the small opening. With the metal connectors of the
   microSD card facing the front of the NOOK Simple Touch, slide the
   microSD card in (the gold connectors should be facing toward you if you
   are holding the NOOK's touchscreen up), and push until it locks into place.
   The NOOK Simple Touch automatically recognizes the card, and you hear a
   beep. Close the metal plate.

2. If the microSD card has not yet been formatted, a screen appears letting you
   know that formatting it will erase everything on the disk. Tap Format Now.
   Tap Format Now again to confirm.

On the Device Info screen (from the Quick Nav Bar, tap Settings, and then tap Device
Info), tap SD Card (only available to tap if a microSD card is installed). This opens
the SD Card screen. Here, you can see information related to the amount of free
memory available on the microSD card.

Tap Unmount SD Card if you want to remove or format the microSD card. The card
unmounts, and you can follow the preceding step 1 to remove it. (Just press the card
in farther and it pops out.)

If you tap Format SD Card, you can format the microSD card, which erases everything on the card. (This option is only available after tapping Unmount SD Card.) A
confirmation screen to format and erase all data on the micro SD card appears. Tap
Format to do so. Tap OK when done.

When you connect your NOOK Simple Touch to your computer, you now see your
microSD card in addition to its built-in memory. (It is the drive called NO NAME.)

NOTE: You can add a microSD card that already has items loaded on it, but
the NOOK Simple Touch folder structure is necessary, so it is easiest to install
a blank microSD card into the NOOK Simple Touch and then plug it into your
computer and load files into the appropriate categories (documents, videos, and
so on).

Now that you have a microSD card installed, how do you access those files? From the
Quick Nav Bar, tap Library and then tap My Files from the type drop-down list (the
far-left drop-down list beneath Library).

Can I Use a High-Capacity microSD Card in My NOOK Simple Touch?
Yes. The NOOK Simple Touch supports microSDHC cards up to 32GB.

CHAPTER 17

Reading on Your NOOK GlowLight and Beyond

Although your NOOK has many unique features and capabilities, when it comes right down to it, its primary purpose is for reading books and other content. One of the benefits of owning a NOOK is that you can carry a complete library with you everywhere you go. If you don't have your NOOK with you, you can also read your ebooks on your PC, Mac, iPhone, iPad, iPod touch, and Android phone (so long as you have the appropriate app for that device).

Various forms of content are available to read on your NOOK, such as NOOK Books, PDFs, and other EPUB ebooks. Appendix A, "Understanding ebook Formats," explains more about the details of ebook formats.

Can I Read Word Documents or TXT Files on My NOOK?

If you want to read Word documents or TXT files on your NOOK, you need to first convert them into a compatible format.

Calibre (calibre-ebook.com) can convert TXT files to the EPUB format for your NOOK. If you want to read a Word document, you should save the file as a PDF file. If you cannot save the Word document as a PDF, first save it as an HTML file, and then use Calibre to convert it for your NOOK.

For more information on using Calibre to convert ebooks, **see** Chapter 24, "Managing Your ebooks with Calibre."

Browsing Your Library

There are two main places for content on your NOOK: the Home screen and My Library.

The Home Screen

The Home screen includes content you have recently read, including new subscription content, new samples, and new ebooks. Tap My Library at the bottom of the Home screen to go to your full library.

TIP: Some notifications, such as new subscription content and LendMe offers, show up as balloon tips in the top information bar on your NOOK's Home screen or above the My Library text. You can access more details on these notifications by tapping the balloon.

The Reading Now section shows the last item you were reading along with which page you are on. Tap the cover to continue reading that content.

In the Now on NOOK section, you see new books at B&N. Tap See All to go to the NOOK Shop or tap the cover to see more details about that NOOK Book, including an option to purchase it. **See** Chapter 21, "Shopping and Visiting B&N on Your NOOK GlowLight," to learn more about shopping on your NOOK.

My Library

My Library contains all the content you purchase from B&N. This includes not only books you purchase, but also magazine and newspaper subscriptions, sample books, free books downloaded from B&N, documents you place on the NOOK, and everything else.

First, consider the basic controls in the Library:

- ▶ **Sync (button is two arrows forming a circle)**: The Sync button forces My Library to update, which means that it downloads any new content that has not yet downloaded and syncs reading location, annotations, highlights, and bookmarks on NOOK Books across NOOK reading devices (NOOK HD+, NOOK HD, NOOK Simple Touch, NOOK for iPad®, and so on).

- ▶ **Search (button is a magnifying glass)**: Tap this to search your Library. When the search screen appears, type your search criteria, and tap the Search key (looks like a magnifying glass on the keyboard). You can scroll through the results (if more than a few). Tap the item to open it. Tap Close to close the search screen and return to My Library. This feature doesn't search inside your content. It searches only the *metadata* for your content. Metadata includes the title, author, publisher, contributors, and subject.

- ▶ **Type**: The default is All, but you can narrow what you see in your Library by choosing what type of content you want to see: All, Books, Newsstand, LendMe, Shelves, My Files, Archived, or Everything Else.

NOTE: Here "All" doesn't actually mean "all content." If you choose All, you are viewing all content *except* for Archived and Everything Else items. However, while searching, archived content that matches your search criteria appears.

To change what you want to see, tap the drop-down list, and then tap your choice. A few of them offer additional actions beyond seeing what's available. Newsstand items show the overall subscription with the number of issues available. Tap the cover to see the individual issues. Tap the individual issue's cover to open it.

LendMe shows your NOOK Books available to lend. Tapping a cover here begins the lending process. **See** Chapter 18, "Lending and Borrowing Books with LendMe on Your NOOK GlowLight," for more information about LendMe.

Shelves enables you to see any shelves you created and enables you to add more. **See** the section "Shelves" later in this chapter for more information about using them.

My Files enables you to navigate the NOOK internal memory for non-NOOK Books content. Tap the folder to navigate to the location you want, and then double-tap the file to open it.

In Archived, tap the Unarchive button on the cover (or to the right of the title's name) to unarchive the title.

Everything Else shows you all your other B&N content that is not compatible with the NOOK GlowLight.

▶ **Sort**: Enables you to sort what you are viewing by the Most Recent items (that is, added to the NOOK), by title, or by author.

▶ **Grid/List View**: These two options determine how you view the content in the Library. (Grid view is a set of six boxes in a grid format, whereas List view is a set of four stacked lines.) Grid shows the covers. List shows the title without the cover.

▶ **My Library**: This is, of course, the main reason for this screen. You can scroll through the My Library and double-tap the cover (or the title if in List view) to see the Title Details screen. **See** "View Item Details and Options" for more information about that screen. Tap the cover (or the title if in List view) to open that ebook.

Items in My Library are in one of three categories:

▶ **Items on your NOOK**: Items on your NOOK are available for reading immediately by selecting the item. They are stored in your NOOK's memory or on a microSD card if one is installed.

▶ **Archived items**: These are items in My NOOK Library on BN.com and that have been downloaded to your NOOK device or app at one point but that have since been removed from your device (not necessarily from the same device or app on which it was downloaded).

▶ **Everything else**: These are items in My NOOK Library that are not compatible with the NOOK. For example, the NOOK HD+ and NOOK HD support apps, but the NOOK GlowLight does not. So My Library shows any apps you have purchased. Other examples include NOOK Books for Kids, some magazines (for example, *National Geographic*), and textbooks, among others.

For more information on using My NOOK Library on bn.com, **see** Chapter 25, "Using My NOOK Library."

When you purchase a NOOK Book, that book is added to My NOOK Library on BN.com and is downloaded to your NOOK.

CAUTION: If you plan to be away from Wi-Fi hotspots, you should make sure that the items that appear in My Library have actually been downloaded to your NOOK.

Some items in My Library might have an indicator banner on the bottom-left corner of the cover or to the right of the title. This icon indicates special properties of the item (such as the ability to lend the item to a friend using the LendMe feature), or it might indicate that an item has been lent to someone or is borrowed from someone.

For more information on the LendMe feature, **see** Chapter 18.

The following icons might be displayed for an item:

▶ **LendMe**: Indicates that the item can be lent to a friend using the LendMe feature.

▶ **On Loan**: Indicates that the item has been lent to a friend. You cannot read this item for a period of 14 days from the lend date.

▶ **Borrowed**: Indicates that the item has been borrowed from a friend. The item will be available to you for 14 days.

▶ **Lent to You**: Indicates that the item is one that a friend has offered to lend to you. After you accept the offer, the item shows a Borrowed banner.

▶ **Sample**: Indicates that the item is a sample ebook from B&N.

▶ **New**: Indicates newly purchased or arrived items.

▶ **Returned**: Indicates that a NOOK Book you borrowed has been returned.

You can also see the buttons Download (actually a cloud with a down-pointing arrow) and Unarchive on the cover in Grid view (or the right of the title in List view). Tap Download to download the NOOK Book from B&N. Tap Unarchive to unarchive the book.

View Item Details and Options

When you double-tap a cover in the Library, you see the Title Details screen. The available options differ depending on the content you select:

▶ **Download**: Displayed only when the content has not already been down-loaded to your NOOK. Tapping Download transfers it using Wi-Fi.

▶ **Read**: Displayed only when the content has been downloaded to your NOOK. Tapping Read opens the content on the reading screen.

▶ **LendMe**: Displayed only when the publisher has enabled the LendMe feature. This menu item enables you to lend the content to a friend.

▶ **Rating**: A series of stars is available so that you can rate your content. Tap the stars, and five large stars display. Touch the star that corresponds to your rating.

> TIP: If you want to remove your rating, tap the leftmost star, and drag your finger toward the left away from the stars.

▶ **Overview**: This displays a description of the item (if available) and other details.

▶ **Reviews**: For B&N content, you can see customer and editorial reviews of that NOOK Book. You can also add a review. **See** Chapter 20, "Using the Social Features of Your NOOK GlowLight," for more information.

▶ **More Like This**: This displays similar titles divided by either People Also Bought or More by This Author.

▶ **Share**: For more information about this feature, **see** Chapter 20.

▶ **Archive**: Removes the selected content from your NOOK's storage. The item is still visible in the Library, but if you want to read the content, you need to unarchive it first.

NOTE: There isn't a way to delete content from your library from the NOOK. To delete content (including sample books), you need to use My NOOK Library at the B&N website. If you delete content there, you will have to repurchase it.

For more information on using My NOOK Library, **see** Chapter 25.

Shelves

You can organize your ebooks into shelves, aligning them into whatever categories you want for easier access to similar ebooks. You can go directly to a shelf of books by pressing the Home button, tapping My Library, and tapping Shelves in the Type list. If you have more than four titles on the shelf, swipe left or right to horizontally scroll through the titles or tap See All to see all the titles on that shelf. Books, magazines, and so on can appear on multiple shelves.

If you have shelves you created and you want to place ebooks onto those shelves, tap Edit. A list of title appears. Scroll to the title or titles you want, tapping the check box along the way. Tap Save to add those titles to the shelf. If you want to remove titles from the shelf, simply tap the check box to clear out the check mark, and tap Save. You can add and remove titles at the same time.

The Sort options for shelves changes to Most Recent and Shelf Name. Just tap the Sort drop-down list, and tap the sort order you want.

To create a new shelf, from the Shelf screen, tap Add Shelf. Type the name of the shelf and tap Save. Add titles (although this is not required). Tap Save.

To remove a shelf, tap Edit for the shelf you want to delete, tap Delete Shelf, and tap OK.

To rename a shelf, tap Edit for the shelf you want to delete, tap Rename, update the name, and tap Save.

Archiving Library Items

As mentioned earlier, you can archive an item by double-tapping the cover and then tapping Archive on the Overview tab. Archiving is a means to remove an item you purchased from B&N from your NOOK. Archived items still appear in My Library but with the Unarchive banner appearing instead of the Download banner on the cover.

When an item is archived, you can still view details on the item, rate the item, and lend the item to a friend using the LendMe feature. However, to read the item, you must unarchive it.

To unarchive an item, tap Unarchive on the cover. The item begins downloading and disappears out of the Archived view.

> TIP: You can manage your ebook library (including archiving and unarchiving items) using My NOOK Library at bn.com. My NOOK Library is covered in detail in Chapter 25.

My Files

My Files contains content you manually copy to your NOOK from other sources. B&N calls the process of manually copying books and other content to your NOOK *sideloading*, and any reading content you sideload onto your NOOK appears in the My Files portion of My Library (and also when you view All content).

You can put files on the NOOK's built-in memory or on a microSD card (NOOK Simple Touch only). When you connect your NOOK to a computer, the folder structure is the same regardless of which memory it is (see Figure 17.1).

FIGURE 17.1   The folder structure for placing your files.

Any content you place in Books appears whenever you sort your library by Books. If you put files in Magazines and Newspapers, when you filter on Newsstand in My Library, those items appear there.

Regardless, you can get to any of your files by filtering to My Files. Tap either NOOK Files (those stored on the built-in memory) or Memory Card (those stored on the microSD card). Tap My Files—and so on until you get to the files you want.

> TIP: If you view My Library, you can switch to My Files by tapping My Files from the Type drop-down list.

View Item Details and Options

When you double-tap a My Files cover, you see the details for the selected item. Details include the publisher, publication date, and so on if available. You also see the file path for the selected item.

> TIP: The file path begins with my media if the selected item is stored in your NOOK's internal memory. If the item is stored in a microSD card, it begins with sdcard.

You have only one option from this Details screen: Open.

> **How Can I Delete Sideloaded Content Because There Isn't a Menu Option to Remove It?**
>
> Sideloaded content must be deleted by connecting your NOOK to your computer and removing the content. The easiest way to manage your sideloaded content is to use Calibre, a free ebook management application. **See** Chapter 24. Before you delete sideloaded content from your NOOK, make sure you have a copy elsewhere. Deleting sideloaded content is not like archiving a NOOK Book.

Reading Books on Your NOOK

If you open a NOOK Book or sideloaded EPUB file for the first time, after you select it, you go to the starting point that the publisher chose for that item. This might or might not be the first page. Some ebooks open on the cover or title page. The publisher of the book decides which page is visible when you first open an ebook.

If you open a NOOK Book that you have read on the NOOK before in any of the NOOK Apps, NOOK Study, or Samsung Galaxy Tab 4 NOOK, you are taken to the last location you were reading. If you open a sideloaded EPUB file you have read on the NOOK before, it opens to the last page you were on. In other words, non-B&N content does not sync across applications.

As you're reading, swipe right across the page to go to the previous page and swipe left across the page to go to the next page.

Of course, there's more to reading books than just reading, right? To see the Reading Tools, quickly tap the reading screen. (B&N recommends tapping the middle of the screen.)

The following are the Reading Tools options:

▶ **Contents**: This opens up a screen to navigate the table of contents, annotations, bookmarks, and lookups. To go to a specific table of contents, note, highlight, or bookmark, simply tap the appropriate tab, and tap the table of content location you want to go to. **See** Chapter 19, "Using Highlights, Bookmarks, and Annotations," for more details about using these features.

▶ **Find**: Tap this option to search the text within this book. Type the text and tap Search (the magnifying glass in the keyboard). The NOOK searches through the book and displays the results, providing the page number and some context for the search word. If you want to go to the location of that search, tap the row and you are taken there. Otherwise, tap the x button in the top right.

When you tap one of the search results, you are taken to the page, and at the bottom of the screen a bar appears where you can change the search term and move back and forth between the results (using the arrow keys). At the far left, you see button with four horizontal lines. Tap that to return to the search results screen.

TIP: Typing lots of uppercase letters? Tap the Shift key twice. (It has a white highlight around the key.) This enables you to enter only uppercase letters. Tap the Shift key again to release the Caps Lock.

▶ **Go To**: Tapping this displays a scrollbar, your location within the book, and two options: Go Back and Enter a Page. To scroll to a specific page, tap the vertical bar, and drag it to the location you want to go to. As you scroll, the page number and location information change to reflect that location. To go to a specific page, tap Enter a Page, type the number of the page, and tap the check mark button. Whether scrolling or going to a specific page, if you want to go back to the position in the book you were at immediately prior, tap Go Back.

▶ **Text**: Tap this to access the font and size options. **See** the "Changing the Text Font and Text Size" section for more details.

▶ **More**: This opens up the Details screen.

To exit the Reading Tools, tap anywhere on the reading screen without those tools appearing.

Finally, while reading, you can press and hold on a word. The Text Selection Toolbar appears. If you want to select more than that single word, drag the selection highlight to the end of the block of text you want to select. For the Highlight, Add Note, Share, and Look Up buttons, **see** Chapter 19. For the Share button, **see** Chapter 20. The "Looking Up Words" section of this chapter discusses looking up words.

Changing the Text Font and Text Size

Your NOOK enables you to easily change the text font and text size while you read.

The text options are available from the Text option on the Reading Tools screen. An array of options display: Size, Font, Line Spacing, Margins, and Publisher Defaults. (If the options are locked down by the publisher, you may have only an option to adjust the text size.)

Your NOOK supports seven text sizes, represented by the A. The current text size A is highlighted. Tap the A for the size you want. You can see the text size adjust behind the text menu.

The current font used has an arrow next to it. To change the font, tap from the six available fonts:

▶ You cannot change the text font if the publisher created the content with a specific font embedded in it.

▶ You cannot change the text font for PDF files. If the creator of the PDF file embedded a particular font, your NOOK uses that font. Otherwise, it uses the default font.

▶ Some ebooks consist of pages scanned as images, usually as PDF files. You cannot change the text font for these ebooks.

NOTE: Tapping Publisher Defaults to On changes all settings on this screen to the options chosen by the Publisher for all content that you read. You can toggle that back to Off at any time.

The Line Spacing options are similar to using single space or double space. The current selection is highlighted. You have three options. Tap the option you want. The reading screen adjusts.

The Margin options determine the amount of white space on the right and left sides of the text. The current selection is selected. You have three options. Tap the option you want. The reading screen adjusts.

Looking Up Words

One of the most convenient features of your NOOK is to quickly look up the definitions of words you don't know. If you're reading a book and encounter a word you don't know or are curious about, press and hold on that word until the Text Selection toolbar appears, which also displays a window with a dictionary entry. You can also tap the Lookup button (the one that looks like a book with A-Z appearing on it). This displays the definition in a larger screen with a larger font size.

> NOTE: Looking up words is not supported for certain types of ebooks—for example, ADE PDFs and PDFs.

Reading Magazines and Newspapers on Your NOOK

In addition to books, B&N provides magazine and newspaper subscriptions for your NOOK that it can deliver if a Wi-Fi connection is available.

For more information on subscribing to content on your NOOK, **see** Chapter 21. Some magazines are not supported for reading on your NOOK (for example, *National Geographic*), so be sure to check the supported NOOK devices and apps on the B&N website.

Unlike books, newspaper content isn't presented in a linear format. Content is often presented as article headlines followed by a small synopsis of each article. To read the specific article, tap the headline for that article. After an article is open, use swipe left and right gestures to navigate between pages just as you do when reading a book.

Tapping the screen displays the Reading Tools, which are the same as the ebook Read Tools.

Newspaper content often contains links that make navigating the content easier. For example, when reading *The New York Times*, you can move to the next or previous articles (as available) by tapping Previous Article or Next Article. Many magazines are set up the same way.

For more information on subscription content, including when your NOOK automatically deletes subscription content, **see** Chapter 21.

This chapter covered a lot of information on reading content on your NOOK. However, your NOOK is only one device of many that provides access to your My NOOK Library. You can also read content on your computer, your iPhone, and other devices.

CHAPTER 18

Lending and Borrowing Books with LendMe on Your NOOK GlowLight

To keep readers from sharing ebooks with all their friends, publishers usually protect ebooks with digital rights management (DRM), which ties an ebook to an individual. Unless that individual can prove that he or she is the authorized reader, the ebook does not open.

The use of DRM is a frequent complaint about ebooks. After all, when readers find a good read, they like to pass it on to friends and family. The number of people with whom you can share a physical book is fairly limited, but because ebooks are digital copies of a book, they can literally be shared with millions of people quite easily via email, Facebook, and any number of other methods.

One of the unique features that B&N added to its NOOK Books is the ability to lend some ebooks to other readers using the LendMe feature. Although there are restrictions when lending and borrowing books, the LendMe feature is a step in the right direction.

Lending Books with LendMe

To lend a book to someone, the book must support LendMe. Not all books do. If a book does support lending, you will see the LendMe logo on the book's page on BN.com, as shown in Figure 18.1. You also see the LendMe banner on the book's cover in the Library on your NOOK and in the NOOK App.

FIGURE 18.1   The LendMe logo appears on a book's page at BN.com if the book is lendable.

> TIP: To see a list of LendMe books on your NOOK, go to the My Library and choose LendMe from the Type drop-down. You are presented with only LendMe NOOK Books. Tap on the cover to begin the lending process.

To lend a book to someone using LendMe, follow these steps:

1. Browse to the book on your NOOK, and double-tap the cover to see the Details screen.

2. Tap LendMe. The LendMe screen appears.

3. Tap With Contacts to select someone from your contacts, or tap On Facebook to send the offer via Facebook.

4. Tap Next.

5. Tap Select a Contact to add a contact to receive this LendMe offer; select the contact and tap Done. Type a message to send with the lend invitation. (The message is optional.) The same goes for Facebook LendMe offers, but Select a Contact is instead Select a Friend.

6. Tap the check mark button.

Your NOOK then displays a message that it's taking care of your LendMe request. When that message disappears, you're taken back to your Library.

What Happens If I Lend My Friend a Book She Already Owns?

If you attempt to lend a book to a friend who already owns the book you're lending, a lending error occurs. On your NOOK, you simply see a message that says, "Sorry, Your LendMe Request Was Not Possible." On the NOOK for PC™ app, you see an error that says, "Lending Error." Unfortunately, B&N doesn't provide any useful information about why the failure occurred, so you're left to wonder if it's because your friend already owns the book or if something else went wrong.

If you see a lending error when attempting to lend a friend a book, check with your friend to see whether she owns the book already. If she does not yet own the book, contact B&N for information on why the LendMe attempt failed.

Choose carefully when lending a book because after you lend a book, you can never lend that particular book to anyone again. However, a book is considered to be on loan only if your friend accepts the LendMe offer. If your friend rejects the offer or if she allows the offer to expire without accepting it, you can lend the book again after it's returned to My Library.

I Want to Lend a Book to One of My Friends. Does My Friend Need to Own a NOOK for Me to Lend Her a Book?

No. Your friend can read an ebook you've lent to her using a NOOK desktop or mobile app. However, your friend cannot read the book unless the email address you used to send the LendMe offer is associated with her B&N account.

The person to whom you've loaned the ebook has 7 days to accept the loan offer. If she doesn't accept within 7 days, the book is returned to your library. The loan offer can also be rejected, in which case the book is returned to your library immediately.

You see notifications in the status bar about your loaned ebook if your friend accepts the loan offer or rejects the loan offer and when the loaned book has been automatically returned to your library. Loan offers and notifications are visible on the status bar and on your NOOK.

While an ebook is loaned, On Loan appears next to the title in the Library, and you cannot read the book. When you loan a book, you also loan your DRM rights to the book. Only one person can possess the DRM rights to a book at one time, so you need to wait until the book is returned to your library before you can read the book again.

If My Friend Finishes a Loaned Book Before 14 Days Have Elapsed, Can She Return the Book to Me Immediately?

Yes. Your friend can click the Return It link that appears in the book's listing in the NOOK App. However, you cannot manually return a book using your NOOK.

If your email goes awry and the offer doesn't arrive to the lendee, you cannot force a re-send of the offer email, and there's no way to cancel the offer. Just wait the seven days for the offer to expire and then send the offer again.

Borrowing Books

When a friend lends you a book, you can see the loan offer in the status bar (or in your NOOK App, on the Samsung Galaxy Tab 4 NOOK, via email, and so on). You have 7 days to either accept the offer or reject it. Tap the talk bubble in the top status bar to see the available LendMe offer. If you have only one offer, the offer appears. Tap No Thanks or Accept depending on what you want to do. If you have multiple offers pending, when you tap the talk bubble, you are presented with a list of offers. Tap View Offer to go to the specific item. Tap No Thanks or Accept.

If you accept a loan offer from your NOOK, that book is also available for the loan period in the NOOK Apps, NOOK devices, and vice versa. However, if you accept the offer from the NOOK App and then try to read the book on your NOOK, it might not realize that you've accepted the offer and might ask you to accept the offer again. When you do, the LendMe request will fail, and you'll see a message telling you that the LendMe request was not successful. When this happens, tap the Sync button from the Library, and your NOOK synchronizes with the loan offer you accepted in the NOOK App. You can then read the book you were loaned without any problems.

The banner on the cover shows the time left. If you don't finish the book within the loan period, you can buy the book (or go into a B&N store and read in the store). When you buy a book that was lent to you, the lent copy is immediately returned to your friend.

CHAPTER 19

Using Highlights, Bookmarks, and Annotations

Take a look at one of your favorite books, and you can likely find notes in the margins and perhaps dog-eared pages. Jotting down notes about passages that impact you or marking pages you want to come back to visit later is how you make books personalized possessions. Fortunately, you don't need to forgo these things when using ebooks because your NOOK enables you to highlight passages and add bookmarks and notes to pages.

Using Highlights, Notes, and Bookmarks on Your NOOK

When you think of highlighting something in a book, you typically think of using a yellow highlighter marker to draw attention to portions of the text. Highlighting on your NOOK is similar to that.

A note in an ebook is simply a highlighted area with a message attached. Therefore, the steps necessary to add, view, edit, and delete notes are the same as the steps for using highlights.

Adding a Highlight or a Note

To highlight text or add a note in an ebook, follow these steps:

1. Press and hold a word. The word appears in a bubble, and that is your signal to raise your finger. The word is highlighted, and the Text Selection toolbar appears.

2. If you want to highlight only that word, move to step 3. If you want to highlight a block of text, notice the highlighted word is bounded by two black bars. Press, hold, and drag one of the bars to the location you want to end or start the highlight.

NOTE: The initial word highlighted must always be the first or last word in the highlight.

3. Tap Highlight to just add a highlight. Tap Add Note if you want to add a note. If you chose the former, the text is highlighted. If you chose the latter, the Add Note screen appears.

4. Type your note and tap the check mark button.

5. The highlight is added, and a Note icon appears next in the margin.

Viewing, Editing, and Deleting Highlights and Notes

The simplest way to edit a note is to tap the highlighted text. A menu appears, giving you several options:

▶ **View Note**: Tap this to view the note. This appears only if a note is attached to that highlight. After you are in the note, you can tap Edit to edit the note.

▶ **Edit Note**: Tap this to edit the text of the note. This appears only if a note is attached to that highlight.

▶ **Add Note**: Tap this to add a note to highlighted text. An Add Note screen appears. Type in your note and tap the checkmark button. This appears only if no note is attached to that highlight.

▶ **Remove Note**: Tap this to remove the note. The highlight remains. This appears only if a note is attached to that highlight.

▶ **Remove Highlight**: Tap this to delete both the note and highlight.

TIP: You can view the note text by tapping the Note icon on the page. From there, you can then tap Edit to edit the text of the note.

To navigate or jump to notes throughout an ebook, from the Reading Tools toolbar (tap the screen), tap Content. Then tap Notes & Highlights. You see a listing of the notes in the ebook. (Scroll if you need to see more.) You see the text that was highlighted, the page number of the note, and the date and time it was last edited. Tap the particular note you want to jump to. The contents screen disappears, and you go to the page with the highlight or note you tapped.

Here are a couple other notes about this screen's contents. Two other options exist: Clear All and Show Notes & Highlights. If you tap Clear All, you delete all notes and highlights in the ebook. If you turn off Show Notes & Highlights (removing the check mark), you turn off the visibility of the highlights and notes. You can turn them back on by turning on Show Notes & Highlights.

Using Bookmarks

Bookmarks enable you to easily return to a particular page. Unlike notes, bookmarks do not have any text associated with them. Bookmarks work in all your ebooks, magazines, and newspapers.

For ebooks, magazines, and newspapers, to add a bookmark on the page you're reading, tap the reading screen, and then tap the icon that looks like a bookmark in the top-right corner. It changes to black. Tap it again to remove the bookmark. Alternatively, you can tap the upper-right corner of the screen to place a bookmark or tap the bookmark to remove it.

To return to a bookmark, from the Reading Tools toolbar, tap Content and then tap Bookmarks. A list of pages containing bookmarks appears. Tap the bookmark you want to go to; your NOOK immediately takes you to that page.

Tap Clear All to remove all bookmarks in that ebook, magazine, or newspaper.

CHAPTER 20

Using the Social Features of Your NOOK GlowLight

As I'm sure you know, Facebook and Twitter are big deals these days—everyone is sharing everything. The NOOK makes this sharing even easier. You can share your reading status and quotes and rate and recommend books. You can share to specific contacts on BN.com, Facebook, and Twitter. Because many of these options overlap and at the same time are scattered across the interface, this chapter focuses on Facebook sharing and the NOOK Friends app. However, sharing on Twitter is nearly identical.

> NOTE: Although the locations for the sharing features are scattered, they make sense in their location. Basically, B&N provides many locations for the sharing features to make it easy to share.

> NOTE: For LendMe coverage, **see** Chapter 18, "Lending and Borrowing Books with LendMe on Your NOOK GlowLight."
>
> Using Facebook and Twitter features requires that you link your Facebook and Twitter accounts to your NOOK. **See** "Social" in Chapter 16, "Customizing and Configuring Your NOOK GlowLight," for linking your accounts.

> NOTE: The social features work only for NOOK Books, magazines, and newspapers purchased from B&N.

You can access the social features in several ways:

- ▶ From the Details screen (remember, you get there by double-tapping the cover image), tap Share.
- ▶ From the Reading Tools toolbar, tap More, and then tap Share.
- ▶ From the Text Selection toolbar, tap Share.

Now let's consider each of these contexts.

Using Share from the Details Screen or Reading Tools Toolbar

Double-tapping a cover either from My Library or from the Reading Tools toolbar displays the View Details Screen. Tap Share and then tap Recommend to see your recommend options: With Contacts, On Facebook, and Via Twitter. Tap Facebook and then tap Next to see the Facebook Recommendation screen—if you are not currently connected to a Wi-Fi hotspot, your NOOK asks you to connect to one.

To post to your Facebook wall:

1. Tap Post to My Wall.

2. Type your message that will appear. As you type, you see the number of available characters (max of 420) go down, giving you an indication of how much space you have left.

3. Tap the check mark button. Your NOOK sends the recommendation to your wall.

After tapping Share from the Details screen, you have some other options: Post Reading Status, Rate and Review, and Like on Facebook.

▶ **Post Reading Status**: This option enables you to post how far along you are in reading this NOOK Book to Facebook or Twitter. A brief headline indicating how far you are into the NOOK Book and its title is followed by the synopsis of the NOOK Book as found on BN.com.

  After tapping Share and tapping Post Reading Status, tap the check box for Facebook or Twitter (or both), and then tap Post. The update is sent.

▶ **Rate and Review**: Tapping this allows you to rate and review the book on BN.com, which appears on the B&N book's specific web page. You must provide both a rating and either a headline or review before you can post. After you tap the check mark button, the information is sent to BN.com.

> TIP: When you are at a book's Detail screen and tap Reviews and are looking at Customer reviews, you will see a pencil icon with a plus above it. You can tap this to Rate and Review a title.

▶ **Like on Facebook**: This option enables you to post to your Facebook wall that you like this book. Tap this link, and your NOOK makes the connection that you like that NOOK Book.

Using Share from the Text Selection Toolbar

Use this share function when you have a quote you want others to see. You can share on Facebook, with a contact, or via Twitter:

1. Press and hold the word you want to start the quote.

2. When the Text Selection toolbar appears, finish highlighting the quote by dragging to the end of the text you want to share.

3. Tap the Share button.

4. Tap On Facebook, and then tap Next.

5. Tap Post to My Wall. Type a message and tap the check mark button.

The appropriate wall is updated.

What About Twitter and Contacts?

NOOK's support for Twitter and Contacts functions identically to Facebook, except that you share with specific contacts via email or your Twitter feed. Twitter has a more limited character count, however.

Using NOOK Friends

NOOK Friends is, to quote B&N, "the place for people who love to share their love for reading!" Here, you can connect with friends to lend and borrow books, see what your friends have been doing, and other things.

Adding NOOK Friends

If you want to add a friend or accept a request, tap the Gear icon and then tap All Settings. From the Settings screen, tap Social, and tap Manage My NOOK Friends. A screen appears with your existing friends. If you tap one of your friend's name, you see a screen that shows which of her books are available to borrow. Tap Requests when someone requests to be your NOOK Friend, which you can accept or decline. Tap Sent to see which NOOK Friends requests you have sent.

To send a request to become a NOOK Friend, tap the plus button. The Add NOOK Friends screen appears.

All Contacts displays to see all your contacts. Tap Invite to invite that contact, and they are sent an email as well as see the request on their NOOK. Tap Suggested to see a filtered list of your contacts that B&N knows already have a B&N account. You can also add a new contact by tapping the plus button. Enter her first and last names and the email address. Leave the Invite as NOOK Friend check box marked to send that contact a request to become a NOOK Friend. Tap the check mark button to send the request and save the contact.

If you want to delete NOOK Friends, **see** Chapter 25, "Using My NOOK Library." You can only delete them at BN.com.

Controlling What LendMe Books Your NOOK Friends Can See

Ever had a friend see a book of yours and request to borrow it, and you felt that you had to loan it even though it was the next book you wanted to read? Well, on your NOOK, you can hide any of your NOOK Books that have LendMe capability so that your friends cannot see it to request to borrow it. When you are ready to lend it (if ever), you can make it visible again.

First, make sure you have an active Wi-Fi connection. Tap the Gear icon, tap All Settings, and then tap Social. Tap Manage Visibility of My LendMe Books. On the screen that appears, you see a list of any LendMe books you own that your friends could request. To turn off a specific book from being seen, scroll to that title, and tap the Show check box so that the check mark disappears. Tap the check box to make the check mark appear again to show that book to your NOOK Friends again.

If you don't want to show any of your LendMe books to your friends, tap the check box with the long label Show All My Lendable Books to My NOOK Friends so that the check mark is removed.

CHAPTER 21

Shopping and Visiting B&N on Your NOOK GlowLight

One of the great features of your NOOK is the capability to sample and buy content from B&N directly from the device. As long as you have a Wi-Fi connection, you can get new content for your NOOK no matter where you are. However, you can also use the B&N website to sample and purchase content for your NOOK.

> NOTE: Only customers with billing addresses in the United States, Canada, or a U.S. territory can order content from the B&N NOOK Store. Citizens of U.S. territories cannot preorder items. UK citizens can purchase NOOK content from http://uk.nook.com/.

Shopping on Your NOOK

To shop on your NOOK, tap the Home button and tap Shop. Your NOOK establishes a network connection using Wi-Fi (assuming it has one) and displays the NOOK Store Home screen, what B&N calls the *shopfront*.

Browsing the NOOK Store

The shopfront is divided into a three sections: Shop, a scrolling list of recommendations and B&N bookseller picks, and Popular Lists. To start browsing, tap Books, Magazines, or Newspapers. Whichever you tap, a screen of categories for that list appears. You can scroll through the categories and tap to dive deeper into a specific category. Eventually (depending on the categories selected), you reach a list of specific titles. You can sort this list by Bestsellers, Most Recent, and so on. **See** the later section "Sampling and Buying Content" for what to do next.

In the middle of the shopfront is a section displaying picks (B&N Recommends, NOOK Daily Find, and so on). These are often based on your past purchase or browsing history. Also some deals are tossed in there as well. This section cycles through a series of screens. You can watch them cycle or swipe through them by tapping the small arrows on either the right or left.

> TIP: You've been browsing and searching for a while, and you want to get back to the shopfront quickly and easily. Tap the Shop Home button at the top of the screen to return to the front page of the NOOK Store.

Searching for Content

If you want to find a particular item in the NOOK Store, tap Search (the magnifying glass) and enter your search terms. Your NOOK displays the results of your search after several seconds. The results show all the items in which your search terms appear in one or more of the following:

- ▶ Title
- ▶ Author
- ▶ Publisher
- ▶ Subject
- ▶ Contributors

When your search results appear, you can view the results by covers in Grid view or by list view. In addition, you can sort by choosing Top Matches, Best Selling, Title, Price, or Release Date by tapping the drop-down list.

Sampling and Buying Content

After you locate and select an item you're interested in, tap the cover to see an overview page that describes the item and shows the rating of the item from other B&N readers. In addition, you see the following options:

- ▶ **Overview**: The default view when you tap a cover. You can tap the stars to give the NOOK Book a rating, tap Share to access the social options, or tap My Wishlist to add this title to your wishlist.

> NOTE: This wishlist is *not* the same wishlist as on BN.com or on your Samsung Galaxy Tab 4 NOOK, NOOK HD+, NOOK HD, NOOK Simple Touch, or any other NOOK GlowLights. Perhaps some day, B&N will synchronize the NOOK GlowLight wishlists with other NOOK wishlists.

▶ **Reviews**: Displays editorial and customer reviews for the item—pick which
one you want from the drop-down list. Editorial reviews often show details
from the publisher along with critic reviews of the item. It can span multiple
pages. Customer reviews are comments from other B&N customers. In fact,
you can enter your own review here. Just tap the pencil icon with a plus
above it. Give the book a number of stars, enter a headline for the review,
and enter the review. When you are finished, tap the check mark button.

▶ **More Like This**: Displays either more titles by this author or more titles
that other people purchased along with the book you are looking at. Tap the
drop-down list to see either set. Tap the cover to see information about
that title.

If you like what you see, you can download a sample to your NOOK by tapping Free
Sample. (Sampling is only valid with NOOK Books.) Samples typically consist of the
first chapter of an ebook. However, it's up to the publisher to decide what to provide
as a sample. In some cases, samples might contain just a few pages. In other cases,
samples consist primarily of front matter, such as the title page, table of contents,
dedication, and so on. One sample I downloaded contained nine pages of front matter
and two pages of actual manuscript—hardly enough to actually get a feel for the
book.

> NOTE: Samples never expire. You can keep a sample for as long as you want.
> Should you decide to eventually purchase the book, the sample is not replaced.
> If you want to remove it, you must delete it.

If you decide to buy a book after reading the sample, tap Buy; the book is then added
to your library. Because samples and full ebooks are completely separate products, a
purchased book does not open at the point where the sample ended. You must manually navigate to the point where you stopped reading the sample.

> NOTE: If a B&N gift card is associated with your account, the cost for items
> purchased from the B&N NOOK Store are applied against that gift card. If there
> is not enough credit left on the card, B&N charges the remaining balance to
> your credit card on file.

If you'd like to remove a sample from your NOOK, you must visit My NOOK
Library at BN.com from your computer or archive the sample in My Library. If you
delete a sample unintentionally, you can download it again.

For more information on using My NOOK Library, **see** Chapter 25, "Using My NOOK Library."

Is It Possible to Accidentally Purchase a Book I Previously Purchased from B&N's NOOK Store?

Your NOOK does not even present the option to purchase a book you already own. If you select a book in the NOOK Store that you already own, you are shown an option to download or read the book, depending upon whether the book is already on your NOOK. However, you will not be shown an option to buy the book.

Some classic titles are released by multiple publishers. Two books of the same title from two different publishers are not the same title, so in these cases, you can purchase the same book twice.

Subscription content also enables you to sample prior to purchasing, but it works a bit differently than it does with ebooks. When you subscribe to a newspaper or magazine, you receive a 14-day free trial. If you cancel your subscription within that 14-day period, you will not be charged. If you cancel after the 14-day trial period, you will be refunded a prorated amount based on when you cancel. You can also buy just the current issue by tapping Buy Current Issue. You will not be subscribed to that magazine or newspaper.

You can use a trial subscription only once for any particular item. For example, if you subscribe to *The Wall Street Journal* and cancel your subscription within the 14-day trial period, and you then resubscribe to *The Wall Street Journal,* you are immediately charged the normal subscription fee because you have already taken advantage of a trial subscription. To help you keep track of when you've used up a trial offer, when you revisit the Details screen for that magazine or newspaper, the Free Trial button is replaced with a Buy Current Issue button.

NOTE: Subscriptions can be canceled only using My NOOK Library at BN.com. You cannot cancel a subscription using your NOOK.

Your NOOK automatically downloads subscription content when it's available. In addition to seeing the new content in the Library, you'll also receive notifications in The Daily for any new subscription content your NOOK downloads.

Using Your NOOK in a B&N Store

As mentioned earlier, B&N stores have a Wi-Fi hotspot, so your NOOK can access free Wi-Fi while in the store. Your NOOK can automatically connect to a B&N hotspot when in the store, but you do need to ensure that Wi-Fi is turned on. (It's on by default.) Once connected, you can read any NOOK Book for free up to an hour a day.

After your NOOK connects to the B&N hotspot, tap Shop from the Home screen. Browse the store (or search for a specific title). Tap the cover of the book, and on the Details screen, instead of Download a Free Sample, a Read in Store button appears. Tap that button to download the book to your NOOK. After it finishes downloading, tap Read to open the book. Reading a book in the store is the same as reading it at home, except that you cannot enter notes or make highlights and a Buy button appears at the top of the reading screen.

CHAPTER 22

Reading Beyond Your NOOK: Mobile Apps

If you don't have your NOOK handy, you can read items from your ebook library using the B&N NOOK mobile apps. B&N provides a version of the NOOK application for iPhone, iPad, iPod Touch, Android phone, and Android tablet—even a NOOK Kids for iPad app. All the apps are free.

The experience the NOOK App provides varies depending on which device you use. On a tablet, the experience is similar to reading on your NOOK HD+. On other devices, the experience is a bit more scaled-down.

To obtain the app for your device, you can do either of the following:

- ▶ Go to http://www.barnesandnoble.com/u/nook-mobile-apps/379003593, click the appropriate link for your device, and then click Download Now. This opens up a web page at either Apple or Google Play. For Apple, click the View in iTunes, and then click Install after iTunes opens. For Google, click Install when the web page opens.

- ▶ From your device, go to the App Store (Apple) or Google Play (Google). Search for NOOK and then click Install. After the app installs and opens, enter your B&N username and password.

"Wait a second," you say, "I have a Samsung Galaxy Tab 4 NOOK an iPhone, and a PC. How does that work with my library?" First and foremost, your reading location in a book or magazine is, assuming you have an active Wi-Fi connection, synchronized to B&N, stored there, and then pushed out to other apps or devices you may have. So if you are reading the latest thriller on your iPhone while waiting for your take-out order, jump to read a chapter on your PC while working in the evening, and then settle down later that night with your Samsung Galaxy Tab 4 NOOK to continue reading, that version of the thriller will open up to the last read page.

Using NOOK Apps on Your iPad, iPhone, or iPod Touch

When you launch the NOOK App from your device, it syncs with your NOOK library and opens your library home page. You have quite a few options on this screen (see Figure 22.1):

▶ **Sync**: Tapping this synchronizes page location, notes, and so on with your NOOK Library.

▶ **Sort**: Tapping these options sorts your list by the designated category.

▶ **Type**: Tapping this lets you see either your All Items, Books, Magazines, Newspapers, My Files, Archived, or Everything Else. By default, your All Items are sorted by most recent.

FIGURE 22.1   The NOOK App interface has a lot of options.

> TIP: Everything Else is all the content that you *cannot* read in that app.

▶ **Settings**: Tapping this lets you see information about the NOOK App. One area in particular is the NOOK Profile. If you have set up profiles on your NOOK HD or HD+, those appear here. Tap NOOK Profile to switch between profiles and also manage what content is available for that profile.

▶ **Search Library**: Tapping this allows you to search your library for a specific book.

> NOTE: The focus of this section is on the iPad app, but the iPhone and iPod Touch apps are identical—just on a smaller screen.

Browsing My NOOK Library

Browsing your library is easy; just swipe up and down with your finger to scroll.

> CAUTION: On the iPhone of iPod Touch, don't be surprised if while you scroll through your library, you accidentally tap the Download icon and download the book to your device.

To read an ebook, you first need to download it to your device. It's easy to tell whether a book has been downloaded. If a Download button appears, you have not downloaded it to your device. Just tap the button to do so. After the ebook has been downloaded to your device, tap the cover to open the book.

If you press and hold a cover, a Details screen appears (see Figure 22.2). Here you can download a book if it is not yet downloaded, open it (tap Read), and archive or unarchive a book. You can also assign that book to a specific profile. You can even delete the book permanently.

Some content is grouped together: a book in a series, subscription content, and so on. For these, you see covers overlapping each other. Tap the overlapping covers to have the screen refresh and show only that grouping of content.

> CAUTION: Deleting a book, newspaper, or whatnot *deletes* it from your NOOK library. To *remove* it from your iPad only, tap Archive.

FIGURE 22.2   The Details screen for a NOOK Book.

Reading Books in the NOOK App

To read an ebook in the NOOK App, just tap the cover image to open it in reading mode. When there, to move to the next page, swipe your finger from right to left. To move to the previous page, swipe your finger from left to right. The reading screen, however, offers more options than just reading (see Figure 22.3).

If you do not see the surrounding bars in the reading screen, just tap the page, and they will appear. Before discussing some of these options, take a quick tour:

- ▶ **Back to Library**: Tapping this returns you to your NOOK library.

- ▶ **Back**: This icon appears when you have tapped a footnote link (refer to the "204 Sailing to Byzantium" in Figure 22.3), going to the footnote. Tapping the Return button takes you back to the page you were originally on.

- ▶ **Contents**: Tapping this opens the table of contents with tabs to see your annotations and bookmarks. You can scroll through any of these items and click the appropriate link to go quickly to that spot in the ebook.

- ▶ **Go to Page**: Tapping this allows you to enter a specific page number.

- ▶ **Text Options**: Tapping this allows you to adjust the specific font, theme, margins, line spacing, font size, justification, rotation, and defaults.

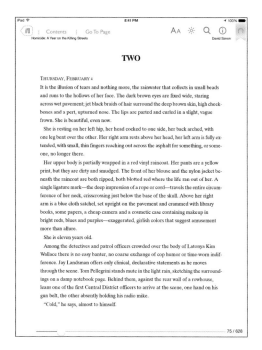

FIGURE 22.3   The NOOK App reading interface.

▶ **Brightness**: Tapping this lets you adjust the brightness.

▶ **Search**: Tapping this lets you search for specific text in this ebook.

▶ **Bookmark**: Tapping this adds a bookmark.

▶ **Book Details**: Tapping this brings up a page with details related to the book.

Two of these screens deserve more attention: Contents and Text Options. Now take a closer look at these.

Using the Contents Screen

After tapping Go To, you see a screen like Figure 22.4. The screen has three tabs: Contents, Bookmarks, and Annotations. Tap the tab you want to navigate to.

You can scroll through any of the tabs. If you have made bookmarks or annotations, they appear in the tab; otherwise, only blank screens appear. To quickly navigate to the chapter, bookmark, or annotation, tap the corresponding item you want to go to. The Contents screen disappears, and the reading screen reappears at the location you tapped to go to.

FIGURE 22.4   The NOOK App's Contents screen.

Adjusting Text Options

After tapping Text Options, you see a screen like Figure 22.5. The general purpose of this screen is to provide settings related to the reading experience in the NOOK App. To close the screen, tap anywhere outside of the Text Options screen.

In an ebook, the publisher often provides a series of defaults (font size, type of font, and so on). Changing the Publisher Defaults option to On sets the settings to use those publisher default settings instead of your own. You can change it to Off any time you want and then customize the screen layout as you see fit.

Clicking the A icon adjusts the font size. The current font size is a teal color. As you tap different sizes, the reading screen adjusts. Depending on what the publisher of the ebook allows, you can further adjust the font. You can scroll through the available list. (A check mark appears to the right of the currently selected one.) You have options between serif and sans serif fonts. Serif is a technical term that refers to the "hanging structure" on a letter. In general, most people find reading serif fonts easier on the eyes. But go with whatever appeals to you.

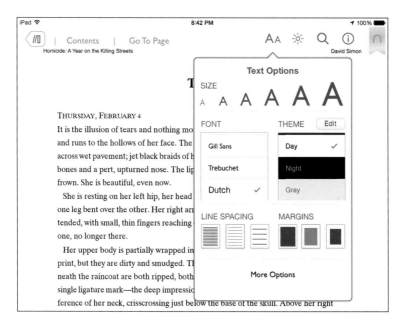

FIGURE 22.5   The NOOK App's Text Options screen.

> NOTE: Of the available font options, Century Schoolbook, Georgia, and Dutch are serif fonts. Ascender Sans, Gill Sans, and Trebuchet are sans serif fonts.

The set of icons beneath the font size determines line spacing. Think of this like single space, double space, and so on. The current setting is colored teal.

Margins determine how close to the edge of the screen the text goes. The more "dark" space in the center, the more the text appears on the screen. The currently selected Margin setting is colored teal.

More Options takes you to a set of four options: Justification, Publisher Defaults, Two Page Landscape, and Animate Page Turns.

The Justification setting is either On or Off (and is Off by default). If On, the text on the right side of the margin ends at the edge (think newspaper columns). If Off, then the line ends on the right wherever—giving it a ragged appearance. You won't see any difference in the reading screen with this option On or Off.

Two Page Landscape is either On or Off. Figure 22.6 shows what both look like. Animate Page Turns changes how changing pages appears. By default, the text just slides left or right. With Animate Page Turns on, turning a page simulates a real book.

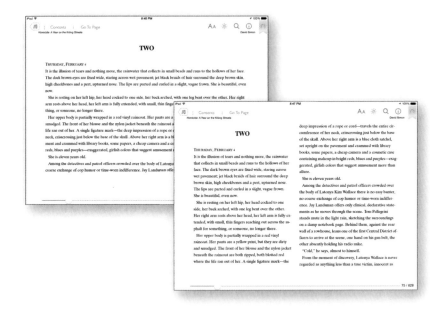

FIGURE 22.6   On the top, Two Page Landscape is Off. On the bottom, Two Page Landscape is On.

Back on the main Text Options screen, toward the top, to the right of Font, you see Themes. You can choose from the predefined themes. (A check mark is next to the currently selected option.) You can also create your own. Tap the plus button next to Theme to see the Create and Edit a Theme screen (see Figure 22.7). If you have already created a theme, the plus button is Edit instead. The bottom part of this screen gives you options for color related to the text, highlights, page, and links. Tap it and you end up in the reading screen color options screen.

The first thing to do is to give your theme a name. Tap in the Theme Name box and type the name. Next, select the particular part of the reading screen you want to change the color on: Text, Links, Page, or Highlights. You have a few color options. In the rainbow area, you can select any color you want. Below that is a gradient that goes from white to black, so if you want to operate only with making items some variant of black and white, you can use this instead of the rainbow area. Beneath that, you can see how your choices will appear on the reading screen. When you adjust the text color, the Preview Text item adjusts—ditto for Link Color and Highlight Color. Tap Save to save your theme.

To edit, tap the Edit button next to Theme, and tap the theme name you want to modify or delete. The Create and Edit a Theme screen appears. Make any changes and tap Save or tap Remove Theme to delete it.

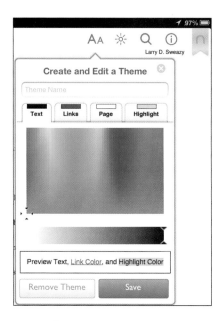

FIGURE 22.7   Create your own theme.

Adding Notes and Highlights in the NOOK App

Adding Notes, Highlights, and Bookmarks in the NOOK App is as easy as using your finger to select the part of the ebook to which you want to add a note or highlight. Here's how to do it:

1. Using your finger, select the word you want to add a Note or Highlight to. If you want to highlight more than one word, tap a single word first, and then use the teal lines to drag left or right to highlight more text. The text will be highlighted according to the Font settings' Highlight color. As soon as you lift your finger from the selection, you get a few options (see Figure 22.8).

2. Tap Highlight to add the highlight and nothing else. The text is highlighted.

3. Tap Add Note to go to the Add Notes screen, where you can type in a note and tap Save. A small sticky note appears in the margin.

4. Tap Look Up to get a definition or search the phrase (see Figure 22.9) if the definition at the top of the screen is not enough. If you select a single word, the definition appears (if one is available). You can also use Google or Wikipedia to launch the Safari browser with the text you selected entered as the search criteria and found (if results are available).

FIGURE 22.8   Adding a note or highlight.

FIGURE 22.9   The Look Up screen.

NOTE: To get definitions, you must have a dictionary installed. (The *Merriam-Webster's Collegiate Dictionary*, 11th Edition, is available for free.) If you have not installed it (you can do this in the Settings menu), and you highlight a single word or tap Look Up, you are offered an opportunity to download and install the dictionary. If you do have the dictionary installed, when you highlight a single word, the definition appears at the bottom of the reading screen. You don't need to tap Look Up.

5. Tap Find to start a search for the word or phrase in the book itself.

The note and highlights are available for easy access using the Contents menu from the reading screen.

To view an existing note, simply tap the sticky note that appears whenever a Note is already in place, and then tap View Note (see Figure 22.10). This same menu enables you to edit the note, delete it, or delete the note and the highlight.

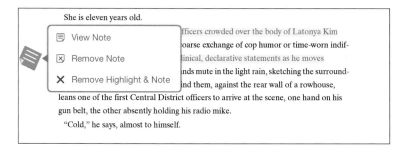

FIGURE 22.10   Changing notes or highlights.

If you have text that is highlighted only, tap quickly on the highlight, and then tap Remove Highlight from the menu that appears.

If you want to add a note to a highlight, tap quickly on the highlight, and then tap Add Note from the menu that appears. Enter your note and tap Save. The sticky note appears in the margin.

Reading Magazines and Newspapers in the NOOK App

In general, reading newspapers is a lot like reading books. However, because the Publisher Defaults are always on and you cannot turn them off, you usually can't alter text options for them.

Magazines, however, function a bit differently. Although you cannot read enhanced magazines on the iPad (for example, *Time*), many magazines are available without video, and so on. Magazines offer thumbnails that you can scroll through. To see that, just tap the screen to get the reading options (see Figure 22.11).

FIGURE 22.11   Reading a magazine.

You can scroll through the thumbnails to see what is covered on those pages. Just tap the thumbnail to go to that page. Tap Contents to see a vertical scrolling list of the magazine's contents or your bookmarks. Tap the article or bookmark you want to navigate to. Tap Brightness to adjust the brightness of the screen.

When reading an article, you can pinch and zoom in or out to see more or less of the page. However, you may find this tedious, which is why the app offers ArticleView. Tap it to start reading the article in a "bubbles" area (see Figure 22.12). If you are on a page with more than one article, ArticleView gives you the option of which article you want to read.

When in ArticleView, you have a couple of options. Tap the reading screen to see the Contents, Text, and Brightness options. The Contents and Brightness function just like the regular magazine reading screen. Text, however, gives you options similar to reading a book (see Figure 22.13). You can also move back and forth between articles by swiping right or left.

FIGURE 22.12   Reading an article.

FIGURE 22.13   A magazine's Text options.

The general purpose of the Text screen is to provide settings related to the reading experience in the NOOK App. To close the screen, tap anywhere outside of the Text Options screen.

Clicking the A icon adjusts the font size. The current font size is a teal color. As you tap different sizes, the reading screen adjusts. Depending on what the publisher of this ebook allows, you can adjust the font. You can scroll through the available list.

The bottom-left set of three icons determines line spacing. Think of this like single space, double space, and so on. The currently selected setting is colored teal.

The bottom-right set of three icons determine how close to the edge of the screen the text goes. The more "dark" space in the center, the more the text appears on the screen. The currently selected Margin setting is colored teal.

Adding a bookmark to a magazine is a bit different than a book. Instead of the bookmark icon appearing in the top right, you need to look at the bottom left, where you see a small triangle with a plus sign. Tap it to fold the page over. That's a bookmark. Tap it again to remove the bookmark.

Reading NOOK Comics

Reading comics in your NOOK App is straightforward. Mostly, you have fewer options. The thumbnail view is available that allows you to scroll through the pages (see Figure 22.14). The Content screen provides the vertical view while also letting you see your bookmarks.

You can use pinch and zoom gestures to zoom in on the page. However, the NOOK App also offers Zoom View, which appears at the top of the screen. When you use this, the screen zooms in on a specific panel (see Figure 22.15). When you swipe left or right, instead of advancing to the next page, you are advanced (or taken back) to the next panel. To turn on Zoom View, simply tap the button. When you use the thumbnails to advance to a different page, you are automatically taken out of Zoom View. You can also tap Zoom View again to leave that particular way of reading the comic. If you tap the Settings icon, you can turn on ZoomView Letterboxing. With this option on, the images around the nonzoomed in part are obscured slightly.

FIGURE 22.14   Reading comics.

FIGURE 22.15   Using Zoom View
in comics.

Reading PagePerfect Books in NOOK App

Much like your NOOK HD+, you can now read PagePerfect books with your NOOK App (see Figure 22.16).

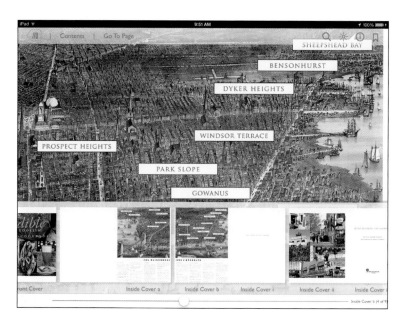

FIGURE 22.16   Reading a PagePerfect book.

In many ways, reading a PagePerfect book is like reading a magazine, although you have slightly different options. The thumbnail scroll is like a magazine's. Just swipe left or right to see the contents. Tap the thumbnail for the page that you want to go to. Tap Contents to see a vertical list of the book's contents, your notes and annotations, or bookmarks.

Tap Go to Page if you want to go to a specific page number. Type the number and tap Go. The screen jumps to that page.

The Search button offers similar search functions as reading a regular book.

You can add notes and highlights to PagePerfect books, but only to those areas that are *not* images.

Finally, you can pinch and zoom in or out like a magazine to read the text or get a better view of the picture.

Working with Profiles on Your NOOK App

You can now use multiple profiles in one NOOK App for the iPad and manage content for all profiles. To access the profile settings, tap the Settings icon and tap the arrow button (see Figure 22.17) for NOOK Profile. The Passcode for Child Profiles means that someone using a child profile cannot switch to other profiles (that is, those that control the content) without entering a passcode. You can turn this requirement on by tapping the switch for Passcode for Child Profiles, entering a four-digit PIN, and reentering that PIN.

FIGURE 22.17   The Settings for the NOOK App.

When you tap the arrow in settings, you see the screen shown in Figure 22.18. Here, you can see all profiles that have been set up (on the Samsung Galaxy Tab 4 NOOK or earlier NOOK HD or HD+). To switch to a different profile, tap the profile and then tap OK. If you are on a child profile and want to switch, you will be required to enter a passcode. If you want to adjust the passcode, tap Edit Child Passcode, enter the old PIN, enter a new PIN, and re-enter that new PIN.

If you want to manage content for a profile, tap Manage Content. The Manage Content screen appears. Tap a profile to manage.

When you tap a profile, the screen adjusts to that shown in Figure 22.19.

FIGURE 22.18   Available profiles.

FIGURE 22.19   Choosing specific content.

In this screen, any of the check marked items are content available to that profile. Tap covers to remove or add availability. If you want all items available or not, tap the All button in the top right. If all items are selected to be available, a check mark appears. If none are selected, a blank check box appears. The minus sign appears if there is a mixture of selected and not selected content.

In addition, you can switch between specific types of content by using the Type list as well as sort it using the Sort list. When you do that, the All function works for that *specific* type of content.

Tap OK when complete and you've managed the content for that profile.

Adding Content to Your NOOK App

You may have noticed in the NOOK Library a filter option titled My Files. The NOOK App now enables you to upload your own content to this area. You can upload EPUB (those without DRM) or PDFs to your NOOK Library.

> CAUTION: Any content you sideload into the NOOK App is not synched across devices.

You have two ways to do this: from the iPad or from your laptop.

From Your iPad

Many apps on your iPad enable you to add an EPUB or PDF file directly to the NOOK App. For example, I am a big fan of Dropbox. I store a lot of my files there because I can easily access them. When you open a PDF or EPUB in Dropbox, you see the Open In/Print button. Tap it, and then tap Open In. A list of apps appears that are applicable to that type of file (see Figure 22.20). Tap Open in Nook to launch the NOOK App and open the file. Doing so also adds the file to your library.

Another method to open this content from on the iPad is from Safari. If you like Project Gutenberg (tons of free books), you can browse their offerings on Safari and open an EPUB file directly into the NOOK App. First, find your book (see Figure 22.21). Tap EPUB, which opens up the screen in Figure 22.22. Tap Open In and choose Open in Nook to launch the NOOK App and open the file. Doing so also adds the file to your library.

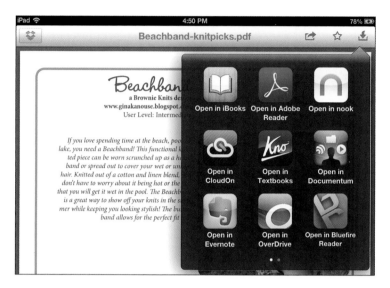

FIGURE 22.20   Opening in the NOOK from Dropbox.

FIGURE 22.21   Found an EPUB file to open.

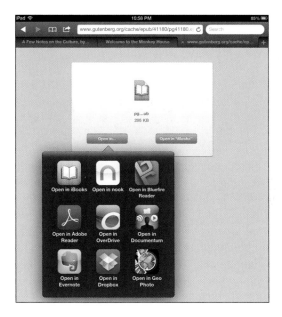

FIGURE 22.22   Opening in the NOOK from the Safari browser.

From Your Laptop

You can also use iTunes on your Laptop to add files. First, connect your device to a power source and start iTunes. From devices, choose the iPad and then select Apps. In this screen, scroll down until you see File Sharing (see Figure 22.23). Scroll through the Apps list and choose Nook. Click Add, browse to the file you want, and click Open. The file is added to the list, and when you synch, it is added to the list of files available in the NOOK App. To delete it, just highlight, and press Delete.

Also, if you have added a file from the iPad, you can see it here, highlight it, and click Save To to save it to your laptop for safekeeping.

Using the NOOK Video App

In 2013, B&N provided NOOK Video, which works on your Android or iOS device. The app is separate from the NOOK reading apps, and you can download it from the Google Play Store or Apple App Store. When you start the app, you will notice that it appears similar to the NOOK reading app (see Figure 22.24).

FIGURE 22.23   Adding content from within iTunes.

FIGURE 22.24   The NOOK Video app's opening screen.

You can sort your videos by Movies or TV Shows as well as sort them by most Recent and Title. Tap the Sync button to sync with your Library. To play a video, tap the cover. You see some details about the TV show or movie (see Figure 22.25).

FIGURE 22.25   A NOOK Video's Details screen.

Here you can choose to download the movie (particularly useful if you will be away from a Wi-Fi connection) or stream it. If this is a TV show, you see a list of episodes. Tap the episode name to see details specific to that episode and options to stream or download the show. If you have already begun a film, tap Resume to begin streaming where you left off. Tap Stream or Download to start watching or download the content. If you tap Download, a progress bar appears. Tap the X button to cancel the download. After a show has downloaded, the Stream button changes to Watch and the Download button changes to Remove from Device. Following are a couple things to note:

▶ When you stream a NOOK Video, it syncs across your devices (for example, on your iOS and Android devices). This means you can pause the film and resume watching from the paused point on a different device.

▶ When you download a NOOK Video, it does *not* sync across your devices.

When you are watching a movie or show (see Figure 22.26), you see traditional options for scrolling to a specific place in the video, controlling the volume, playing, pausing, jumping back 30 seconds, and so on. Tap Done to return to the video's Details screen.

FIGURE 22.26   Watching a video.

Using NOOK Apps on Your Android Device

When you launch the NOOK App on your Android device, it immediately syncs with your NOOK library. You have quite a few options on this small screen (see Figure 22.27):

▶ **Shop**: Tapping this synchronizes page location, notes, and so on with your NOOK Library.

FIGURE 22.27   The NOOK App interface has a lot of options.

▶ **Help**: Tapping this launches Chrome to the NOOK Reading Apps FAQ page.

▶ **Settings**: Tapping this opens a number of options you explore later.

▶ **Sync**: Tapping this synchronizes page location, notes, and so on with your NOOK Library.

▶ **Sort**: Tapping these options sorts your list by the designated category.

▶ **Type**: Tapping this lets you see either your All Items, Books, Magazines, Newspapers, My Files, Archived, or Everything Else. By default, your All Items are sorted by most recent.

> TIP: Everything Else is all the content that you *cannot* read in that app.

▶ **Search Library**: Tapping this allows you to search your library for a specific book.

> **NOTE:** As of this writing, B&N has disabled reading some subscription content on the NOOK App (particularly newspapers). If you want to read content other than ebooks, you need to use either NOOK for PC app, NOOK Study app, or NOOK.

> **NOTE:** The focus of this section is on the Android phone app; although the tablet app is identical—just on a bigger screen.

NOOK App Settings

Tap Settings from the main screen to show a variety of options (see Figure 22.28).

At the top, it shows you which account you are logged in under. Tap Logout to log out if you want to log in as someone else.

The credit card information is the same as the one tied to your BN.com account. Tap Edit if you want to update or enter new credit card information for making purchases.

In the Page Settings area, you have a few options:

- ▶ **Animated Page Turns**: This option simply turns on or off the appearance of a page turn when reading a book. If it is on, you see the page curl and lift before showing the next page. With it off, one page of text simply slides off and is replaced with another. The animated page turns take a bit more processing power, so on older devices, page turning may take longer with those on. Mostly, though, it's a matter of aesthetics.

- ▶ **Lock Page Orientation**: Tapping this shows you three options: Automatic (default), Portrait, and Landscape. If you leave it in Automatic, how you hold the phone determines the orientation. Choosing Portrait or Landscape *locks* the NOOK App on the phone from switching when you alter the position of the phone.

- ▶ **Hide Status Bar**: Tapping this lets you either display or not display the time and battery life. When reading a book, if you hide the time and battery life, you get a larger screen to read on, from the bottom bar where that information disappears. Leave the box unchecked to keep the battery life and time bar visible.

- ▶ **Two Page Mode**: Tapping this lets you determine how the reading screen appears when in landscape mode. If this is off, the reading screen is one column. If on, the reading screen splits into two columns.

FIGURE 22.28   The NOOK App's settings.

▶ **Zoom View Letterboxing**: Tapping this controls how the screen appears
when using Zoom View in comic books. Without the Zoom View letterboxing off, the surrounding panels are still visible, but with this setting on,
when you zoom from panel to panel, the panels not part of the focus are
hidden.

In the Other Settings area, you have two options:

▶ **Download over WiFi Only**: This setting enables you to control when to
download large files. Some comic books and magazines can exceed 20MB,
and you may not want to use up valuable data over the cellular network. In
that case, turn this setting on, and any files larger than 20MB must wait until
a Wi-Fi connection is established.

▶ **Dictionary Options**: Use this setting to control which dictionary (if more
than one exists) to use. If you have a dictionary installed, it shows here. Just
tap to see what your available dictionaries are or download another free one
(currently, only the *Merriam-Webster's Collegiate Dictionary*, 11th Edition,
is available—to use that, you must download it).

Browsing My NOOK Library

Browsing your library is easy; just swipe up and down with your finger to scroll.

To read an ebook, you first must download it to your device. You can easily tell whether a book has been downloaded. If a Download button appears, you have not downloaded it to your device. Just tap the button to do so. After the ebook has been downloaded to your device, tap the cover to open the book.

For subscription content (magazines and newspapers), the items are "put together." You can see this when multiple covers appear behind the front cover. Tapping the screen opens up a detail screen that shows more of the available content (see Figure 22.29). Tap the cover again to close it.

FIGURE 22.29   Seeing available subscription items.

If you press and hold a cover, a Details screen appears (see Figure 22.30). Here you can download a book if it is not yet downloaded, open it (tap Read), buy it if it is a sample, and archive or unarchive it. You can even delete the book permanently.

You can also see what other customers have said about the book by tapping Customer Reviews.

If you have added notes, highlights, or bookmarks, you can also see them from the Details screen by tapping the Notes, Highlights, Bookmarks tab. You can then tap the note, highlight, or bookmark to open the book to that location.

FIGURE 22.30   The Details screen for a NOOK Book.

CAUTION: Deleting a book, newspaper, or whatnot *deletes* the book from your NOOK library. If you want to *remove* the book from your iPad but keep the book, tap Archive.

Reading Books in the NOOK App

To read an ebook in the NOOK App, just tap the cover image to open it in reading mode. When there, to move to the next page, swipe your finger from right to left. To move to the previous page, swipe your finger from left to right. The reading screen, however, offers more options than just reading (see Figure 22.31).

If you do not see the surrounding bars in the reading screen, just tap the page, and they appear. Before discussing some of these options, take a quick tour:

▸ **Home**: Tapping this returns you to your NOOK library.

▸ **Back**: This icon appears when you tap a footnote link. Tapping the Return button takes you back to the page you were originally on.

FIGURE 22.31   The NOOK App reading interface.

▶ **Contents**: Tapping this opens the table of contents with tabs to see your annotations and bookmarks. You can scroll through any of these items and click the appropriate link to go quickly to that spot in the ebook. Also, if you know the page you want to go to, type it into the top text box and tap Go To.

▶ **Search**: Tapping this lets you search for specific text in this ebook. **See** the section "Looking Up Words."

▶ **Text**: Tapping this allows you to adjust the specific font, theme, margins, line spacing, font size, justification, rotation, and defaults. **See** the section "Adjusting Fonts."

▶ **Brightness**: Tapping this lets you adjust the brightness.

▶ **Details**: Tapping this brings up a page with details related to the book.

Two of these screens deserve more attention: Contents and Text.

Using the Contents Screen

After tapping Go To, you see a screen like Figure 22.32. The screen has three tabs: Contents, Notes & Highlights, and Bookmarks. Tap the tab you want to navigate to.

FIGURE 22.32 The NOOK App's Contents screen.

You can scroll through any of the tabs. If you have made bookmarks or annotations, they appear in the tab; otherwise, only blank screens appear. To quickly navigate to the chapter, bookmark, or annotation, tap the corresponding item you want to go to. The Contents screen disappears, and the reading screen reappears at the location you tapped to go to.

Looking Up Words

If you're reading a book and encounter a word you don't know or are curious about, press and hold on that word until the Text Selection toolbar appears. Tap Look Up. A window appears with a dictionary entry (see Figure 22.33). You can also tap Wikipedia or Google. Tapping takes you to the browser, opens up the corresponding website, and enters that word as the search criteria. If you want, you can look up another word by tapping in the Edit Your Search box and editing the word and tapping return.

To search your ebook for a specific word or phrase, tap the Search button, and then type the text you want to search. A keyboard and text entry box appears. Type your search words and tap Search. If it finds your word, your NOOK Tablet displays the locations of that word in a scrollable window (see Figure 22.34). The scrollable window provides a bit of context. Tap the location of the word you want to go to. You are taken to that location, the word is highlighted, the scrollable window disappears, but you still see the search text box. You can tap the bottom-left button to redisplay the scrollable window, or you can tap the left or right keys next to the search word to go to and highlight the next appearance of that word. Tap the X, or tap the reading screen to exit search mode. If you want to search for a different word or phrase, tap in the box that contains your original search term.

FIGURE 22.33 Your dictionary goes wherever your NOOK App goes.

FIGURE 22.34 Searching your ebook is easy.

Finally, if you select a word while reading, from the Text Selection toolbar, you can tap Find. Your NOOK Tablet performs a search for that word or phrase in that ebook, displaying the results like any other search.

Adjusting Fonts

After tapping Text, you see a screen like Figure 22.35. The general purpose of this screen is to provide settings related to the reading experience in the NOOK App. To close the screen, tap anywhere outside of the Text screen.

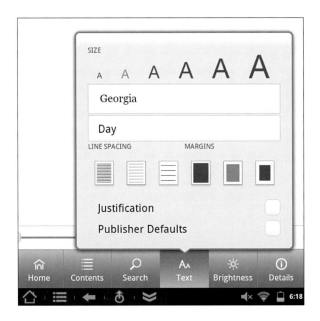

FIGURE 22.35   The NOOK App's Text Options screen.

Clicking the A icon adjusts the font size. The currently selected font size is a teal color. As you tap different sizes, the reading screen adjusts.

Depending on what the publisher of this ebook allows, you can adjust the font. You can scroll through the available list. (A check mark appears to the right of the currently selected one.) You have options between serif and sans serif fonts. Serif is a technical term that refers to the "hanging structure" on a letter. In Figure 22.35, if you look at the word "Georgia," notice the little hanging things off the top of the G? That's a serif. Sans (French for "without") serif fonts lack these structures. In general, most people find reading serif fonts easier on the eyes. But go with whatever you want.

> NOTE: Of the available font options, Century Schoolbook, Georgia, and Dutch are serif fonts. Ascender Sans, Gill Sans, and Trebuchet MS are sans serif fonts.

Beneath the type of font, you can choose from a number of themes, which determine the font and page colors. The current selection has a check mark next to it. Scroll to the one you like and tap it to switch.

The three icons below the theme for line spacing determine how much space is between the lines. Think of this like single space, double space, and so on. The current setting is colored teal.

To the right of line spacing, margins determine how close to the edge of the screen the text goes. The more "dark" space in the center, the more the text appears on the screen. The currently selected Margin setting is colored teal.

The Justification setting is either On or Off (and is Off by default). If On, the text on the right side of the margin ends at the edge (think newspaper columns). If Off, then the line ends on the right wherever—giving it a ragged appearance. I have yet to see any difference in the reading screen with this option On or Off.

If you'd like, you can turn on Publisher Defaults, which set the font, size, spacing, and so on to what the Publisher feels is optimal.

Adding Notes and Highlights in the NOOK App

Adding Notes, Highlights, and Bookmarks in the NOOK App is as easy as using your finger to select the part of the ebook to which you want to add a note or highlight. Here's how you do it:

1. Using your finger, select the word you want to add a Note or Highlight to. If you want to highlight more than one word, you can either drag your finger to the end point or tap a single word first and then use the teal lines to drag left or right to highlight more text. As soon as you lift your finger from the selection, you get a few options.

2. Tap Add Highlight to add the highlight and nothing else. The text is highlighted.

3. Tap Add Note to get a text box. Type your note and tap Save. A small sticky note appears in the margin.

4. Tap Look Up to get a definition or search the book (**see** the earlier section "Looking Up Words").

The note and highlights are available for easy access using the Contents menu from the reading screen.

To remove or edit an existing note, simply tap highlighted text; tap either Remove Note or Edit Note. If you choose the latter, the text box appears with your existing note, which you can change. Tap Save to update it.

If you have text that is highlighted only, tap quickly on the highlight, and then tap Remove Highlight from the menu that appears. You can also choose to add a note. Enter your note and tap Save. The sticky note appears in the margin.

Reading Magazines and Newspapers in the NOOK App

In general, reading newspapers is a lot like reading books. Generally, however, you cannot alter the text options because the Publisher Defaults are always on, and you cannot turn them off.

Magazines, however, function a bit differently. Although you cannot read enhanced magazines on an Android device (for example, *Time*), many magazines are available without video, and so on. Magazines offer thumbnails that you can scroll through. To see that, just tap the screen to get the reading options (see Figure 22.36).

FIGURE 22.36 Reading a magazine.

You can scroll through the thumbnails to see what is covered on those pages. Just tap the thumbnail for the page you want to go to. Tap Contents to see a vertical scrolling list of the magazine's contents or your bookmarks. Tap the article or bookmark you want to navigate to. Tap Brightness to adjust the brightness of the screen.

When just reading an article, you can pinch and zoom in or out to see more or less of the page. However, you may find this tedious, which is why the app offers ArticleView. Tap it to start reading the article in a "bubble" area (see Figure 22.37). If you are on a page with more than one article, ArticleView gives you the option of which article you want to read.

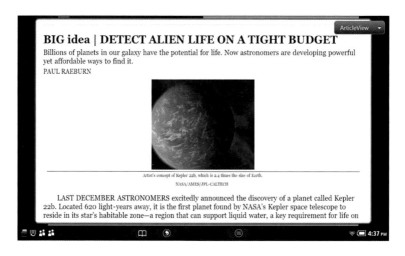

FIGURE 22.37   Reading an article.

When in ArticleView, you have a couple options. Tap the reading screen to see the Contents, Text, and Brightness options. The Contents and Brightness function just like the regular magazine reading screen. Text, however, gives you options similar to read-ing a book (see Figure 22.38). You can also move back and forth between articles by swiping right or left.

You can adjust the font size. The general purpose of this screen is to provide settings related to the reading experience in the NOOK App. To close the screen, tap any-where outside of the Text Options screen.

Clicking the A icon adjusts the font size. The current font size is colored red. As you tap different sizes, the reading screen adjusts. Depending on what the publisher of this ebook allows, you can adjust the font. You can scroll through the available list.

The bottom-left set of three icons determines line spacing. Think of this like single space, double space, and so on. The current setting is colored red.

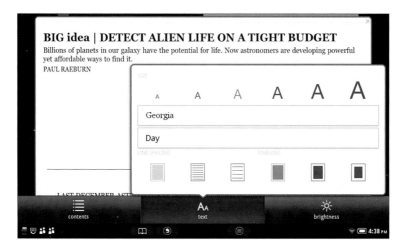

FIGURE 22.38   A magazine's Text options.

The bottom-right set of three icons determines how close to the edge of the screen the text goes. The more "dark" space in the center, the more the text appears on the screen. The currently selected Margin setting is colored red.

Adding a bookmark to a magazine is a bit different than a book. Instead of the bookmark icon appearing in the top right, you need to look at the bottom left, where you can see a small triangle with a plus sign. Tap it to fold the page over. That's a bookmark. Tap it again to remove the bookmark.

Reading NOOK Comics

Reading comics in your NOOK App is straightforward. Mostly, you have fewer options. The thumbnail view is available that allows you to scroll through the pages (see Figure 22.39). The Content screen provides the vertical view while also letting you see your bookmarks.

You can use pinch and zoom gestures to zoom in on the page. However, the NOOK App also offers Zoom View, which appears at the top of the screen. When you use this, the screen zooms in on a specific panel (see Figure 22.40). When you swipe left or right, instead of advancing to the next page, you are advanced (or taken back) to the next panel. To turn on Zoom View, simply tap the button. When you use the thumbnails to advance to a different page, you are automatically taken out of Zoom View. You can also tap Zoom View again to leave that particular way of reading the comic.

FIGURE 22.39   Reading comics.

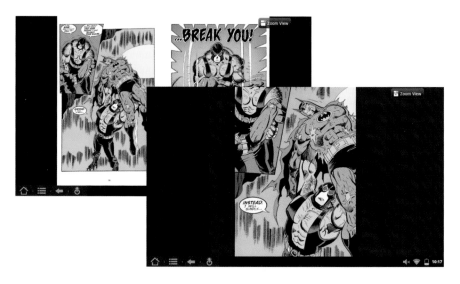

FIGURE 22.40   Using Zoom View in comics.

Adding Content to Your NOOK App

You can add non-DRM EPUB files to your NOOK App. The procedure is simple:

1. Connect your Android device to your laptop.

2. When its drive appears in Finder (Mac) or File Explorer (Windows), open the NOOK folder.

3. Open the My Documents folder.

4. Drag or copy and paste any EPUB files you want into that folder.

5. Disconnect your device.

When you open the NOOK App, you will have access to them. You can narrow down into them by filtering to just My Files.

Shopping from the NOOK App

You can shop for new books, magazines, and newspapers directly in the NOOK App. Tap the Shop button to open the NOOK Shop (see Figure 22.41). This screen is divided into two parts. At the top, the tag Customers Who Bought This Also Bought gives an indication of what those covers mean. The leftmost cover is something that you have purchased in the past. Based on what others have purchased, you see a list of those items. You can scroll through them to see the full list. If one of the titles interests you, tap the cover to see a detailed info screen about that title.

FIGURE 22.41   The NOOK Shop.

The bottom part of the screen defaults to the B&N Top 100 sellers list. You have several options here. First, you can change the list of what you're viewing by tapping the drop-down list and selecting from the available options (see Figure 22.42).

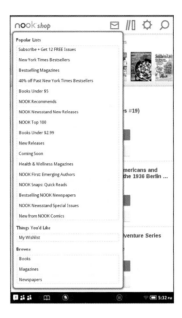

FIGURE 22.42   A multitude of ways to browse the NOOK Shop.

If you tap one of the Browse categories (Books, Magazines, and Newspapers), a screen pops up with additional categories. You can continue to drill down to a list of titles to browse. If you tap My Wishlist, you see items that you have added to your wishlist. Note that this wishlist is separate from your BN.com or NOOK device wishlists.

In the listing of titles, you can tap the price button to purchase the book. The button changes to Confirm. Tap it again to complete the purchase. If you tap Free Sample, it is downloaded immediately to your library. Samples typically consist of the first chapter of an ebook. However, it's up to the publisher to decide what to provide as a sample. In some cases, samples might contain just a few pages. In other cases, samples consist primarily of front matter, such as the title page, table of contents, dedication, and so on. One sample I downloaded contained nine pages of front matter and two pages of actual manuscript—hardly enough to actually get a feel for the book.

> NOTE: Samples never expire. You can keep a sample for as long as you want.

Also, you can tap Add to Wishlist, which adds the title to your wishlist. When you view the wishlist, you can purchase books from that list by tapping the Purchase button and then tapping Confirm. This removes the item from your wishlist and adds it to your library. Also, you can tap Remove to remove that title from your wishlist.

While browsing titles, if you tap the cover, you are taken to a Details screen (see Figure 22.43).

FIGURE 22.43   Details screen.

From this screen, if you tap the Purchase button and then Confirm, you'll buy the book and add it to your library. You can choose to get a free sample from here and add it to your wishlist. The Overview tab provides a description. You can tap Customer Reviews and Editorial Reviews to see what others have to say. On the Customer Reviews tab, you can add your own review, which will be posted to BN.com. Tap Write a Review. The Rate and Review screen appears. Provide a star rating, a headline, and your review. (You must provide all three.) Tap Post when you finish.

To exit the Details screen, tap the X in the upper-right corner.

The Details screen for magazines and newspapers are a bit different (see Figure 22.44).

FIGURE 22.44   A magazine's Details screen.

If you want to buy the current issue, tap the Current Issue button, and then tap Confirm. This adds that issue to your library. You do not automatically receive the next issue. For that, you must subscribe. If you have never subscribed to the newspaper or magazine, you can tap Free Trial, which opens a Confirm Your Order screen (see Figure 22.45).

When you subscribe to a newspaper or magazine, you receive a 14-day free trial. If you cancel your subscription within that 14-day period, you will not be charged. If you cancel after the 14-day trial period, you will be refunded a prorated amount based on when you cancel.

You can use a trial subscription only once for any particular item. For example, if you subscribe to *The Wall Street Journal* and cancel your subscription within the 14-day trial period, and you later resubscribe to it, you will be charged immediately because you have already taken advantage of a trial subscription. When you revisit the Details screen for that magazine or newspaper, the Free Trial button is replaced with a Subscribe Now button.

NOTE: Subscriptions can be canceled only using My NOOK Library at BN.com. You cannot cancel a subscription using your NOOK App.

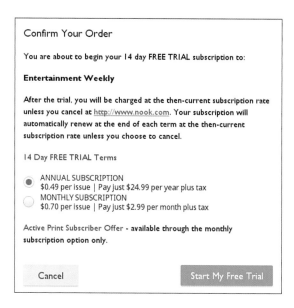

FIGURE 22.45   Confirming if I want to start a trial.

Finally, if you want to search the NOOK Shop for a title, an author, or whatnot, tap the Search button (the magnifying glass), enter your search term(s), and tap Go on the keyboard. You see results displayed onscreen just like the B&N Top 100 list.

To get back to your library, tap the Library button.

Working with Profiles on Your NOOK App

You can now use multiple profiles in one NOOK App for the iPad and manage content for all profiles. To access the profile settings, tap the Settings icon and tap the arrow button (refer to Figure 22.28) for NOOK Profile. The Passcode for Child Profiles means that someone using a child profile cannot switch to other profiles (that is, those that control the content) without entering a passcode. You can turn this requirement on by tapping the switch for Passcode for Child Profiles, enter a four-digit PIN, and re-enter that PIN.

When you tap the arrow in settings, you see the screen shown in Figure 22.46. You can tap Switch Profile or Manage Content. To switch to a different profile, tap Switch Profile, which shows the profiles as seen in Figure 22.47. Tap the profile you want and then tap OK. If you are on a child profile and want to switch, you will be required to enter a passcode. If you want to adjust the passcode, tap Edit Child Passcode, enter the old PIN, enter a new PIN, and re-enter that new PIN.

FIGURE 22.46   Switch or manage profiles.

FIGURE 22.47   Choose a profile.

If you want to manage content for a profile, tap Manage Content and then tap the profile for which you want to manage the content. The screen adjusts to that shown in Figure 22.48.

FIGURE 22.48   Choosing specific content.

In this screen, any of the check marked items are content available to that profile. Tap covers to remove or add availability. If you want all items available or not, tap the All button in the top right. If all items are selected to be available, a check mark appears. If none are selected, a blank check box appears. The minus sign appears if there is a mixture of selected and not selected content.

In addition, you can switch between specific types of content by using the Type list as well as sort it using the Sort list. When you do that, the All function works for that *specific* type of content.

Tap OK when complete and you've managed the content for that profile.

Using the NOOK for Kids App for Your iPad

When the Barnes and Noble NOOK Color was released November 19, 2010, one of its signature features was NOOK Kids Read to Me ebooks. These books featured a narrator (and not a fake, mechanical-sounding one) if you wanted it. Moving from page to page, a child could hear the words read to them. Tapping the text reread that particular segment. Thumbnail views of each page mimicked the visual magazine representation. The downside of these books is that they were only available for the NOOK Color. (This was all prior to the NOOK Tablet's, NOOK HD+'s, and NOOK HD's releases.)

Fortunately, Barnes and Noble released the NOOK for Kids app for iPad, which enables the same experience with NOOK Kids Read to Me ebooks whether you have a NOOK Color or an iPad.

Installing and Setting Up NOOK Kids for Your iPad

Find the NOOK Kids app in iTunes, whether on your computer or on the iPad (see Figure 22.49). (In that case, use the App Store.)

FIGURE 22.49   The NOOK Kids app in the iTunes store.

After you find the app, install it. If you downloaded it via iTunes, sync your iPad to load the app. With your iPad on, tap the NOOK Kids app icon.

The first time you start the app, you will be asked to enter your Barnes & Noble account information and name the library (for example, Raleigh's Library)—see Figure 22.50.

You are ready to start browsing and reading NOOK Books.

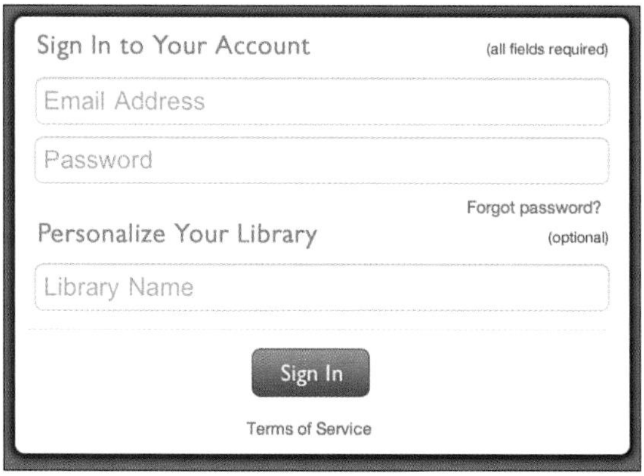

FIGURE 22.50 Enter your account information to start.

Browsing Your B&N Library

After you have installed the NOOK for Kids app and so long as you are connected via Wi-Fi or 3G/4G, your B&N NOOK Books library will appear on the shelves (see Figure 22.51), for example, anything that is a NOOK Kids Read to Me ebook or NOOK Book for Kids (that is, ones without the Read to Me feature but are "traditional" children's books, like *Curious George Goes to the Ice Cream Shop*). You may also notice NOOK Books that don't fit these categories directly: *The Adventures of Tom Sawyer* or *Grimm's Fairy Tales*. I have been unable to discern why those appear but others do not; although I assume that Barnes and Noble considers them appropriate children's books. No matter, you can control which titles you want to appear in the NOOK Kids app (**see** "Using the Parents Button," later).

> NOTE: Double-check BN.com when you purchase kids books that say Read to Me if you want the Read to Me feature.

To download the book to your iPad so that you can read it, tap the Download button. You can tap the red x button to stop the download (see Figure 22.52).

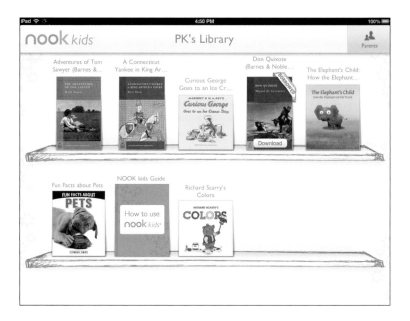

FIGURE 22.51   Browsing the library.

FIGURE 22.52   Downloading a NOOK Book.

To scroll up and down in your library, press the screen, and while holding your finger to the screen, drag your finger up or down.

If you tap the Refresh button, any new purchases appear or archived items disappear.

You have one other option here: Parents. The "Using the Parents Button" section covers this.

Reading a NOOK Kids ebook

To open a book, tap the book's cover in the library. Essentially, there are two types of books that you can read in the NOOK for Kids app: your traditional young children's book with a focus on images and text, and more straightforward texts, like *The Adventures of Tom Sawyer*. Both are covered here, but focus first on the former.

> NOTE: NOOK Kids Read and Play NOOK Books are not compatible with the NOOK for Kids app.

Reading NOOK Books for Kids

These books, such as *The Elephant's Child: How the Elephant Got His Trunk*, always open and are read in landscape view (that is, wider rather than taller). Many of these books have the Read to Me feature available. (These books are labeled as NOOK Kids Read to Me on BN.com.)

When you open these types of books, you are presented with two options: Read by Myself and Read to Me (see Figure 22.53). If the book is not a NOOK Kids Read to Me book, you have only the option Read by Myself, which means just that—no audio reading of the book occurs.

If you choose Read to Me, as you advance from page to page, you hear a person reading the text to you. You can pause the text, and you can replay the text. If you do not make a choice and flip to the first page of the book, the default is Read to Me.

The basics are this: To advance a page, swipe the screen from right to left. To go back to a previous page, swipe the screen from left to right. Double-tapping the text places the text in a balloon, and you have a play button at the corner of the text (see Figure 22.54). Tapping this play button reads that portion of the text. If the button has a square in it, tapping that pauses the reading. If you chose Read to Myself, you can double-tap the text and press the play button to have it read the recording to you.

If the book is not a Read to Me book, if you double-tap the text, it is shown in a balloon without the play or pause button.

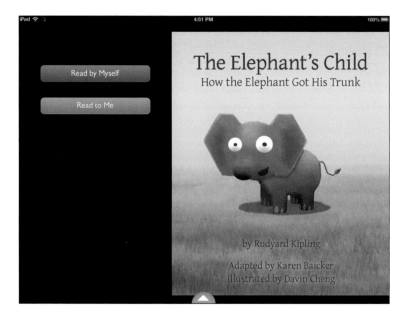

FIGURE 22.53   The opening page for a NOOK Kids Read to Me ebook.

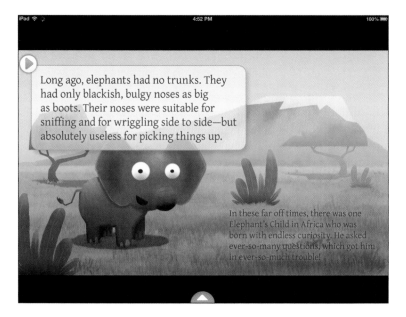

FIGURE 22.54   You can replay specific portions of the text.

As you read these books, you notice an upward arrow button at the bottom of the page. If you tap this, a variety of reading options appears at the bottom of the page, and thumbnails of the pages appear (see Figure 22.55):

▶ **Library**: Tap Library to return to your B&N library.

▶ **Play/Pause**: Plays or pauses the reading for that page. If you choose Read to Myself, this option does not appear here, but you can double-tap the text and choose the play button to play the recording.

▶ **Pages**: Tap this to hide the thumbnails if they are visible or show them if they are hidden.

▶ **Brightness**: Adjust the brightness of the screen.

▶ **Thumbnails**: The current page you are on is marked with a blue outline. Press, hold, and drag the thumbnails back and forth to scroll through them. Tap a thumbnail to advance to that page. As you scroll, you see a small light gray bar increase or decrease as you advance or retreat through the thumbnails. This is an indication of your overall location in the book.

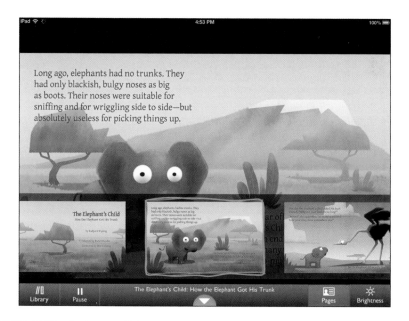

FIGURE 22.55   Options available while reading.

Reading NOOK Books

These books, such as *The Adventures of Tom Sawyer*, open in either landscape or portrait mode. When there, to move to the next page, swipe your finger from right to left. To move to the previous page, swipe your finger from left to right. The reading screen, however, offers more options than just reading (see Figure 22.56).

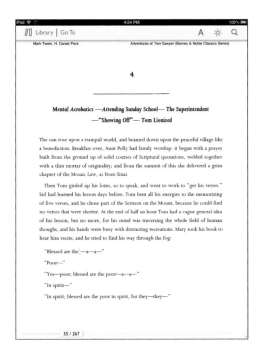

FIGURE 22.56   Options when reading regular NOOK Books.

If you do not see the top light teal bar and the bottom scroll bar in the reading screen, just tap the page and they appear. Before exploring some of these options, take a quick tour:

- ▶ **Library**: Tapping this returns you to your NOOK library.

- ▶ **Go To**: Tapping this opens the table of contents with links to see your notes and annotations and bookmarks. You can scroll through any of these items and click the appropriate link to go quickly to that spot in the ebook.

- ▶ **Bookmark**: Tapping this adds a bookmark to this page.

- ▶ **Search**: Tapping this lets you search for specific text in this ebook.

- ▶ **Brightness**: Tapping this lets you adjust the brightness.

► **Font**: Tapping this allows you to adjust the specific font, justification, colors, and font size.

► **Scroll Bar**: Tapping and holding this lets you move quickly from page to page.

Adjusting Fonts

After tapping Fonts, you see a screen like Figure 22.57. The general purpose of this screen is to provide settings related to the reading experience in the NOOK App for regular NOOK Books. Tapping outside the Fonts screen closes it, returns you to the reading screen, and makes any changes that you have indicated.

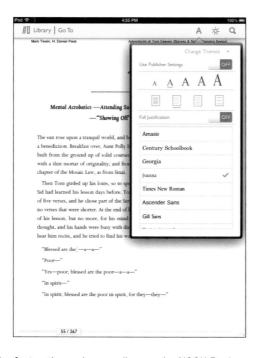

FIGURE 22.57   The font options when reading regular NOOK Books.

Tapping Change Themes changes the screen, which actually means text color, background color, and highlight color. You have five themes you can choose from. Tap the theme, and either tap Back to adjust more font items or touch the reading screen.

Back at the Fonts screen, you can choose Use Publisher Settings. In an ebook, the publisher often provides a series of defaults (font size, type of font, and so on).

Changing this option to On sets the settings to those publisher default settings. You can change it to Off at any time you want.

Tapping the A icon adjusts the font size. The current font size has an underline beneath it.

The set of icons beneath the font size determines line spacing. Think of this like single space, double space, and so on. The current setting has a line beneath that icon.

The Full Justification setting is either On or Off (and is Off by default). I have yet to see any difference in the reading screen with this option On or Off.

Depending on what the publisher of this ebook allows, you can adjust the font. You can scroll through the available list. (A check mark appears to the right of the currently selected one.) You have options between serif and sans serif fonts. What is this? Serif is a technical term that refers to the "hanging structure" on a letter. Referring to Figure 22.57, if you look at the A icons, notice the little base at the bottom of each leg of the A? That's a serif. Sans (French for "without") serif fonts lack these structures. In general, most people find reading serif fonts easier on the eyes.

> NOTE: Of the available font options, Amasis, Century Schoolbook, Georgia, Joanna, and Times New Roman are serif fonts. Ascender Sans, Gill Sans, and Trebuchet MS are sans serif fonts.

Adding Notes, Highlights, and Bookmarks in the NOOK for Kids App for iPad

Adding notes, highlights, and bookmarks in the NOOK for iPad app is as easy as using your finger to select the part of the ebook where you want to add a note or whatever to. Here's how you do it:

1. Using your finger, press and hold until you see the word your finger is on become highlighted; then select the text you want to add a Note or Highlight to. (If you just want that word, you can lift your finger.) The text will be highlighted according to the Font settings' Highlight color. As soon as you lift your finger from the selection, the Note & Highlights screen opens (see Figure 22.58).

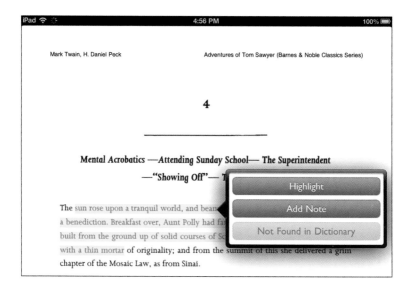

FIGURE 22.58   Adding a note or highlight.

2. Tap Highlight to add the highlight and nothing else.

Tap Add Note to go to the Add Notes screen where you can type in a note and tap Save Note.

If you select a single word, the Search Dictionary is an available option. Tapping it brings up a dictionary entry for the word. Tapping outside the definition screen takes you back to the reading screen.

3. The note and highlights are available for easy access using the Go To menu from the reading screen.

Using the Go To Menu

Speaking of the Go To menu, you use this menu to access the NOOK Book's table of contents or any note and highlights you have added.

While reading a NOOK Book, tap Go To to access the table of contents (see Figure 22.59). Tap any location in the table of contents to go to that spot in the NOOK Book.

Tap Notes & Highlights or Bookmarks to access any of these that you have added to the NOOK Book. Tap the specific one you want to go to.

FIGURE 22.59   Accessing the table of contents.

Using the Parents Button

You need to explore the final areas of the NOOK for Kids iPad app: Parents. The Parents options provide a way to limit which books appear in the library and control password access. Tapping Parents first asks you to enter your password. After you do that, you see a new screen that defaults to the Manage Kids' Library section (see Figure 22.60).

On this screen, you can control which books appear in the library and are stored on the iPad. For example, if you want to allow *The Aeneid* to be read in the NOOK for Kids iPad app, you can tap the check box in the Show in Kids' Library column.

If you want to remove a book from the library in the NOOK for Kids app, you can tap the check box so that the check mark no longer appears. In addition, you can tap Remove to remove the file from the app. (You can always re-add it by downloading it again.)

When you tap Settings, you get the Settings screen (see Figure 22.61).

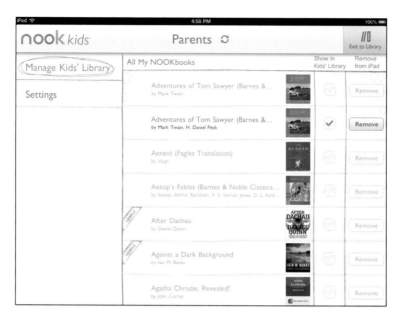

FIGURE 22.60   The Manage Kids' Library screen.

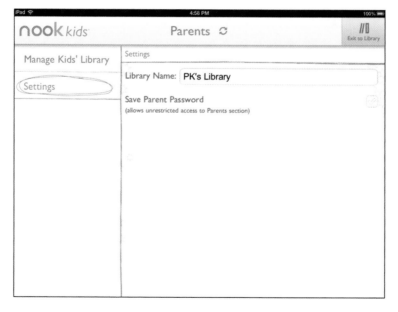

FIGURE 22.61   The Settings screen.

If you choose Save Parent Password, anyone accessing the Shop or Parents button does not need to enter a password. If you choose to not save the password (by removing the check mark), any time users tap the Shop or Parents button, they are required to enter the password. In other words, if you don't want your kids to control what ebooks appear in the Library, do not save the password.

Also, here you can change the Library Name.

As you can tell, the NOOK for Kids app for iPad is an easy-to-use app, but its primary distinction is that it enables you to use the Read to Me features for kids books whether you have a Samsung Galaxy Tab 4 NOOK or not.

CHAPTER 23

Reading Beyond Your NOOK: Desktop Apps

In this chapter, you look at the NOOK Apps B&N provides for reading NOOK Books, Newspapers, and such on your desktop or laptop: NOOK for PC/Mac, NOOK Study, and NOOK for Web. If you don't have your NOOK handy, you can read items from your ebook library using these apps.

You can download the NOOK App for your PC or another device by going to http://www.barnesandnoble.com/u/nook-mobile-apps/379003593, clicking the appropriate NOOK App device link, and clicking the Download Now button.

If you have multiple NOOKs and NOOK Apps, B&N keeps them all synchronized (assuming you have active Wi-Fi connections for each device) so that when you jump from device to device, you can pick up right where you left off.

Using the NOOK for PC App

After you install the NOOK for desktop—whether for the PC or Mac—app, when you first launch the app, you'll be asked to sign in to your B&N account. Enter your username and password, and click Sign In if you already have an account on BN.com. If you don't have an account, you can click Create an Account to create one.

Browsing Your B&N Online Library with the NOOK for PC App

After you sign in to your account, the NOOK for PC app checks in with My NOOK Library and synchronizes samples, last pages read, and so on. You then see a series of buttons along the left side (see Figure 23.1).

By default, the NOOK for PC app displays all items. However, you can filter the view to show only ebooks, emagazines, enewspapers, archived items, and manually added content (what B&N calls "my stuff") by clicking the appropriate option in the My Library menu.

FIGURE 23.1   The menu buttons in the NOOK for PC app mirror several of those on your NOOK.

Along the top of the NOOK for PC app are buttons to manually refresh your library, control the views of your library, sort your library, and search your library, as shown in Figure 23.2.

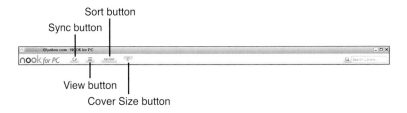

FIGURE 23.2   Function buttons at the top of the NOOK for PC app enable you to control how you view your library.

Clicking the Sync button synchronizes your B&N NOOK Library with the NOOK for PC app. Use this to synchronize your notes and page location.

The View button controls how your ebook library appears in the NOOK for PC app and shows what view you are currently in (three lines for list view and six boxes for grid view). By default, the NOOK for PC app shows your library in list view. In this view, a small image of the cover of each item displays along with items such as the author, the last read date, and so on. You can switch to a grid view that shows only large images of each item's cover by clicking View button, as shown in Figure 23.3.

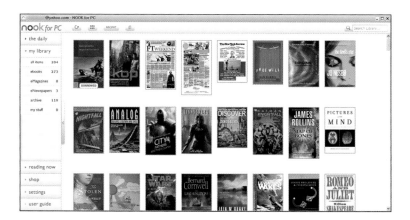

FIGURE 23.3   Viewing My Library in grid view.

When you select to show your items in grid view, the Cover Size button enables you to control the size of the cover image that displays. (The button shows a small rectangle.) The smallest size is slightly smaller than the size displayed when in grid view, and the largest size is approximately twice the size of the covers shown in grid view.

> NOTE: Most covers provided with ebooks and other content look terrible when you select the largest available size in list view because they're not intended for display at such a large size.

You can sort your online library in the NOOK for PC app by clicking the Sort button, which defaults to Recent but changes to Title and Author as you continue to click it.

As you accumulate a library of digital content, the NOOK for PC app enables you to easily find content by searching for it. When you click inside the Search Library box, you're given a choice to search for a title, an author, a publisher, or all three. Select an option, enter your search text, and either click the magnifying glass or press Enter to search your library.

> TIP: Searches are filtered based on how your library is filtered. For example, if you select eMagazines from the My Library menu, searches show only magazines that match your search terms, so if you actually want to search your entire library, make sure you click All Items in My Library.

If you want to view all the items in your NOOK library instead of just those that match your search terms, click the X inside the Search Library box. Doing so clears your search term and shows all the items in your online library.

Shelves on the NOOK for Mac App

On the NOOK for Mac app, you can also create shelves. Just click Create Shelf. The Create a Shelf dialog box appears. Enter a name for the shelf and select an icon. You can add a title to the shelf by clicking and dragging a title from the My Library screen.

At the bottom of the screen, you see the My Archive, Settings, Info, Sync, and Notification buttons. Click My Archive to see your archived items. **See** the "Configuring the NOOK for PC App Settings" section to learn about these settings. The Info option enables you to check your system, review the privacy policy, and so on. Clicking the Sync button forces the NOOK App to sync with your other NOOK devices and apps. If you receive LendMe offers, you see it appear in the Notification button. Click it to see the offer. You can choose to Accept or Reject.

Viewing the Daily in the NOOK for PC App

Clicking the Daily menu button displays the Daily. Assuming you are connected to the Internet, it updates with the latest articles and loan offers. Click Read Now to read the particular article, which appears in a small box. Clicking Close hides the article from view.

NOTE: On the NOOK for Mac app, the Daily does not exist. Instead, you have just My Library.

For a loan offer, you can click Accept or Decline. Or you can click Details, which refreshes the screen to show just that book, some additional details, and buttons to Buy Now and More by Author. Clicking either of these last two options opens your browser to the book page (where you can purchase it) or to a listing of that author's titles.

Shopping for ebooks in the NOOK for PC App

Clicking the Shop button opens up your web browser at BN.com. For more information about shopping for ebooks, **see** "Shopping on Your Computer" in Chapter 12, "Shopping and Visiting B&N on Your Samsung Galaxy Tab 4 NOOK."

Item Options in the NOOK for PC App

Click the More Options button (see Figure 23.4) or hover your mouse pointer over an item (see Figure 23.5) in My Library to see several options:

▶ **Read Now**: Opens the item in the NOOK for PC app. If the item hasn't been downloaded to your computer, the NOOK for PC app downloads it first and then opens it.

▶ **LendMe**: Displayed only for items you can lend to friends. When clicked, it opens a dialog box for entering the email address of a friend to whom you'd like to lend the item. **See** the section "Using LendMe in the NOOK for PC App," for more details about the LendMe feature.

▶ **Download**: Displayed when the item hasn't been downloaded to your computer. When clicked, the item is downloaded to your local computer, and Download changes to Remove Local Copy.

▶ **Remove Local Copy**: Displayed when the item has been downloaded to your local computer. When clicked, the item is removed from your local computer. If you want to read it at a later time, you need to download it again. Note that this does not remove the items from your NOOK library; it removes it only from the particular computer you use.

▶ **Move to Archive**: Moves the item to your archive. Archived items appear in the Archive category in My Library.

▶ **Unarchive**: Displayed only for archived items. When clicked, the item is moved from the archive to your main digital library.

FIGURE 23.4   Available options for when in list view.

FIGURE 23.5   Available options for when you hover over a cover.

▶ **Details**: Opens a screen that provides a bit more information, including buttons for Remove Local Copy, Move to Archive, Read Now, and More by Author.

> TIP: Archiving or unarchiving an item in the NOOK for PC app on your PC also archives or unarchives the item for all your NOOK devices and apps.

For subscription content for which you have more than one copy available to read, when you click Details, a new screen appears (see Figure 23.6). From here, you can pick the specific issue you want to read, download, or archive.

FIGURE 23.6   Subscription content details.

Reading Books in the NOOK for PC App

To read a book, click the cover or click Read Now from the available options described previously. Your book opens, hiding the My Library, My Daily, and so on bar (see Figure 23.7). You can always see My Library again by clicking the large gray box with the right pointing arrows. This slides the My Library bar over (see Figure 23.8). While you're reading content, the NOOK for PC app displays the Reading Now menu, as shown in Figure 23.8. Using the Reading Now menu, you can easily navigate to the last page read, access the table of contents, and access bookmarks, annotations, and highlights for the item you're reading.

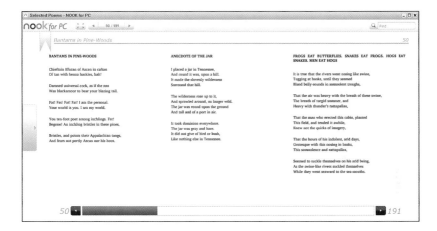

FIGURE 23.7 How a book opens in NOOK for PC.

FIGURE 23.8 Reading a book with My Library visible.

While reading, you navigate the pages by pressing the arrow keys (right and down advance a page; left and up retreat a page) or clicking the arrows in the scrollbars at the top or bottom of the screen. In the top scrollbar, you can click the page number and enter a new page number to be taken directly to that page.

At the top of the screen, the Full Screen button adjusts the screen by removing the clutter (see Figure 23.9). Press Esc or click the button again (its arrows now point toward each other) to return to the default reading screen.

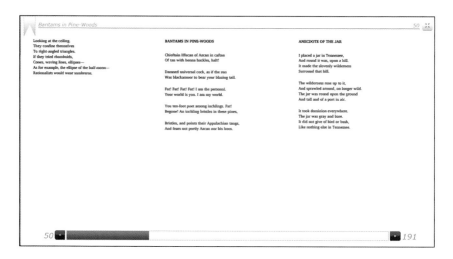

FIGURE 23.9   Reading in Full Screen mode.

In the Search box, you can type a word or phrase to search the book on. Type the text you want to search on, and press Enter. If a result is found, you are taken to that page with the word highlighted. Click the magnifying glass to advance to the next instance of that word found in the book. When no more instances of that word are found, a small dialog box appears that states, No Matches Found. If you type a word that does not appear in the book, a dialog box appears that states, No Matches Found.

If you want to navigate to a particular chapter or location in the book, you can use the Table of Contents option. Just click that, and the table of contents appears next to the reading screen (see Figure 23.10). You can scroll through this table of contents using the scrollbar. Just click the entry you want to navigate to, and the reading screen jumps to that location. Click the X button to close the table of contents.

FIGURE 23.10   Using the table of contents to navigate the book.

Before moving to notes, highlights, and bookmarks, a couple features are available to you while reading: definitions and Wikipedia lookups. To access either of these features, highlight the text in question in the reading screen by clicking your mouse at the starting point, dragging to the end point, and releasing the mouse button. A pop-up menu appears (see Figure 23.11). At the bottom of that menu, you have two options: Look Up with Dictionary.com and Look Up with Wikipedia. Selecting either option opens up your browser with the highlighted term or phrase automatically entered as the search criteria and found (if applicable) at the respective site. Of course, your selection determines what is found—for example, selecting a phrase does not produce any definition results.

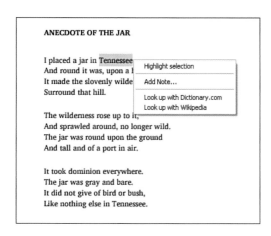

FIGURE 23.11   Selecting text gives you options.

When reading magazines and newspapers, reading functions is essentially the same. One difference is that newspapers and magazines are typically set up with a linkable front page or list of contents (see Figure 23.12). In this image, each of those items is an article. You can click Spanish Premier Suffers Setback to jump to that article (see Figure 23.13).

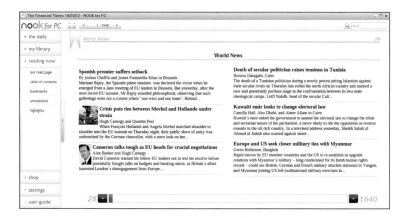

FIGURE 23.12   Reading a newspaper.

FIGURE 23.13   Reading an article.

In Figure 23.13, you can quickly navigate to the list of contents by clicking the World News link. You can also advance quickly to the next article by clicking Next Article. (If you were in the second article of this section, you would see a Previous Article link on the top-left portion of the screen.) In addition, you can use the arrow keys and scrollbars to navigate from article to article in a page-by-page method.

NOTE: Want to adjust the font size you are reading? **See** the section "Configuring the NOOK for PC App Settings."

Using Highlights, Notes, and Bookmarks in the NOOK for PC App

You can also use highlights in the NOOK for PC app. However, you cannot add highlights or notes to subscription content.

Adding Highlights and Notes

To add a highlight to an ebook in the NOOK for PC app, click your mouse on the starting point where you want your highlight. While holding the mouse button, drag your mouse to the ending point for the highlight. When you do this, the NOOK for PC app highlights the text and displays a pop-up menu (see Figure 23.14). To make the highlighted text an actual highlight, click Highlight Selection.

If you want to add a note, click Add Note from the pop-up menu. Type your note, and then click OK. If you want to add a note to text that is already defined as a highlight, highlight a portion of that text again. The pop-up menu offers a couple extra options (see Figure 23.14). Click Add Note to add a new note to the existing highlight. Add the text for your note, and then click OK.

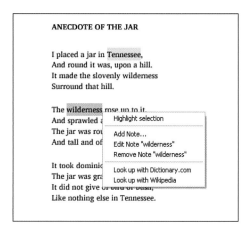

FIGURE 23.14   Editing an existing note or highlight.

Viewing Highlights and Notes

To view highlights, click Highlights under the Reading Now menu. Highlights that don't have notes associated with them can be found by clicking Highlights. If a note is associated with the highlight, click Annotations in the Reading Now menu to see the note. You can quickly jump to any note or highlight by clicking the specific note or highlight.

Can I Change the Green Color the NOOK or PC App Uses for Highlights?
You can't change the color of highlights on the PC.

Editing and Deleting Highlights and Notes

To edit a note associated with a highlight, highlight a portion of that text that composes the note, and click Edit Note. Enter the new text for the note, and click OK. To delete the note, select Remove Note; then click Yes when asked to confirm that you want to delete the note. Follow the same steps to remove a highlight that doesn't have a note associated with it.

Using Bookmarks

To add a bookmark to a page in the NOOK for PC app, click the ribbon with pointed ends in the corner of the page. When you do, the ribbon drops down onto the page, and your bookmark appears in the bookmark pane when you select Bookmarks from the Reading Now menu. To remove the bookmark, click the ribbon again.

You can easily navigate to a particular bookmark by clicking the bookmark in the bookmark pane.

Importing Books into the NOOK for PC App

All books in your B&N online library are automatically added to the NOOK for PC app. If you want to read a book you purchased from another source or your own content, you can add it to the NOOK for PC app by clicking the My Library, the My Stuff menu, and then the Add New Item button (see Figure 23.15).

NOTE: You can import only eReader format (PDB files) and EPUB format ebooks along with PDFs into the NOOK for PC app.

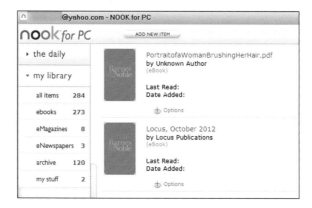

FIGURE 23.15   Click this button to add non-B&N ebooks and content.

If the book you import contains DRM, you will be asked for your name and credit card information when you attempt to read the book in the NOOK for PC app. You need to supply this information only the first time you read the book.

Can I Read Books in Formats Other Than eReader and EPUB in the NOOK for PC App?

Kind of. To read a book in the NOOK for PC app, you must first convert the book to either eReader format or EPUB format. You can use Calibre to convert books into a format compatible with the NOOK for PC app, provided the book is not protected with DRM. To learn how to use Calibre, **see** Chapter 24, "Managing Your ebooks with Calibre."

Configuring the NOOK for PC App Settings

Clicking the Settings menu lets you change the appearance of content in the NOOK for PC app and change your account settings.

To change the appearance of content, click Settings and then click Reader Settings. From this screen, you can change the font size and margin spacing used in the NOOK for PC app. Clicking the font size adjusts the sample text size to give you an idea of how it will appear when reading an actual ebook. The Margins option is controlled by clicking and dragging the Indicator icon or clicking anywhere along the bar. Toward the right increases the amount of white space on either side of the text. Toward the left decreases the amount.

NOTE: Account Settings appears by default when you click Settings.

To change account settings, click Account Settings. You can sign in or sign out of your B&N account from this screen. You can also choose whether recent purchases are downloaded automatically. The other option you have is Autohide Navigation When Opening Reading Now. By default, this is selected, and what it means is that when you are reading an ebook, the Daily, My Library, and such options on the left disappear. (You can get it back by clicking the left-facing arrow bar.) Otherwise, the menu is always available.

Using LendMe in the NOOK for PC App

On the NOOK for PC app, you can not only read books that you have borrowed using the LendMe program but also offer books to friends and family who have a NOOK device or app.

Any offers you receive (that is, books offered to you to borrow), appear in the Daily initially (see Figure 23.16). You can accept or decline the offer by clicking the appropriate button. If you accept, the book is added to your library with the banner Borrowed on the cover.

FIGURE 23.16   Offers available to you.

If you would like to lend a book, the book must first be in the LendMe program. If it is, you see a LendMe button in the Details (see Figure 23.17). To lend the book, click the LendMe button, which opens up a screen like Figure 23.18.

FIGURE 23.17   The LendMe button.

FIGURE 23.18   Sending a LendMe offer.

Here, enter the recipient's email address and an optional message. Your email address is filled out automatically from your account information. Click Send. The offer is then sent to your friend to accept or decline.

Using the NOOK Study App on PC

NOOK Study is an app for the laptop or desktop developed by Barnes & Noble for reading and marking textbooks while at the same time prepping for tests, papers, and so on. Although intended for students, the NOOK Study app is a useful, feature-rich program. For PC users, you do not need both apps, though having both doesn't cause any problems.

Following are the feature highlights. (The NOOK Study app for both the PC and Mac are essentially identical, so the focus is on the PC version for the rest of this section.)

▸ Syncing with your online library.

▸ Viewing multiple books at once and dual-book view.

▸ Customizable courses, which is a fancy way to say, "You can organize your books into categories."

▸ Enhanced note and lookup features.

These are covered while looking at the program.

Downloading, Installing, and Setting Up the NOOK Study App

To use this software, you need an Adobe Digital Editions (ADE) account. Go to adobe.com/products/digitaleditions/ to create one if you do not already have one. It's free!

You can find the NOOK Study app at barnesandnoble.com/nookstudy/download/index.asp. Download the appropriate version for your operating system. After the file has downloaded to your computer, double-click the file, and follow the instructions.

> NOTE: On the Mac, you first need to unzip the file. Then double-click the setup file.

After NOOK Study has installed, start the program. When you first start it, you are asked to agree to the License Agreement. Click Agree. You are then asked to enter your B&N account information. (This is the same account you use to purchase books on BN.com.) You can also create an account by clicking Create Account. If you have an account, click I Have an Account, and enter the account information. Next, enter your Adobe ID and password. Finally, enter your school. That's it! You are now ready to use NOOK Study.

> NOTE: If you are not a student and just want to use NOOK Study, enter a school near you. I, so far, have not gauged any effect on how the school matters.

Navigating NOOK Study

When you open NOOK Study (see Figure 23.19), it syncs with your My NOOK Library, so if you were on page 400 of *Moby-Dick* on your NOOK for iPhone® app, when you open *Moby-Dick* on NOOK Study, it opens at page 400.

FIGURE 23.19   The My Library screen.

Unlike the NOOK App for PC, there is no My Library, Shop, and such buttons. Instead, your library (called My Library) is shown. At the top of the screen, you have four buttons:

▶ **Reading Now**: Clicking this takes you to the reading pane, where all ebooks you have open appear in tabs (much like the omnipresent browser tabs).

▶ **Shop**: Clicking this opens a dialog box. Enter a title, author, or ISBN, and click Search Now. Your browser opens, goes to BN.com, and performs a search based on what you entered.

▶ **Notifications**: If you receive a LendMe offer, you see it appear in the Notification button. Click it to see the offer. You can choose to Accept or Reject.

▶ **Settings**: Clicking this enables you to modify your account settings, check for updates, and such.

These four buttons are always present and available.

Navigating NOOK Study's My Library View

While at the My Library screen, choose to see all your books and documents. You can also choose a particular course, which filters your viewing list to just books in that course. If you haven't yet done so, you can create a course. To create a course:

1. Click Add Course.

2. Give the course a name.

3. To change the icon of the course, click the Folder icon next to the course name, and select the one you want (see Figure 23.20). (You'll notice these are thematic according to probable types of courses: Law, Science, Economics, Classics, and so on.)

FIGURE 23.20   Changing the folder icon.

4. You can now select books from your library and drag them to the course to add books to that course. Note, doing this does not remove them from the All Books & Docs view.

After you finish with the course or if you need to make changes at any point in time, this is easy to do:

1. Click the course name, and click the right-pointing arrow that appears. When you do this, you see two options: Edit and Remove This Course.

2. Click Remove This Course to delete the course. NOOK Study asks you to confirm that you want to delete the course. You are not deleting the books from your library, just deleting that particular course.

3. Click Edit to edit the name for the course.

You have a few more options on this screen. You can choose to view My Archive. From here, you can unarchive books or documents.

The Sync button forces a sync with My NOOK Library, which means that the existing page you were reading is sent to your library. When you next open your NOOK for iPad app or NOOK Color, you will be taken to that same page.

In the view of your books, you see some features similar to the NOOK for PC app. You can choose to Sort your books by Title, Author, Last Read, Markup Count, or Recently Added.

You can also choose what type of books and documents you are looking at in this view by choosing the Filter drop-down list. Your options here are All, Books, Textbooks, Newsstand (both magazines and newspapers), and My Files.

You use the Search Library box to search the entire contents of your NOOK Study library. If you type **conscious**, NOOK Study searches for that word in all titles, notes, and text. If you click the down arrow in the Search Library box, you can filter the results (see Figure 23.21). For example, if you turn off the check mark next to Title, Author, and ISBN, NOOK Study does not search those items. Clicking the results found link below the title displays the results in detail where the search term was found in that particular book (see Figure 23.22). Click the specific result to go to that page in the book.

FIGURE 23.21   NOOK Study searches not only the titles but also the notes you've added and the full text.

FIGURE 23.22   Specific results for a search.

You can also choose to see your books in either grid or list view. In grid view, clicking the book cover opens the books for reading. If you have not downloaded the book yet, it will download first. If you hover your mouse over the cover, you can see an "i" button in the bottom-right corner of the cover. Clicking it gives you a variety of options depending on if you have downloaded the ebook or issue, added notes, and so on. If you haven't downloaded the book yet, you are also given an option to download the book.

Book Info is straightforward (see Figure 23.23): It takes you to a page with some information about the book along with options to Read Now, Download, Remove the Local Copy, and Archive it (or unarchive it if you have archived it).

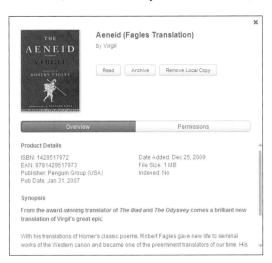

FIGURE 23.23   The Book Info screen.

In list view, clicking the cover image opens the book for reading. The Book Info link takes you to the Book Info page that is the same as what you get from the grid view. If you have added notes to the ebook, to the far right, you see a list of links for the type of notes you have made. Clicking one of the types of notes opens the ebook with the Notes view open, which is discussed in the section "Using the Highlights, Notes, and Look Up Features of NOOK Study."

If the content is subscription content, the options are slightly different. First, if you have multiple copies of a magazine or newspaper, when you click the cover image, a drop-down appears displaying all the issues available to you (see Figure 23.24). Click the one you want to read.

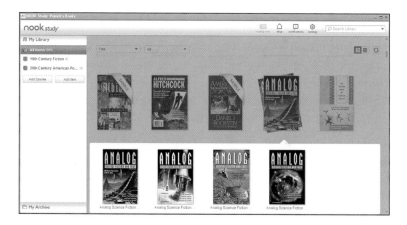

FIGURE 23.24   Click the issue you want to read.

If you click to go to the Subscription Info screen (the equivalent to the Book Info screen), the main Overview screen provides a description just like the Book Info screen. But here, things begin to differ (see Figure 23.25). If you click Manage Subscriptions, your browser opens to BN.com's My Account page. Scroll down and click Manage Subscriptions to cancel or modify a subscription.

If you click Read, the magazine or newspaper opens for reading. Click Previous Editions to see a list of the issues you have. Place your mouse over issue date, and you see options to read, remove the copy from your computer, and archive. If you click Archive, you remove it from this view. However, if you were in My Archive, the Subscription Info's Previous Issues screen would give you the option to Unarchive the issue.

FIGURE 23.25   The Subscription Info screen.

Reading Your Books in NOOK Study

Clicking the Now Reading button or a book cover takes you to the reading view (see Figure 23.26). Although initial impressions may be that this functions the same as the reading view in the NOOK App for PC, that impression quickly disappears when you see the variety of options you have available.

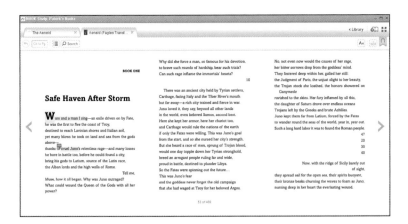

FIGURE 23.26   The reading screen in NOOK Study.

First and foremost, you can have multiple books open at once and navigate between them by clicking the tabs. Beyond that you have a host of buttons and options to explore, so dive into those features.

Dual Book View

You can look at books side by side to compare. Say you wanted to compare the Latin and English versions of *The Aeneid*. Easy.

1. Open one of the books, and then click the Dual Book button. The Dual Book View screen appears.

2. Either scroll or search for the book you want to open. (You can open the same book you initially started with in Dual Book View.)

3. The second book opens and you get two reading screens, both with the same options (see Figure 23.27). The book that you are in (that is, the one where if you press the arrow key to turn the page and the page turns) is the one that you click in.

FIGURE 23.27 Reading two books side by side.

4. You can then interact with each book individually just like you do regularly reading.

When you finish looking at the books in Dual Book view, click the Chain icon that connects the two tabs of the books. Each book then appears on its own tab.

Font

Click the Font button to adjust the font and font size for the book (see Figure 23.28). The size you currently have selected is highlighted in gray, as is the font you have currently selected. To change either, just click what you would like. The screen adjusts automatically.

FIGURE 23.28   Adjusting font settings.

Page Turning

Pull your mouse over the reading area of the screen. Two arrows appear on both sides of the screen. You can click the page right or page left buttons to turn the page (or use the arrow keys on your keyboard). Or you can enter the page number in the Go to Pg box.

Contents View

Click this to open a screen on the left side of the reading screen to see a table of contents, notes and highlights, and bookmarks for this ebook (see Figure 23.29).

The table of contents is a scrollable list that you can use to navigate the book. If you want to go to a specific location indicated in the table of contents, click it and the reading screen jumps to there.

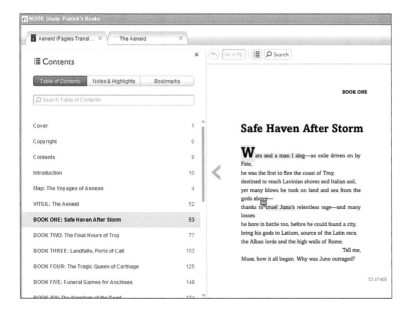

FIGURE 23.29   Viewing notes while in the reading screen.

The notes and highlights are presented in tabular format. The Type column indicates the type of note (Highlight, Asterisk, or Question). The Page column provides the page number of the note.

NOTE: For more about entering notes and highlights and the associated options, **see** "Using the Highlights, Notes, and Look Up Features of NOOK Study."

TIP: For the Type, Page, Added, and Tag columns, if you click the column header, you can sort the table based on that column's information.

The Excerpt column provides a snippet of text where the note is located. The Added column provides the date the note was added. The Tags column lists any associated tags you indicated in the note. Clicking the individual notes displays the note on the page and provides note details.

At the bottom of the Notes and Highlights section, you can see the full note and any links associated with it. In addition, you can Export or Print your notes. If you choose

Export, you can sort them by the page they appear on, type, the color, or date added. You can export to a Word or text file.

You can also search for specific content in the notes by entering search criteria.

When you access the bookmarks, you see a list of all the bookmarks in the book. Click the bookmark link to go to it in the reading screen.

Full Screen Mode

Click this to open the book to take up the entire screen. Press Esc to close full screen mode.

Search

Use this button to search for a word or phrase in the ebook.

Using the Highlights, Notes, and Look Up Features of NOOK Study

Adding notes and highlights to ebooks in NOOK Study is easy, and you have a variety of options. To add a highlight, follow these steps:

1. With the ebook open, select the text you want to highlight with the cursor. A pop-up menu appears (see Figure 23.30).

2. Click Apply Markup. You can choose Highlight, Underline, Asterisk, or Question from the menu. Other than using them for three different types of highlighting, the distinction is the icon used:

> **Highlight**: No icon.
>
> **Asterisk**: Asterisk icon.
>
> **Underline**: Text is underlined.
>
> **Question**: Question mark icon.

To add a note, follow these steps:

1. With the ebook open, select the text you want to highlight with the cursor. A pop-up menu appears.

2. Click Add Note. The Add Note dialog box appears (see Figure 23.31).

3. Set the Markup Style to Highlight, Underline, Asterisk, or Question.

4. Enter the text of your note.

5. Add tags if you want them.

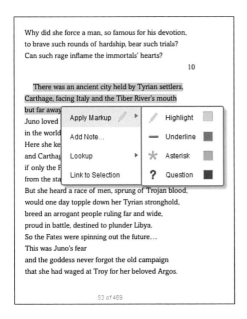

FIGURE 23.30 Text selection tools.

NOTE: Tags can be useful for identifying notes with a similar type or theme. These can then come in handy if searching notes.

FIGURE 23.31 The Add Note dialog box.

6. Add a hyperlink to outside research or articles. Just paste a link here and click Attach.

7. Click Save.

You can always edit the note by clicking the note in the reading screen.

NOOK Study also provides some lookup features. Just like creating a note, select the text on which you want to perform a search at one of seven websites (see Figure 23.32):

▶ Search This Book

▶ Dictionary.com

▶ Google

▶ Google Scholar

▶ YouTube

▶ Wikipedia

▶ Wolfram Alpha

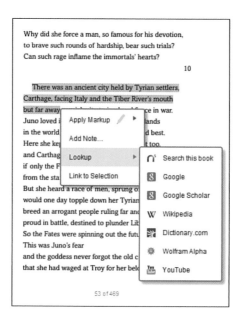

FIGURE 23.32 A multitude of lookup sites.

The final option you have after you select text is Link to Selection. NOOK Study creates a link that you can send to other NOOK Study users, and when they receive it, they can link to it and go directly to that page in their NOOK Study.

Using LendMe in NOOK Study

With NOOK Study, you can use B&N's LendMe feature. You can access the LendMe options, assuming LendMe is available for that NOOK Book, either from the plus sign menu or the Book Info screen. Clicking LendMe in either location opens the LendMe dialog box (see Figure 23.33).

FIGURE 23.33   NOOK Study's LendMe dialog box.

Enter the email address of the person you want to lend the NOOK Book to, enter a personal message if you want, and click Send.

The normal LendMe rules apply.

Using Print to NOOK Study

If you have a PowerPoint or Word document you want to add to your NOOK Study library, you can easily do so. When you installed NOOK Study, it placed a print driver on your computer. So, if you are in PowerPoint or another program and you want to add that file to your NOOK Study library, choose File, Print. In your printer options, choose Print to NOOK Study (see Figure 23.34). (On the Mac, choose PDF in the bottom left, and click Print to NOOK Study from there.) Click Print. The file is automatically placed into your NOOK Study library.

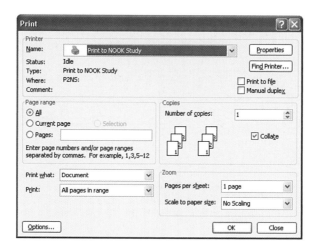

FIGURE 23.34   Printing to NOOK Study in Word.

Adding Your Own Files to NOOK Study

If you have a PDF or EPUB file you want to add to NOOK Study, click Add Item, navigate to the file, and click Open. The file is added to your library, and you can manipulate it like any other document.

Using NOOK for Web

NOOK for Web is a browser-based way to read your NOOK Books. NOOK for Web is connected to your account and lets you read NOOK Books without having any of the iPhone, iPad, or Android apps, the PC or Mac NOOK or NOOK Study applications, or even a NOOK device. You can buy NOOK Books and read them on your computer without downloading them. The good news is, if you own a NOOK or use any of the apps or applications, your NOOK library is synched, so jumping from device to device retains your reading location (but not, currently, bookmarks, notes, or highlights).

To use NOOK for Web, you need a PC or Mac running one of the following browsers:

Chrome on PC or Mac
Internet Explorer
Safari on PC, Mac, iPad, or iPhone
Firefox on PC or Mac

Currently, you cannot use NOOK for Web using an Android tablet browser, though B&N says those will eventually be supported.

You also need a B&N account if you do not already have one: https://mynook. barnesandnoble.com/index.html. Just click the Create an Account now link. When you have an account, you can start reading with NOOK for Web.

Opening NOOK Books in NOOK for Web

You have a few ways to read content in NOOK for Web. If you are on a product page (see Figure 23.35), you can hover your mouse over the cover until Open This Book appears. Click Open This Book, and NOOK for Web starts. If you own the NOOK Book, you have access to the entire book. If you do not own it, the sample (the first 10–20 pages) appears in NOOK for Web.

FIGURE 23.35 Click Open This Book to start NOOK for Web.

NOTE: Now the bad news. Not *all* NOOK Books can be read in NOOK for Web, though the vast majority can be. Also, magazines, newspapers, textbooks, NOOK Books for kids, enhanced NOOK Books, PagePerfect NOOK Books, and comics cannot be read in NOOK for Web.

However, probably the most common way you will access your NOOK Books in NOOK for Web is through your library at BN.com. From BN.com, click My NOOK.

When the My NOOK page loads (see Figure 23.36), click Library.

FIGURE 23.36   Click Library to go to a listing of your NOOK Books.

Scroll and click until you reach the NOOK Book you want to open. You can use the features at the top to help make finding the book you want faster. You can sort the content differently or filter the content. By default, All Items is selected, but clicking any of the other check boxes shows *only* that set of content.

When you see the NOOK Book you want to read, click the Read Instantly button (see Figure 23.37) to open that book in NOOK for Web. You can also click the cover to start NOOK for Web.

FIGURE 23.37   Click Read Instantly to open the NOOK Book in NOOK for Web.

Reading in NOOK for Web

When you start NOOK for Web, the NOOK Book opens either to the publisher's default starting position (if this is the first time you are opening this on *any* device) or to the last location you were reading whether that was in NOOK for Web or on any NOOK App, application, or device. Now let's get oriented to this screen (see Figure 23.38).

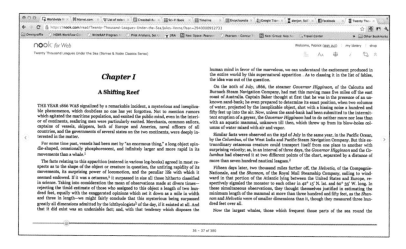

FIGURE 23.38   NOOK for Web's reading screen.

Contents

The Contents menu displays that book's table of contents (see Figure 23.39). Simply click the table of contents entry you want to advance to. The browser screen refreshes to that location.

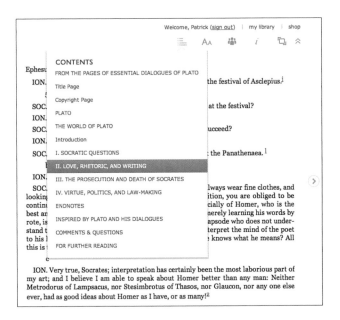

FIGURE 23.39   The Contents menu for a NOOK Book.

Text

The Text menu shows text display options (see Figure 23.40). To adjust the size of the text, click the A you want. The current size displays in a turquoise color. When you click the size, the text changes in the background. To change the font (the current font displays in a turquoise color), click the font you want. It changes in the background. Choose the font you want first; then adjust the size.

If you want to use the Publisher's Defaults to display text size and particular font, click the Publisher's Defaults check box. You can always click it again to turn it off.

By default, NOOK for Web displays books in a two-column format. If, however, you prefer to see only one column, click Single Page Layout, which shifts the view from two columns to one column.

Share

The Share menu displays the different options you have to share your reading experience.

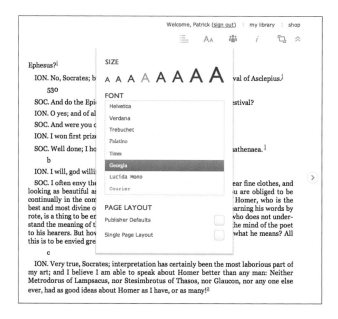

FIGURE 23.40   The Text menu for a NOOK Book.

NOTE: The share features assume you have linked at least your Facebook, Twitter, or Gmail accounts. If you have a NOOK device or app, you may have already linked accounts, but if you have not or want to link more (or unlink), go to https://mynook.barnesandnoble.com/friends.html. Click the Link Accounts button and enter the required information.

If you click Rate and Review, a dialog box appears (see Figure 23.41). Indicate a number of stars for the review, type in a headline for your review (for example, Fantastic trip through philosophy!), and enter your review. The review will be shared on BN.com, where other B&N shoppers can see what you have said. In addition, if you click the Facebook or Twitter buttons, the review will be shared on those respective sites as well with the accounts linked to your BN.com account. Click Submit Review when you are ready to share with BN.com.

If you click Recommend, the Recommend dialog box appears. You can recommend this book via Facebook, Twitter, or email. Click the Facebook tab to recommend on Facebook. It defaults to displaying the recommendation as a post on your timeline. If you want to recommend to one of your Facebook friend's timeline, click the people button, and select the friend from the drop-down menu. Type your message and click Recommend.

FIGURE 23.41   Rate and Review a NOOK Book.

Click the Twitter tab to recommend on Twitter. Enter your recommendation and click Recommend.

Click the Email tab to recommend via email. Select from the drop-down list the email you want, type your message, and click Recommend.

Click Like on Facebook if you want to post on your Facebook timeline that you like that book. If you have liked it already, the menu option here is Unlike on Facebook. Click it to unlike it.

About

The About menu displays two options: Book Details and More Books Like This. If you click Book Details, a dialog box appears (see Figure 23.42). The information here is standard stuff: author, title, format, and cover. You can read the Overview, which is a short description of the book. You can also click Customer Reviews to see what others have said. If you click Find Other Formats, the B&N product page for this book appears so that you can buy the hardcover, trade paperback, audio, or whatever format it is available in. If you click Learn About NOOK, your browser switches to the NOOK device product page.

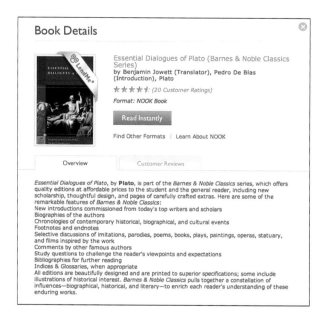

FIGURE 23.42   The Book Details dialog.

If you click More Books Like This, a dialog appears. This dialog has two options: More Like This and More by This Author. More Like This shows book that B&N thinks are similar. If you click one of the covers, NOOK for Web opens a sample of that book, with a Buy Now button should you want to purchase it. If you click More by This Author, you see more titles by that author. Click the cover to open a sample in NOOK for Web.

Full Screen

If you click Full Screen, the window around the reading screen (that is, the browser's menus and Open and Close buttons) and anything outside that window disappear (see Figure 23.43). All the functionality is the same, but it provides a more pristine reading experience. (When you first start, switch to full screen; you may see a message that tells you if your browser is in full screen; this disappears in a few minutes.) To exit full screen, either press Esc on your computer or click Full Screen again.

Simple View

If you click Simple View, the Contents, Font, Share, About, Full Screen, My Library, and Shop links disappear, and Simple View changes to a nondescript two downward arrows in gray. Click those to leave Simple View.

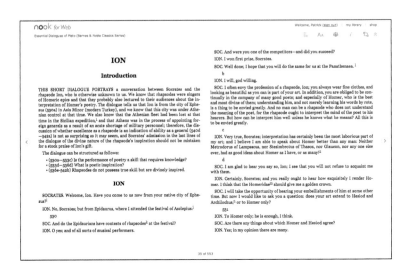

FIGURE 23.43   Reading a NOOK Book in Full Screen.

To advance forward or backward in the book, you have a few options. First, you could use the Contents menu and click the location. Second, you can click either the previous page or next page buttons either side of the text to advance or retreat a single page. Press the left or right arrow buttons on your computer to do the same. Third, you can use the Page Scroll feature at the bottom of the page. With this, you can either click directly some place on the scrollbar and your screen jumps immediately to that page, or you can click and hold the turquoise circle and drag to the location you want and release the mouse button.

If your book contains footnotes, those will look like hyperlinks (colored blue). You can click the footnote, and it takes you to the location. Click the corresponding link in the footnotes to go back. For example, if you click footnote B in the main body, when you go to the footnotes, you see B next to the actual footnote. Click that B to go back to the main text.

The last few options at the top of the screen are a welcome note, My Library, and Shop. You can click Sign Out to sign out. Doing so, takes you back to BN.com. You can click Sign In to sign in under a different account or just re-sign in. If you started reading a sample without being signed in, Sign Out is, instead, Sign In. Click that to sign in. If you click My Library, you are taken to My NOOK Library at BN.com. Click Shop takes you to BN.com's NOOK Book Store where you can browse and shop for more NOOK Books.

That's all there is to NOOK for Web. You can access your NOOK Books without having a NOOK device or app.

CHAPTER 24

Managing Your ebooks with Calibre

I have a huge library of ebooks. Because I get my ebooks from many different sources, they are spread out all over my hard drive. My ADE books are in one folder, books I've bought from Fictionwise are in another folder, my Project Gutenberg books in yet another, and so on. All my files on my computer are backed up, so I'm not concerned about losing them, but it sure is easier to manage them when they are all in one location.

A while back I discovered Calibre, a free application for managing an ebook library. Calibre is incredibly powerful, but it's also easy to use. In this chapter, you learn to use Calibre to manage your library; edit the metadata for your ebooks so that they show up correctly on your NOOK and NOOK Simple Touch; get cover art when covers are missing; and sideload books to your NOOK Simple Touch.

Configuring Calibre

You can download Calibre from calibre-ebook.com. There's a version for practically every type of computer on the market today. After you install Calibre, you need to specify a location for your Calibre library. When you add books to Calibre, it copies the ebook to your Calibre library. That way, all your ebooks are kept in one location.

To set up your Calibre library, simply launch Calibre, and it starts the Welcome Wizard. In the first step of the wizard, specify where you want Calibre to store your ebooks. You can choose any disk location you want, or you can leave it at the default setting.

Is There Any Advantage to Using a Custom Location for My Calibre Library?

In some situations, yes. Let's put it this way: There's no disadvantage to using a custom location for your Calibre library unless the location you specify is a network location you don't always have access to or you use Calibre's built-in Content Server feature.

In the next step of the Welcome Wizard, select Barnes & Noble from the list of manufacturers, and then select Nook from the list of devices, which looks like a generic NOOK. Calibre uses your choice here for the default conversion settings. In other words, because you are choosing a NOOK as your reading device, Calibre knows it needs to convert ebooks to EPUB format when it sideloads ebooks onto your NOOK Simple Touch.

In the final step of the Welcome Wizard, Calibre displays links for tutorial videos and the Calibre user's guide. The videos are an excellent way to learn all the features of Calibre. But if you just need to manage your library and sideload ebooks onto your NOOK Simple Touch, you can skip them for now. (You can also access them at calibre-ebook.com/help.)

> NOTE: You cannot sideload books to your Samsung Galaxy Tab 4 NOOK. Instead, you must load the books first to a microSD card and transfer the books via Bluetooth and then move them to the NOOK\Books folder using My Files on the NOOK.

Adding Books to Your Calibre Library

When you first start using Calibre, your library is empty. To add books to your library, click the Add Books button on the toolbar. Select the books you want to add, and then click Open.

> TIP: You can select multiple ebooks before you click Open; all the ebooks you select are added to your Calibre library.

> **Can I Add NOOK Books I've Purchased for My Samsung Galaxy Tab 4 NOOK, NOOK HD+, NOOK HD, or NOOK Simple Touch to My Calibre Library?**
>
> Absolutely! Although Calibre does not allow you to read books protected by DRM, you can manage protected books with Calibre. That includes managing the book's metadata and adding a cover graphic.

When adding ebooks protected with DRM, you need to make sure that they are in either eReader or EPUB format. However, unprotected ebooks can be in any format.

When you sideload unprotected ebooks to your NOOK Simple Touch, Calibre automatically converts them into the correct format.

> NOTE: Your NOOK device cannot read eReader (PDB) formatted ebooks.
> Those books need to be converted to EPUB format, which you *cannot* do if they
> are secure eReader files.

Editing Metadata

As you add books to your library (see Figure 24.1), you might notice that some books have missing or incorrect metadata. For example, the book's title might not be formatted correctly or the listing in Calibre might be missing the author's name. You can edit the information Calibre uses for the book's listing by editing the book's metadata. You'll almost certainly want to be sure that your metadata is correct for all your ebooks because your NOOK device also uses metadata to display information about the ebooks.

FIGURE 24.1   The Calibre main window.

To edit metadata for an ebook, first select the ebook in Calibre, and then click Edit Metadata on the toolbar. Calibre displays the current metadata for the book you selected (see Figure 24.2). At this point, you can manually change the metadata or let Calibre retrieve metadata from either Google or ISBNdb.com.

To let Calibre automatically retrieve metadata for your ebook, click the Download Metadata button at the bottom of the Edit Meta Information dialog. Calibre uses the metadata shown in the dialog box to attempt a lookup on the book. If the metadata that already exists isn't sufficient, Calibre lets you know.

FIGURE 24.2   The Calibre Metadata Information screen.

> **TIP:**   If Calibre cannot retrieve metadata for a particular book, enter the ISBN number (you can usually get it from BN.com or Amazon.com) for the book and try again. I've never experienced a problem when the ISBN number was entered first.

By default, Calibre searches Google for metadata. In most cases, Google has the metadata you need, but if it doesn't, click the Change Metadata button next to the Download Metadata button. Here you can find many options for other metadata sources. Click the ones you want to use, and for each one click Configure Selected Source. Complete the necessary information.

> **TIP:**   If you need to edit the title or author of an ebook, you can double-click the title or author name (and other metadata as well) in the Calibre library, type the new information, and press Enter.

If you want to update the metadata for a lot of titles, simply select them all, click the down arrow next to Edit Metadata, and click Download Metadata and Covers. You can choose to download only the metadata, only the covers, or both.

Adding Covers

Because books you sideload onto your NOOK Simple Touch are kept in My Documents, you can't browse them by cover. However, you can see the cover on the touchscreen while you're reading the book—assuming a cover image is available. Sideloaded books on your NOOK Simple Touch, however, do show the cover when you view them in the Library.

> NOTE: Recall that sideloaded books and content are ebooks and documents you have from sources other than B&N (for example, Fictionwise, Project Gutenberg, and so on).

Calibre can download covers for your ebooks automatically. You can even add covers to ebooks protected with DRM from the B&N NOOK Store or from another ebook store.

The easiest way to flip through cover images for your ebooks is to enable browsing by covers in Calibre. Click the Browse by Covers button (as shown in Figure 24.3) to enable this feature. You can then click either side of the current cover to flip to another cover or use the arrow keys on your keyboard to flip through your covers. To return to full library view, click the Browse by Covers button again.

FIGURE 24.3   The Browse by Covers button makes locating missing covers much quicker.

> TIP: You can also browse ebooks by tags using the Browse by Tags button immediately to the right of the Browse by Covers button. Tags are part of the metadata for an ebook, so you can edit how an ebook is tagged by editing the metadata.

To add (or replace) the cover image for an ebook, select the ebook, and then click Edit Metadata. Click the Download Cover button to add a cover image.

You can add cover images to multiple books by selecting more than one book in the Calibre library. On Windows, you can press Ctrl+A to select all your books (use Command-A on a Mac). If you want to select multiple books that are listed contiguously, click the first book, then hold the Shift key, and click the last book. If you want to select multiple books that are not contiguous, click the first book, and then hold the Ctrl key as you select the other books.

After you select all the books to which you'd like to add covers, click the down arrow to the right of the Edit Meta Information button, and select Download Only Covers from the menu. Calibre automatically downloads covers for all the books you selected.

Sideloading Books with Calibre

Sideloading books onto your NOOK Simple Touch with Calibre is fast and easy. After you connect your NOOK to your computer, Calibre detects it and displays an icon for it in the area directly under the toolbar. If you have a microSD card installed in your NOOK device, Calibre displays an icon for both your NOOK device and the microSD card.

NOTE: When you connect your NOOK device to a Windows computer, Windows assigns drive letters to your NOOK device and to the microSD card if one is installed. Calibre assumes that the first drive letter assigned to your NOOK device is its main memory and the second drive letter is the microSD card. However, sometimes Windows assigns the first drive letter to the microSD card; when it does that, Calibre incorrectly identifies your NOOK device's main memory and the memory card.

To resolve this problem, you need to explicitly assign drive letters to your NOOK device and its microSD card inside of Windows. For information on how to change drive letters in Windows XP, see www.online-tech-tips.com/computer-tips/how-to-change-the-drive-letter-in-windows-xp-for-an-external-usb-stick-or-hard-drive/. For Windows 7, see http://www.howtogeek.com/96298/assign-a-static-drive-letter-to-a-usb-drive-in-windows-7/.

TIP: Sometimes Calibre, if it is already open when you plug in your NOOK device, won't recognize it as being installed. Close Calibre and restart it.

To sideload one or more books onto your NOOK Simple Touch, make sure your device is connected to your computer. Select the books from your library, and click

Send to Device on the toolbar. Calibre automatically converts any ebooks that are not already in a format compatible with your NOOK device and then transfers them to your NOOK Simple Touch. By default, Calibre transfers ebooks to your NOOK Simple Touch's main memory, but you can choose to transfer them to the microSD card if you want. Simply click the down arrow next to the Send to Device button, and select Send to Storage Card A from the menu (see Figure 24.4).

FIGURE 24.4   The Send to Device menu.

> TIP: You can also select Set Default Send to Device Action and select Send to Storage Card A. From then on, clicking the Send to Device button automatically sideloads any selected ebooks to your NOOK Simple Touch's microSD card.

Depending on what action is necessary, Calibre might take a while to sideload books. Calibre indicates that it's working and how many jobs it's currently processing using the Jobs indicator in the lower-right corner of the main window. If you click the Jobs indicator, a dialog appears where you can see details on what Calibre is doing.

> **If I Update Some Metadata Information for an ebook That's Already Sideloaded onto My NOOK Device and Sideload It onto My NOOK Simple Touch Again, Will It Overwrite the Existing Copy on My NOOK Simple Touch?**
>
> Yes. Both Calibre and your computer use the filename of an ebook to identify it as a unique ebook. If you change metadata information (such as the title, author, and so on) of an ebook that is already on your NOOK Simple Touch, sideloading it onto your device will overwrite the existing copy. Essentially, you're just updating the metadata of the copy on your NOOK device.

There is one exception to this. If you sideload an ebook to your NOOK device's main memory and the same ebook is already on its microSD card, you will have a duplicate copy of the book and it will show up twice in your library.

Can I Read My ebooks Using Calibre?

You can read an ebook on your computer using Calibre as long as the ebook isn't protected with DRM. To read an ebook with Calibre, select the ebook, and click the View button on the toolbar. A new window appears for you to read the ebook.

Subscribing to News Content in Calibre

Calibre also has an excellent news subscription feature that makes it easy to subscribe to various news feeds that you can then sync to your NOOK Simple Touch. To access this feature, click the Fetch News button, select a news feed, and set the subscription options that determine how often the feed is downloaded. Keep in mind that for feeds to download, Calibre must be running.

TIP: I particularly like this feature (subscribing to news content in Calibre). I have print subscriptions to *The London Review of Books* and *The New York Review of Books*, which I paid for long before I got my NOOK. Although I could subscribe again to *The New York Review of Books* at BN.com, I would be paying for two subscriptions...so I use Calibre to fetch that news (using my account information from *The New York Review of Books* website). When my print subscription runs out, I will switch to the BN.com subscription...but for now, I pay for only one.

Calibre uses a collection of properties known as a "recipe" to subscribe to a particular news feed. If you don't see a news feed that you're interested in, you can find others and submit requests for new recipes by browsing to http://bugs.calibre-ebook.com/wiki/UserRecipes.

Converting ebooks in Calibre

Calibre can convert a wide variety of formats. Although your NOOK can read Word documents, these are not treated as "real" ebooks by the NOOK device. That means you cannot add notes or highlights, bookmark pages, and so on. So, although you can read those formats, you may want to convert them to the EPUB format so that they get the full ebook treatment.

Calibre's conversion options are rich, and I won't go into the details here. The standard default DOC to EPUB, HTML to EPUB, and such work quite well. To convert a document, follow these steps:

1. Add the document to your Calibre library if you haven't already. Do this just like adding a book: Click the Add Books button.

2. Select the book you want to convert.

3. Click the Convert Books button.

4. Click OK.

If you want more details about the vast number of options for conversion, go to calibre-ebook.com/user_manual/conversion.html.

> NOTE: PDFs are the most problematic documents to convert because of the way they are created. So, if the results are less than satisfactory, you might tweak some of the settings to see if you can get better results.

In this chapter, you've seen how powerful Calibre is for managing your ebook library. You've also seen how easily you can edit the metadata for your ebooks, add missing covers to your ebooks, and sideload ebooks onto your NOOK Simple Touch.

CHAPTER 25

Using My NOOK Library

All your B&N content is saved on the bn.com website in B&N's My NOOK Library. Using My NOOK Library, you can browse through your B&N content, lend and borrow books with LendMe, move items to and from your archive, see what your NOOK friends are up to, and delete items from your B&N library. You can even start reading your books. (**See** the section "Using NOOK for Web," in Chapter 23, "Reading Beyond Your NOOK: Desktop Apps.")

Accessing My NOOK Library

You can access My NOOK Library by browsing to http://mynook.barnesandnoble.com (see Figure 25.1). You can also get to this from the BN.com homepage by clicking My NOOK at the top of the screen. Log in if you have not already. From here, you can see recommendations, recent purchases, NOOK Friends activities, and links to your Library, Friends, Recommendations, and Manage My NOOK. You can now work your way through the top links. If you have a few other ways to access the same things (for example, to see your Library), you can click the Library link at the top or the Go to Library link right above titles.

Library

When you click Library, you see a variety of options and ways to interact with it (see Figure 25.2). The first option is Sort. Click this to sort by Most Recent, Title, or Author.

By default, all items in your B&N online library that have not been archived display in My NOOK Library. You can filter the view by clicking Books, Magazines, Newspapers, Apps, or Textbooks. You can also view any items that have been archived by clicking the Archived Items option.

Two views are available in My NOOK Library: Line view or Grid view. To switch between the two views, click one of the View buttons, as shown here, in the Layout category—the one that is a lighter gray is the one not in use.

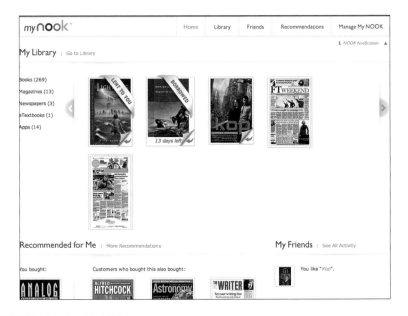

FIGURE 25.1   The My NOOK opening page.

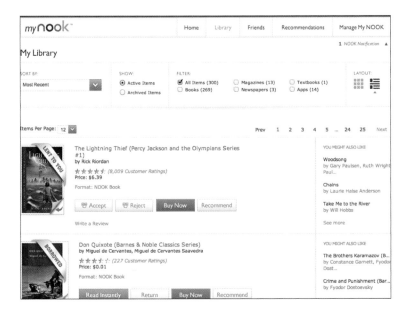

FIGURE 25.2   My NOOK Library page, where you can see all your purchases.

You can interact with individual books. You can download or recommend any books listed here that you've already purchased. You can also write a review, move to your archive, or delete permanently from your library. If the book is a sample or borrowed, you also have a Buy button. If it is a magazine or newspaper, you can manage your subscription.

> CAUTION: Be careful about deleting items. If you delete an item from your library, it will be removed from all your NOOK devices and apps where you access your B&N content. The only way to get it back is to buy it again. Archiving is the safe bet.

To archive an item, click the Move to Archive link. The item is moved to your archive on your NOOK device and apps as well. To move the item back to your library, click Archive under Show, find the item in the archive, and click Move to Active.

> TIP: Think of My NOOK Library as another way that you can view your NOOK Book library. When you interact with content via My NOOK Library, you also impact the content on your NOOK devices and apps.

Recommending and Reviewing Tools in My NOOK Library

You can Recommend or Write a Review of a book or magazine. If you click the Recommend button, you see the Share This Title dialog (see Figure 25.3). You can choose between emailing someone directly, posting to your Twitter, posting to your Facebook wall, or posting to a friend's Facebook wall. Select the option, enter the recipient if appropriate, enter a message, and click Recommend.

If you click the Write a Review link, you see the Rate and Review dialog (see Figure 25.4). No matter what, you are posting a review to BN.com, but you can also choose to copy that review to Facebook or Twitter. Click the number of stars you are giving to the book, type in a headline, write a review, and click Submit Review.

> NOTE: If you cannot post a review to Facebook or find Facebook friends to recommend that book to, you may need to link your accounts. Click a book cover, which opens a new page. Click the Link Accounts button on the left. Click the buttons for which you want to link accounts, and follow the instructions.

FIGURE 25.3   Recommend a title to a friend.

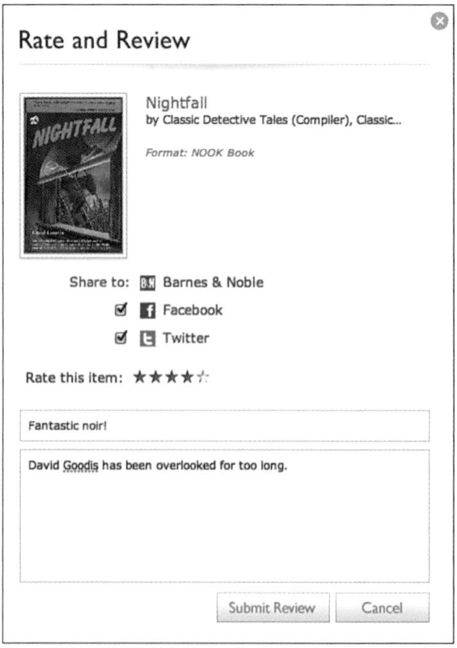

FIGURE 25.4   Write and share a review.

Managing Subscriptions in My NOOK Library

For a magazine or newspaper, you can click Manage Subscription, which opens a
page like that in Figure 25.5. If you click the Cancel Your Subscription link, you are
asked to confirm that you do want to cancel it. Click Confirm to do so, and your subscription is canceled.

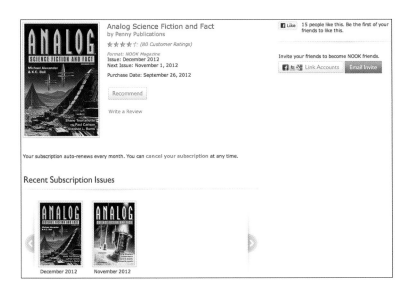

FIGURE 25.5   The Manage Subscription page.

Downloading Content from My NOOK Library

You can download NOOK Books and subscription content from My NOOK Library
for reading on your computer or for local archival purposes. You can download items
to your computer and then sideload them onto your NOOK device later. However, if
you do this, the item does not show up in My B&N Library on your NOOK. Instead,
it shows up in My Documents just like all other sideloaded content.

When you download ebooks to your computer, you can then add them to your Calibre
library. (**See** Chapter 24, "Managing Your ebooks with Calibre.") This is a convenient
way to ensure that you have a backup of your B&N content in case you accidentally
delete an item.

Can I Send an Item to My NOOK Device from My NOOK Library?

You cannot manually send an item to your NOOK device from My NOOK Library. However, because My NOOK Library is actually just another way to view your B&N online library, you should always see the same content on your NOOK devices and apps.

Friends

When you click Friends, you open the portal to interacting with your NOOK Friends from My NOOK Library (see Figure 25.6). This page is divided into three sections: actions you can take (listed under the My Friends heading), a list of yours and your friends' activities, and ways to add friends.

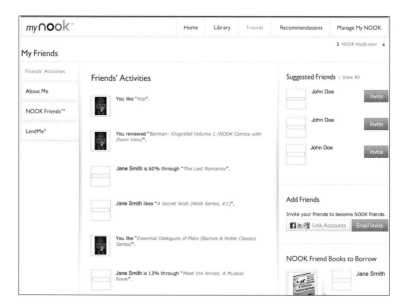

FIGURE 25.6   My NOOK Library Friends page.

You have four options available under the My Friends section:

- ▶ **Friends' Activities**: The default view on this page and the one shown in Figure 25.6.

- ▶ **About Me**: Gives you some information about yourself. The primary purpose of this page is to show or hide books in your library that are LendMe eligible. If you want to hide a book so that a friend cannot request to borrow it, click the Hide option. If you want to hide *all* LendMe books from your friends, turn off the check mark for I Authorize My Friends to See My Lendable Books.

▶ **NOOK Friends**: Here you can remove friends (click Delete), see suggested friends, or invite others. To follow up on the suggestions from B&N, click the Invite button. The invitation is sent immediately. If you want to email a friend, click the Email Invite button, enter the address and message, and click Invite. Also, if you have been sent a friend request, you can review it here and accept or decline.

▶ **LendMe**: From here (see Figure 25.7), you can lend, borrow, and deal with pending LendMe requests. If you want to borrow a book, click Borrow. (If multiple friends have the book, you can click Borrow from the specific friend you want to borrow from.) The request is sent immediately.

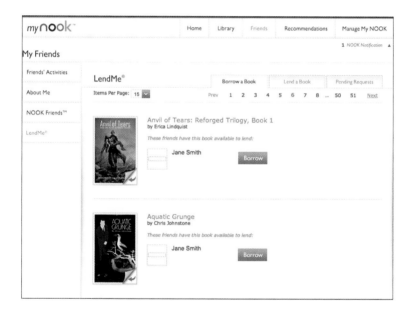

FIGURE 25.7 The LendMe page on My NOOK Library.

Click the LendMe tab to actively loan a friend a book. Click the LendMe button and enter the email address, or pick the Facebook friend. Enter a message and click Lend. The request is sent.

If you have received a lend offer, click Pending Requests to accept or decline that offer. In addition, you see a NOOK Notification beneath the

Manage My NOOK link at the top. Click that and you see a screen similar to Figure 25.8, where you can accept (click Borrow) or decline (click Ignore) the offer.

FIGURE 25.8   Accept or decline a LendMe offer.

Recommendations

When you click Recommendations, you arrive at the Recommendations page (see Figure 25.9). This page is actually a way to see book, magazine, and newspaper recommendations based on your previous purchases, bookseller picks, trending books, and so on. Click the cover to go to that book's page for more information.

Manage My NOOK

When you click Manage My NOOK, you arrive at the page with all your NOOKs. Hover your mouse over the NOOK, and you can see a few options (see Figure 25.10). Click Manage Payment Settings to change your credit card information or add gift cards.

FIGURE 25.9   My NOOK Recommendations page.

FIGURE 25.10   Managing your NOOKs.

Using NOOK Press to Sell Your ebooks

NOOK Press is a B&N website that enables you to submit and edit your ebook for sale through the B&N NOOK store. When people visit BN.com and browse or search for ebooks, yours will be available. If they buy it, the book is downloaded to their NOOK, where they can lend it, share quotes on Facebook—like any other NOOK Book.

Setting Up NOOK Press

Setting up and using NOOK Press is easy:

1. Go to http://www.nookpress.com.

2. Click Get Started Now.

3. Enter the requested information and click Create an Account. If you are a NOOK Press user, you can click I Have a NOOK Press! Account and Want to Sync It to bring over your ebooks you published with NOOK Press.

4. A screen appears and informs you that you will receive an email for account confirmation instructions.

5. When you receive the email, click the link provided. Your browser opens and confirms that your account has been confirmed.

6. Sign in and click Log In.

Important Information about NOOK Press Terms and Conditions

Normally, you might just blindly click I Agree or Accept when you see the kind of legalese included in the NOOK Press Terms and Conditions, but it is important that you understand something about NOOK Press before you agree to this.

B&N can update the pricing and payment terms whenever it wants. At the time of this writing, you, the publisher, can set a price for your content anywhere from $.99 to $199.99. For books priced $2.99 to $9.99, the publisher receives a 65% royalty. For books priced from $.99 to $2.98 or from $10.00 to $199.99, the publisher receives 40%.

B&N also requires that the publisher comply with the Content Policy. So, if B&N deems your content offensive, harmful, legally obscene, and so on, it can choose not to sell your content. It then provides some specific examples but certainly does not cover all areas.

You cannot include the following in the Product Data:

- ▶ Hyperlinks of any kind, including email addresses.
- ▶ Request for action (for example, "If you like this book, please write me a review.").
- ▶ Advertisements or promotional material (including author events, seminars, and so forth).
- ▶ Contact information for the author or publisher.

B&N will make your product available in the Read In and LendMe programs. In addition, 5% of the book's content will be provided as a sample for people to download to their NOOK Tablet, NOOK Color, and such, to try before they buy.

A whole lot of other information is in this agreement (covering such things as withdrawing a book from the NOOK Press program, book rejection and reformatting, and so on), so I highly recommend reading through all the legalese before agreeing. This is your content, so treat this document as what it is: a contract.

Before you can upload any books, you need to create a vendor account:

1. From the NOOK Press Projects screen (see Figure 26.1), click the arrow next to your name and click Vendor Account. The My NOOK Vendor Account screen appears.

2. Click Provide Contact Information. Update the information on the resulting Contact Information screen, and click Save Changes. You are taken back to the My NOOK Vendor Account screen.

3. Click Publisher Information. Update the information on the resulting Publisher Information screen, and click Save Changes. You are taken back to the My NOOK Vendor Account screen.

4. Click Payment & Tax Information. Update the information on the resulting Payment & Tax Information screen, and click Save Changes. You are taken back to the My NOOK Vendor Account screen.

You are now ready to start uploading content and sell it.

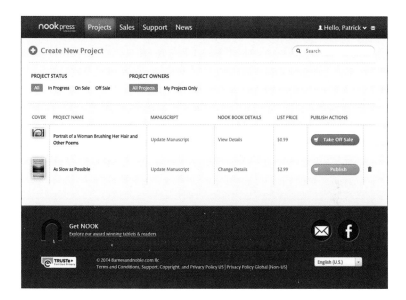

FIGURE 26.1   The My Projects screen on NOOK Press.

Putting Content into NOOK Press

Now that your account is set up, you can load up your first title. If you have a Word, EPUB, text, RTF, or HTML file, you can upload it. Click the guidelines link to open a new window with ways to format the file. (For example, for Word documents, don't use page breaks to separate chapters; instead, use section breaks.)

1. Click Create New Project and enter a Project Name. Click Create My Project.

2. You can click Start Writing if you want. To upload your ebook, click Upload Manuscript File, and click Choose a File to Upload. Navigate to the file, and click it.

3. Click Upload Manuscript File. The screen lets you know that it is importing your file. If the file you chose is not an EPUB file, NOOK Press converts it to an EPUB file, which can take a while. The result is shown in a screen like Figure 26.2.

FIGURE 26.2   Your manuscript is uploaded and converted to an EPUB file.

From here, you have several options:

▶ **Edit Manuscript**: Click this to make changes to the uploaded manuscript.

▶ **Replace Manuscript**: Click this to upload a new file. This replaces all work you may have made with Edit Manuscript.

▶ **Invite Collaborators**: Click this to invite copy editors, beta readers, and so on to review your manuscript prior to publishing it. **See** "Inviting and Working with Collaborators" later for more information about this feature.

▶ **Preview NOOK Book**: Click this to read a preview version of the book in B&N's web-based NOOK reader.

To make changes to your book, click Edit Manuscript. The Manuscript Editor loads (see Figure 26.3). One of the first things to notice is that this screen looks quite a bit like Word. Let's orient ourselves to this screen:

▶ **Options**: These options allow you to upload a new manuscript file, preview the book in B&N NOOK Reader for Web, and save the file.

▶ **Formatting**: These options allow you format the text by adding bold, italic, adjusting size and color, and so on. This all functions just like you would expect in Word or similar word processing software. We'll look at the Image, Split Chapter at Cursor, and Add Internal Link options in "The Extra Formatting Options" section.

▶ **Quick Outline**: This lists the chapters and allows you to reorder chapters, delete chapters, add new chapters, or add front matter. We look at all these in more detail in "The Quick Outline" section.

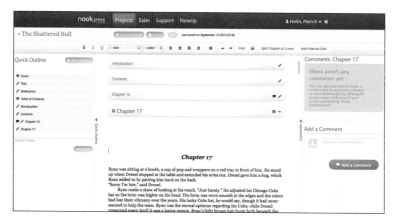

FIGURE 26.3 The Manuscript Editor.

- ▶ **Text area**: Here is where you can add, delete, and otherwise adjust text. Highlight words and add italic just like Word. We explore more of these options in "The Text Area" section.

- ▶ **Comments**: We explore this functionality in the "Inviting and Working with Collaborators" section.

The Quick Outline

This section presents a number of options. The outline lists the chapter names. If you hover over the chapter name, three icons appear on the chapter level (see Figure 26.4):

- ▶ Click the pencil icon to open that chapter in the Text area to edit the text.

- ▶ Click the double-headed arrow to reorder the chapter. When you click it, your cursor changes to two crossed arrows. While holding the mouse button, drag up or down in the outline to relocate the chapter within the outline.

- ▶ Click the trash can icon to delete that chapter.

If you want to add a chapter, type the name of the chapter in the text box Chapter Name and click Add Chapter. The chapter is added.

You will want a front matter for your book, and it should accomplish two things: First, this is where the "legal" stuff goes…the title, the author's name, a statement about copyright, and so on. I recommend taking a look at a published book and seeing what kind of information is there. Second, the front matter is a place to dedicate the book to a friend or loved one as well as include your biography.

FIGURE 26.4   Adjusting the chapters.

To add it, click Add Front Matter. The Add Front Matter dialog appears (see Figure 26.5). Click the plus sign icon next to the items you want to add. You will see them appear in the Quick Outline area. When you are done adding front matter elements, click Done, and the Add Front Matter dialog disappears. After you add them, notice that the Cover and Table of Contents do not have a pencil icon but an eyeball icon. That means these two are read-only items. Adding a cover is discussed later in the "Adding a Cover" section. The Table of Contents is created based on the chapter names. So for each chapter you add, you get an addition to the Table of Contents. You can modify the title, dedication, and introduction just like any other chapter element.

FIGURE 26.5   Adding front matter.

If you want to hide the Quick Outline, click the small left-pointing arrow labeled Quick Outline. If it is hidden, you can show it by clicking the right-pointing arrow.

The Text Area

This area of the screen works much like Word. You can type or delete text, change text to italics, and so on. In the Text area, the bar above the chapter allows you to change the chapter name (click the icon to the left of the chapter name), save your work on that chapter (click the disk icon), or delete the chapter (click the minus sign).

> NOTE: If you upload a Word document, NOOK Press tries to keep the format-ting the same as the Word document. However, this process is not always exact. Feel free to use basic Word formatting features (Heading 1, Heading 2, and so on), but I would not go overboard, for you will want to review the imported version in NOOK Press thoroughly.

The Extra Formatting Options

To the right of the familiar text formatting options, you have a few other tools to cre-ate your ebook. The left-pointing arrow undoes the most recent action. The right-pointing arrow redoes the action that you just undid.

If you want to find or replace text in your book, click the Find button. The Find & Replace dialog appears (see Figure 26.6). This dialog works much like the Find and Replace dialog in Word. When the text you entered is found, it is highlighted in yel-low in the Text area.

FIGURE 26.6   Finding stuff in your manuscript.

If you want to include an image in your book, place the cursor where you want the image to appear and click Image button. The Insert Image dialog appears (see Figure 26.7). Click the Choose an Image to Upload button. Browse to the location, highlight the image, and click Upload Image. The filename of the image appears. When you click it, you see a preview and two options become available: Delete Image and Insert Image at Cursor. Click Insert Image at Cursor. Don't worry if the image is gigantic on the page. When it appears in the ereader, it will be sized appropriately.

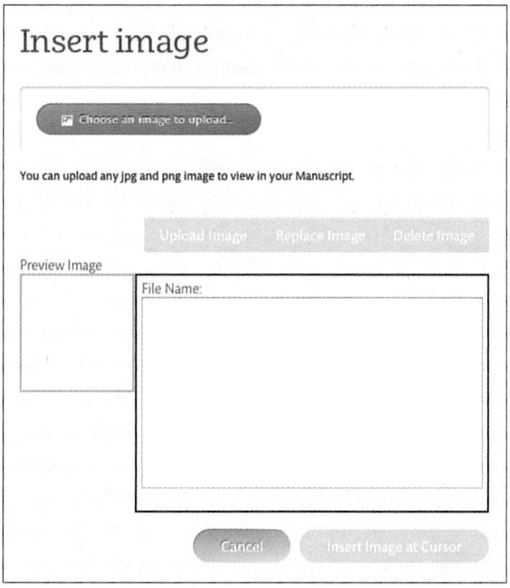

FIGURE 26.7 Inserting an image into your ebook.

If you entered a lot of text and you decide you want to split that text from one into two chapters, you can use the Split Chapter at Cursor button. Place the cursor in front of the text for the new chapter. Click the Split Chapter at Cursor button, and the Splitting Chapter dialog appears (see Figure 26.8). Enter a chapter title and click Split. You'll see the chapter appear in the Quick Outline.

One of the great things about ebooks is that you can put in links that the user can tap. Perhaps you have footnotes or chapter or section references. To make the link, highlight the text you want to create the link from. Then click the Add Internal Link button, and you receive a message that says Click the Target Text Inside the Manuscript to Set the Link. Navigate to the link and click it. The text you had highlighted turns to a hyperlink. To remove the link, highlight the text and click the Add Internal Link button.

If you want to see how all this looks, click Preview, which opens a new window or tab in your browser and displays the book in the B&N NOOK for Web app. Be sure to go through this carefully, adjust the font sizes, and so on.

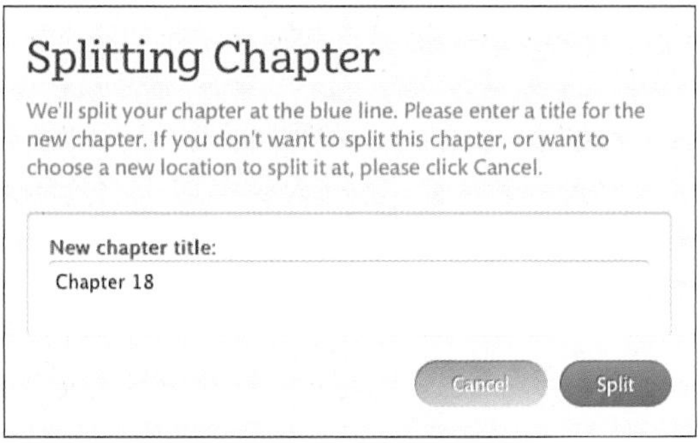

FIGURE 26.8 Splitting a chapter within the Manuscript Editor.

Inviting and Working with Collaborators

Prior to NOOK Press, having people review and comment on your ebook required you to do so outside of the system. NOOK Press now has that functionality built in.

The first thing to do is to invite collaborators. Either from the Edit Manuscript screen, click the title in the upper-left corner and then click Invite Collaborators, or from the Projects screen, click Update Manuscript and then click Invite Collaborators. In each case the Collaborators screen opens (see Figure 26.9). You need to invite collaborators, so enter the name of the person you want to invite, enter his email address, and enter a message (that's optional). Click Send Invitation. Note that collaborators can read the ebook as well as comment on it, but they cannot edit it.

If you have already invited someone, you can cancel his invitation on the Invite Collaborators screen as well by clicking the Cancel Invitation in the Pending Invitations area.

Those whom you invite receive an email with a link for them to click. When they follow that link, they are taken to a screen, as shown in Figure 26.10. When they click Login and Accept Invitation or Sign Up and Accept Invitation, they can see all the projects to which they have access. Click View Manuscript. The collaborators can click Read and Comment, which opens the now familiar Text area screen. The collaborators can navigate this screen much like the creator. However, the collaborators cannot adjust the manuscript. They can read through it and comment on it. If they want to add a comment, they simply type it in the Comments box and click Add a Comment (see Figure 26.11). The collaborators can delete a comment by clicking the x button in the top-right corner of the comment. The comment is then invisible to the author.

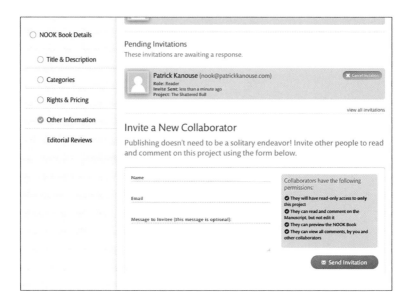

FIGURE 26.9   Invite collaborators to review your manuscript.

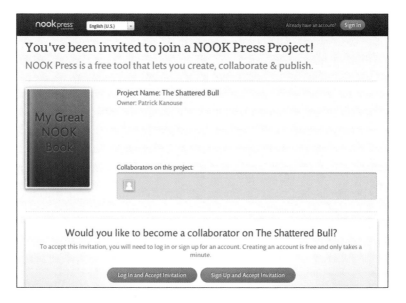

FIGURE 26.10   You have been invited to collaborate on a NOOK project.

FIGURE 26.11   Adding a comment to a manuscript.

You will be informed of collaborators adding comments via the Notifications button at the top right next to your name—the button looks like an envelope. As comments are added, the bubble increases in number. You can click the Notifications button, which takes you to the Notifications screen (see Figure 26.12).

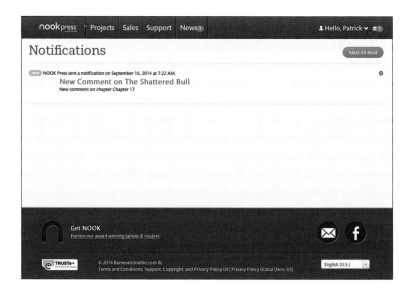

FIGURE 26.12   Your notifications.

To see the comment, click the notification about a comment, and then click the link on the screen that appears. On the Notifications screen, you can also click the close button on the right to remove that notification (but not the comment) or click Mark All Read.

You can also see comments from within the Text area screen. Any chapters with comments will have the Comment icon (refer to Figure 26.3). Open that chapter to see the comments, which you can remove by clicking the X on the comment.

Adding a Cover

As more authors self-publish, cover images are ever more important for catching the potential reader's eye. Although NOOK Press cannot help you create and then modify the cover, you can use it to upload it. To add or replace a cover, from the Projects screen, click the cover icon or image for the project to see the Cover Image screen (see Figure 26.13).

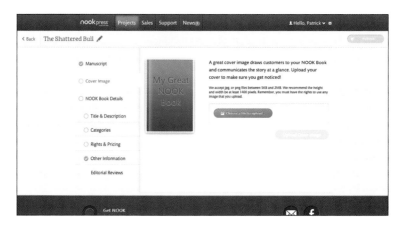

FIGURE 26.13   The Cover Image screen.

NOOK Press accepts JPEGs or PNG files that do not exceed 5MB. NOOK Press recommends that the height and width of the image be at least 1400 pixels. This doesn't mean you need to have a square cover; rather, just make sure that the short side of the cover is at least 1400 pixels.

To add a cover, click Choose a File to Upload, browse to the file, click Open, and then click Upload Cover Image. After the cover is uploaded, you can replace the cover image by uploading a new cover or you can crop it. If you click Crop Original Image, the screen in Figure 26.14 appears. To crop, click one of the gray squares and drag it until you have the crop you want. (You can see it in the thumbnail and large previews.) Click Crop Cover Image to crop it or Cancel to go back to the previous screen without altering the cover.

That's all there is to adding a cover.

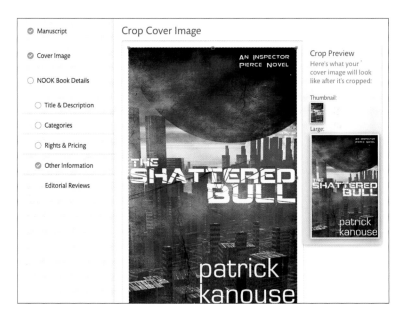

FIGURE 26.14 Cropping your cover.

NOTE: Why the thumbnail and large previews? NOOK Press is providing a view into how your cover will look to potential customers. The large cover preview is what they will see at barnesandnoble.com as they shop for books. If they are shopping from their NOOK, they'll very likely see the thumbnail if they are sorting through search results in the list view. In addition, the thumbnail is how the cover may appear after they have purchased it. Because of the size of the cover that potential customers see, make sure they can read the title and author beyond just looking great.

Adding Details and Publishing

So now that you have your manuscript in NOOK Press, have reviewed it, and have added a cover, you are nearly ready to publish. After clicking View Manuscript, click Set Details to see the screen in Figure 26.15.

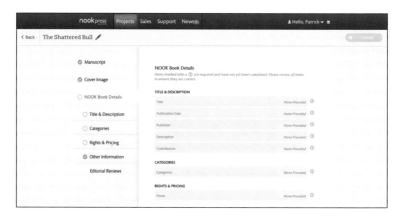

FIGURE 26.15 The NOOK Book Details screen.

This is a summary of what has been completed. To start entering information, click Title & Description in the left column, or click Title in the center of the screen to see the Title & Description screen. Enter the information and click Save & Next.

> NOTE: You can click Save on any of these screens to come back to the information and update it or complete it later.

If you have contributors beyond yourself (for example, a photographer), click Add Another Contributor. The Description section is what appears on the book page in the B&N store. Be thoughtful here. Do you need an ISBN? You do not, but if you have one, you can enter it on this screen.

When you are ready, click Save & Next to go to the Categories screen. On this screen, you can enter up to five categories. When users browse books, they are set up in categories, so the more categories you have, the more browse locations are available for your book.

Add keywords and separate them by commas. Keywords are ways potential readers will see your book when they search the B&N store. Complete the rest of the information and click Save & Next to go to the Rights & Pricing screen. Here you enter your price and let B&N know if it can be sold only in the U.S. or worldwide. If you allow worldwide sales, when you enter a U.S. price, NOOK Press provides conversion prices for British Pounds and the Euro. If you want digital-rights management (DRM) added to your book, click Yes.

> NOTE: If you add DRM to your ebook, it makes it more difficult for people to share it with others (though it is not impossible). It also makes it more difficult for the reader to read on any device they choose, regardless if they have the NOOK Apps or software.

Click Save & Next to go to the Other Information screen. Review the options and click Save & Next to go to the Editorial Reviews screen. If you have editorial reviews, enter the requisite information here. Click Save.

After you have all the information entered, you are ready to publish. You can click the Publish button at the top, or you can click Publish from the Projects screen.

After you have published a book, when you return to the project page, you see a slightly altered screen (see Figure 26.16).

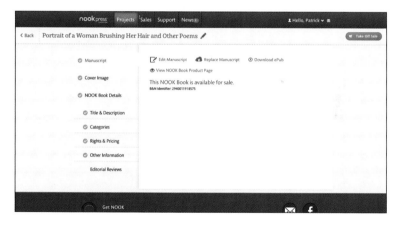

FIGURE 26.16   The Project Page *after* you have published a book.

In particular, take note of two items:

▶ **Download EPUB**: Click to download the EPUB file for your book. You can then use this to deliver to other eBook retailers.

▶ **View NOOK Book Product Page**: Click this to go to the B&N website's specific page for your book.

Speaking of the My Projects Screen

We've been here a few times (see Figure 26.17), so it is worth our time to review some of your actions here.

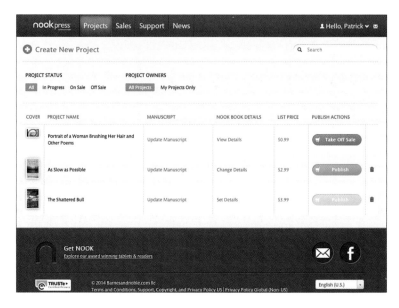

FIGURE 26.17   The NOOK Press Project Status screen.

Under Project Status, you can filter what you see on this screen to All (which is the default), In Progress, On Sale, or Off Sale. You can also filter to see only your projects or all projects that you are either the owner of or a collaborator on. For each individual project, you have a few options:

- ▶ **Update Manuscript**: Click to make changes to the manuscript.

- ▶ **View, Change, or Set Details**: Click to update title, price, and so on.

- ▶ **List Price**: Click to update the price.

- ▶ **Take Off Sale/Publish**: Click to either remove the book from sale or to publish it and make it available for sale.

- ▶ Click the trash can icon to delete that project.

Click Sales to get sales reports.

Finally, click Support to get help. NOOK Press features online chat representatives available from 9 a.m. to 9 p.m. Eastern Monday through Friday.

Click News to get any updates from NOOK Press (for example, sales reporting being unavailable for certain time periods, and so on).

That's it, really, to using NOOK Press. It is now even easier to publish your books on B&N.

CHAPTER 27

Reading Beyond Your NOOK: NOOK App for Windows 8

The NOOK reading app for Windows 8 lets you read your ebooks, magazines, and newspapers on your Surface, Surface 2, or PC.

NOTE: For the purposes of this chapter, I am going to use the touch gestures associated with Windows 8 tablets, but you can use a mouse to interact with all options as well.

The Basics

To obtain the app from the Windows Store, from the Charms bar, search for NOOK in the Store. Tap NOOK from the results to get to the NOOK App screen. Tap Install. You'll see a notice that your NOOK App is installed, adding a tile to the Start screen.

Like any tile on the Start screen, press and hold the tile to see various options (see Figure 27.1). It features the standard tile options: pinning/unpinning, uninstalling, making smaller or larger, and turning off the live feature.

Tap the tile to launch the NOOK App. You are asked to enter your NOOK account or sign up for one. You can also use your Microsoft Account. Enter your information and tap Sign In. If you don't have an account, tap Don't Have an Account? Sign Up and enter the requested information.

The screen loads and syncs your library with all your other devices and apps, so you can jump from your NOOK HD, where you were reading the spine-tingling horror novel, and pick up where you left off in the NOOK App on your Windows 8 tablet.

Your screen now changes to the Home screen, which prominently displays My Library (see Figure 27.2).

FIGURE 27.1   The NOOK App tile options.

FIGURE 27.2   The NOOK App Home screen.

My Library on the opening screen features the five most recent downloads and read items. Swipe left to see B&N shop options: popular lists, bestsellers, and so on.

Tap My Library to see a list of your NOOK content. This is broken down to All, Books, Magazines, Newspapers, and Comics. To the far right, you can see unsupported content, archives, and import. For import, tap it to select a location to upload the file from.

From the Charms bar's Settings selection, you have a few options. About gives you some details regarding which version of the app you have installed and provides a link to NOOK Support. Tap Dictionaries to download a dictionary when looking up a word. If you tap Account and Payment, you can see who this NOOK App is currently registered to, as well as see existing gift card balances and add to a balance, change the default credit card used for the account, and sign out. Tapping Rate and Review takes you to the Windows Store where you can give a rating and write a review of the Nook App for Windows 8 that will be posted to reviews for the app.

Browsing Your NOOK Library

Browsing your library is easy. After you tap Books, Magazines, and so on, just swipe left or right with your finger to scroll.

To read an ebook, you first need to download it to your device. You can easily tell whether a book has been downloaded. If a cloud icon with a down-pointing button appears in the top-left corner of the cover, you have not downloaded it to your device. Just tap the button to do so. After the ebook has been downloaded to your device, tap the cover to open the book.

If you swipe down on a cover, an Options bar appears (see Figure 27.3). Here you can view details, pin to the Start screen, archive the book, or sync that book. Also, if that cover is a sample, you see an option titled Full Version Available, which, after you tap it, opens a screen for you to purchase the full version.

FIGURE 27.3 The Options bar for a NOOK Book.

> TIP: Want to archive a bunch of books quickly? Swipe down on the cover of the first one. The Options bar appears. Then swipe down on additional covers. Tap Archive when you have selected all the books you want to archive.

Tap View Details to see the Details screen (see Figure 27.4).

FIGURE 27.4   The Details screen for a NOOK Book.

This screen differs a bit from type of content to type of content. For books, you have a Read option with a short description. To the right, any customer reviews that have been written are available. (Tap Reviews to see the full complement of reviews and the full review.) Additionally, you see what other customers who purchased this item have purchased and what else the author has written; tap the cover to open the store. For magazines and newspapers, you also see a View Issues button, which you can tap to be taken back to the appropriate library displaying the full complement of issues you own.

For magazines, newspapers, and comics, the library functions are nearly identical.

From any of the libraries, tap the text next to Sort By to sort by Most Recent, Title, or Author (see Figure 27.5).

If you tap Home, you go back to the Home screen. If you tap Shop, you are taken to the NOOK Store. You are in the Library, so the button in the Library screen does not offer much functionality, but, if you were reading a book or magazine, you could tap Library to be taken back to the Library. In the top right, you see what you are currently reading. Tap the cover to open that book.

FIGURE 27.5 Sort options.

At the bottom, you see some Filter and Sort options, along with a Sync button. If you tap Filter, you see the following choices:

▶ **Sync**: Tap this to sync to your library, bookmarks, annotations, and reading location.

▶ **Import**: Tap this navigate to content you want to import into the NOOK App.

▶ **Archived**: Tap this to see a list of archived books, magazines, and so on. You can swipe down on a cover and tap Unarchive to remove it from this list.

▶ **Unsupported**: Tap this to see a list of your content that is not supported at this time for reading on the NOOK App for Windows 8.

TIP: Want to search your library easily? From the Charms bar, tap Search and begin typing in your search criteria. A list of results appears. Tap the result you want to open in the NOOK App.

Reading Books, PagePerfect Books, and Newspapers in the NOOK App

To read an ebook in the NOOK App, just tap the cover image to open it in reading mode. When there, to move to the next page, swipe your finger from right to left. To move to the previous page, swipe your finger from left to right. The reading screen, however, offers more options than just reading (see Figure 27.6), which you can access by swiping down from the top of the screen or up from the bottom of the screen.

FIGURE 27.6   The NOOK App reading interface.

Newspapers, however, offer a tweak on the swiping-through-pages paradigm (though you can still do that). Figure 27.7 shows a typical section page of a newspaper.

The front page (and section pages) offer links to the articles. In Figure 27.7, "New York bracing for new workweek" is the article headline followed by a bit of teaser text. You can tap the article's headline to jump right to that article. When reading an article, you typically have links at the top of the page that transport you quickly between articles and back to the section page.

If you do not see the surrounding bars in the reading screen, just tap the page, and they appear. Before discussing some of these options, take a quick tour:

▶ **Annotations**: Tapping this opens a list of annotations in this book. Tap an annotation to jump to that location. Tap Clear All to remove all annotations from this ebook. Tap Hide Annotations to make them invisible without deleting them.

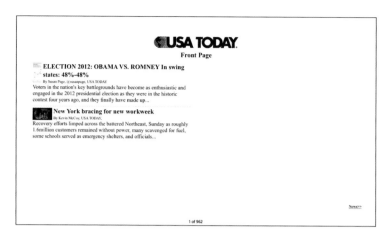

FIGURE 27.7   *USA Today*'s news section page.

▶ **Bookmarks**: Tapping this opens a list of bookmarks in this book. Tap a bookmark to jump to that location. Tap Clear All to remove all bookmarks from this ebook.

▶ **Home**: Tapping this returns you to the Home screen.

▶ **Shop**: Tapping this takes you to the NOOK Store.

▶ **Library**: Tapping this returns you to your NOOK library.

▶ **Table of Contents**: Tap it to open the Table of Contents (see Figure 27.8). You can scroll and tap the appropriate link to go quickly to that spot in the ebook.

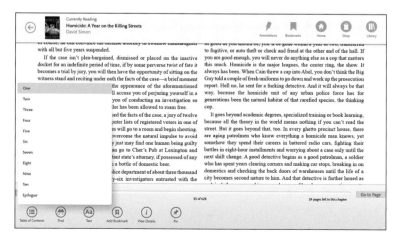

FIGURE 27.8   The NOOK App's Contents screen.

▶ **Scroll Bar**: Press and hold the button and drag to move quickly through the book. You can also tap a spot on the scroll bar to jump farther along. You can tap Back to Page to quickly return to the page you were on before leaping forward or backward. Tap Go to Page to enter a specific page number.

▶ **Find**: Tap to search for a word or phrase in this ebook.

▶ **Go Back**: This icon appears when you have jumped to a different page using the Table of Contents, a bookmark, or the Go to Page option. Tap it to go back to where you just came from.

▶ **Text**: Tapping this allows you to adjust the specific font, theme, margins, line spacing, font size, justification, rotation, and defaults.

▶ **Add Bookmark**: Tapping this adds a bookmark to the current location in the ebook. You'll see a blue bookmark with the NOOK logo appear in the top right. This becomes Remove Bookmark when a bookmark already appears on that page.

▶ **View Details**: Tapping this brings up a page with details related to the book.

▶ **Pin or Unpin**: Tapping this opens the Pin screen, which allows you to pin this book directly to the Start screen. If this book is already pinned to the Start screen, tap Unpin and then Unpin from Start to remove it from the Start screen.

Adjusting Text Options

After tapping Text Options, you see a screen like Figure 27.9. The general purpose of this screen is to provide settings related to the reading experience in the NOOK App. To close the screen, tap anywhere outside of the Text Options screen.

The top-left set of icons determines line spacing. Think of this like single space, double space, and so on. The current setting is colored blue. Tap whichever you prefer. The screen adjusts.

Margins determine how close to the edge of the screen the text goes. The more "dark" space in the center, the more text that appears on the screen. The currently selected Margin setting is colored blue.

Depending on what the publisher of an ebook allows, you can adjust the font. You can scroll through the available list. (A dot appears to the right of the currently selected one, which is also colored blue.)

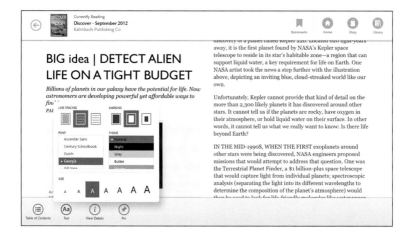

FIGURE 27.9   The NOOK App's Text Options screen.

The Themes option provides a set of backgrounds and font colors. The default is normal, which is a white page with black text. The currently selected option has a dot to the left of the name and is colored blue. Select the theme you want, and the screen changes.

If you'd like, you can set Publisher Defaults to Yes, which sets the font, size, spacing, and so on, to what the publisher feels is optimal. You can change it to Off any time you want.

Clicking the A icon adjusts the font size. The current font size is a blue color. As you tap different sizes, the reading screen adjusts.

Reading PagePerfect Books

PagePerfect books function the same way as regular ebooks, except for two things:

- ▶ **No Text**: You cannot adjust font and margin settings in PagePerfect books, so the Text option is not available.

- ▶ **Zoom**: When reading, you can pinch and zoom in or out to get closer into the text. You can also double-tap the screen to zoom in quickly and double-tap again to zoom back out.

Reading Magazines and Comics in the NOOK App

While you cannot read enhanced magazines (for example, *Time*), many magazines are available without video, and so on. Magazines offer thumbnails that you can scroll through. To see that, just tap the screen to get the reading options (see Figure 27.10). Reading comics is very much like reading magazines.

FIGURE 27.10   Reading a magazine.

> NOTE: Some magazines function more like newspapers when reading; for example, *Analog Science Fiction and Fact*.

You can scroll through the thumbnails to see what is covered on those pages. Just tap the thumbnail you want to go to that page. Tap the downward arrow next to the cover to see a vertical scrolling list of the magazine's contents. Tap Bookmarks to see the bookmarks you've added to the magazine and tap a bookmark to jump to that page.

When reading an article, you can pinch and zoom in or out to get closer into the text. You can also double-tap the screen to zoom in quickly and double-tap again to zoom back out.

For magazines, tap Article View to get a reading screen that emphasizes the text (see Figure 27.11). Reading this is a lot like reading a book. Tap Magazine View to leave Article View.

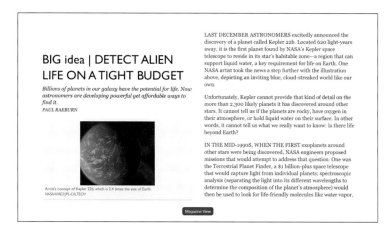

FIGURE 27.11   Article View while reading a magazine.

Shopping from the NOOK App

You can shop for new books, magazines, and newspapers directly within the NOOK App. You can get to the NOOK Store in one of two ways:

- **From the Home screen**: Scroll right until you see the Shop section.

- **From the Options bar**: Tap Shop.

Either way, you land at the NOOK Store (see Figure 27.12). This screen is divided into several parts.

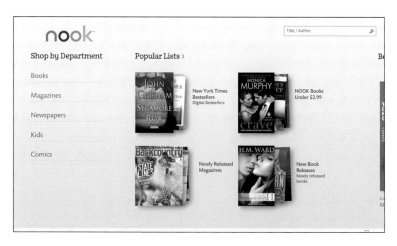

FIGURE 27.12   The NOOK Store.

You can tap Books, which takes you right into a list of current bestsellers. You can scroll right to see even more options. The basic gist of all of these is a series of lists: Most Popular Magazines, Favorite Comics, National Book Aware Nominees, and so on. You can tap each category to drill further down and see what content is available for purchase.

Additionally, you have NOOK channels, which are lists of related titles. Channels are descriptive and—I have found—useful ways of categorizing titles. Instead of just a big collection of history books, you have History by Plot, Notorious American History, and History Buff. The Channels descriptions are themselves evocative of the types of content you will find. Additionally, Channels allow for titles from multiple genres to appear (Science-Fiction Science-Fact is a good example).

Farther to the right, you have large categories: Books, Magazines, Newspapers, Kids, and Comics. Again, you can drill down further to get to specific listings. Once there, you can tap the downward arrow to see more categories (see Figure 27.13). These are further refinements. Tap to your heart's content.

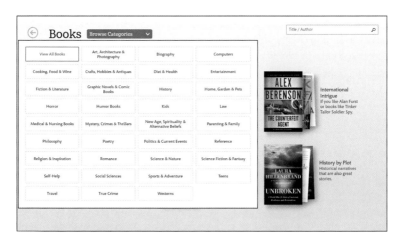

FIGURE 27.13   Refining categories in books.

If you want to search the NOOK Store for a specific title, from the Charms bar, enter the criteria in the Search box and tap Search.

Once you get to a book you like, tap the cover and you are taken to a Details screen (see Figure 27.14).

Reviews gives you an idea of what others have to say about the book. Customers Also Bought shows books that others have purchased who also purchased the one you are looking at. More by This Author shows additional titles that that author has written.

FIGURE 27.14   Book Details screen.

If you want to sample the content before purchasing, tap Free Sample, and a sample downloads to your app and other devices. If you want to buy the book, tap the Buy button and then tap Confirm. The Free Sample and Buy buttons are replaced by the single Read button.

> NOTE: Samples never expire. You can keep a sample for as long as you want.

Magazines and newspapers offer Free Trials instead of Free Samples (see Figure 27.15).

If you tap Free Trial, you get the current issue free, which is downloaded to your app and devices. After 14 days, you are charged an ongoing rate for the subscription. If you want to cancel your subscription, you need to cancel your subscription at BN.com. If you want to buy the current issue, tap Current Issue and then tap Confirm. This adds that issue to your library. You will not automatically receive the next issue. For that, you must subscribe. If you have never subscribed to the newspaper or magazine, you can tap Free Trial and then tap Confirm to begin your trial.

When you subscribe to a newspaper or magazine, you receive a 14-day free trial. If you cancel your subscription within that 14-day period, you are not charged. If you cancel after the 14-day trial period, you are refunded a prorated amount based on when you cancel.

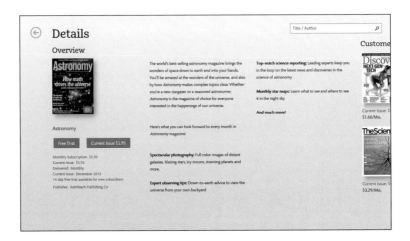

FIGURE 27.15   Magazine Details screen.

You can use a trial subscription only once for any particular item. For example, if you subscribe to *The Wall Street Journal* and cancel your subscription within the 14-day trial period, you are charged beginning immediately if you were to subscribe to *The Wall Street Journal* again because you have already taken advantage of a trial subscription.

> NOTE: Subscriptions can be canceled only using My NOOK Library at BN.com. You cannot cancel a subscription using your NOOK App.

What About LendMe?

At the time of writing, you can read LendMe titles that others loan you, but you need to accept the request on a NOOK device or at BN.com. When you do so, the book downloads to your NOOK App for Windows 8.

Unfortunately, you cannot offer to lend books to any of your friends from the app itself. You can from a NOOK device or BN.com, and when you do so, you cannot read the book until the lending period expires—just like a normal LendMe book.

Understanding ebook Formats

An Overview of ebook Formats

You can use the following types of ebooks on your NOOK:

- ▶ EPUB (including Adobe Digital Editions)
- ▶ PDF

NOTE: If you purchased books from Fictionwise or eReader.com, B&N converted all purchases and put them onto your NOOK device.

Can I Read Word Documents or TXT Files on My Samsung Galaxy Tab 4 NOOK?

If you want to read Word documents or TXT files on your NOOK Tablet and treat them as ebooks versus Word documents, you need to first convert them into EPUB files.

Calibre can convert TXT files to the EPUB format for your NOOK. If you want to read a Word document, you should save the file as a PDF file or convert to EPUB, or use the Hancom Office set of tools on your NOOK. If you cannot save the Word document as a PDF, first save it as an HTML file, and then use Calibre to convert it for your NOOK Tablet.

For more information on using Calibre to convert ebooks, **see** Chapter 24, "Managing Your ebooks with Calibre."

EPUB Format

EPUB (electronic publication) is an open-source format for ebooks. That means the format isn't owned by any single entity, making it an ideal format for electronic books. EPUB ebooks have a file extension of .epub, but EPUB files are actually Zip files (a compressed collection of files) that contain content files for the book along with other supporting files that specify the formatting.

> NOTE: The EPUB format was created to replace the Open eBook format, a format that was widely used in the first ebook readers.

EPUB ebooks are actually just HTML files—just like the files used for web pages. The same technologies used in displaying web pages are used to display EPUB ebooks. If you rename an EPUB book and give it a .zip file extension, you can open the file to see all the files contained in the EPUB archive.

> NOTE: You can use Sigil, a free EPUB editor, to open EPUB books without changing the file extension to .zip. You can get Sigil at https://code.google.com/p/sigil/.

EPUB ebooks can be protected with *digital rights management (DRM)*, which is designed to prevent unauthorized users from accessing digital content such as ebooks. When you purchase a book on your NOOK or from BN.com, that content is tied to your BN.com account using DRM. B&N uses its own DRM mechanism for books purchased from B&N, but your NOOK also supports Adobe Digital Editions DRM.

Using Adobe Digital Editions

Adobe Digital Editions (ADE) is software that manages ebooks that use ADE DRM. Your NOOK GlowLight is compatible with ADE DRM and can be configured as an authorized device in the ADE software.

> NOTE: You can download ADE software free from adobe.com/products/digitaleditions/.

NOTE: You cannot use Adobe Digital Editions software to authorize or load ADE books to the Samsung Galaxy Tab 4 NOOK. Instead, you must load the books first to a microSD card and transfer the books via Bluetooth and then move them to the NOOK\Books folder using My Files on the NOOK. However, you can *read* ADE books on your NOOK so long as you authorize the device in the NOOK Settings>Books screen.

You can use Adobe Digital Editions to sideload ADE books to any other NOOK device.

To authorize your NOOK for ADE DRM, connect your NOOK GlowLight to your computer while ADE is running. When you do, you see a dialog box informing you that your device was detected and needs to be authorized (see Figure A.1). Click the Authorize Device button to authorize it.

FIGURE A.1   Authorize your NOOK GlowLight to use ADE ebooks.

NOTE: Sometimes I have to connect the NOOK GlowLight before starting ADE.

After your NOOK GlowLight is authorized, ADE displays an icon for your NOOK in the bookshelf on the left side of the main window. If you click that icon, you see all the content on your NOOK that is compatible with ADE. Any content in EPUB or PDF format is available for reading directly in ADE.

NOTE: ADE does not yet distinguish between the different NOOKs. It simply refers to it as NOOK.

TIP: I have a few ADE books I have purchased that I could not read on my iPhone or iPad because apps such as Stanza, eReader, and others did not support ADE books. However, the Bluefire eReader app does support ADE, so check it out.

Sideloading Adobe Digital Editions

To sideload ADE content to your NOOK GlowLight, connect your NOOK to your computer, and launch ADE if it's not already running. Drag the ebook from your ADE library to the NOOK icon in the bookshelf.

ADE supports both protected PDF files and protected EPUB files.

TIP: One of the most popular ebook stores for ADE books is ebooks.com.

When ADE books are copied to your NOOK, ADE creates a folder called Digital Editions, and the books are copied to this folder. Unlike protected books from eReader.com and Fictionwise, ADE ebooks don't require you to enter any information to open them. As long as your NOOK is an authorized device, you can open ADE EPUB books.

TIP: When you sideload content onto your NOOK, you find the items in My Documents. You need to tap Check for New Content before the new item is visible in My Documents.

You don't need to use ADE to sideload ADE EPUB books onto your NOOK. I prefer using Calibre to manage all my ebooks and use it to sideload ADE books. **See** Chapter 24 for more information about Calibre.

Sources for ebooks Other than B&N

EPUB Sources

You can buy EPUB books or download free EPUB books that you can read on your NOOK from numerous places. Here are just a few:

- ▶ Gutenberg.org
- ▶ Feedbooks.com
- ▶ eBooks.com
- ▶ Google Play (play.google.com/store/books)
- ▶ Smashwords (www.smashwords.com)
- ▶ BooksOnBoard (www.booksonboard.com)
- ▶ Kobo Books (www.kobobooks.com)
- ▶ Diesel eBook Store (www.diesel-ebooks.com)
- ▶ Powells.com
- ▶ Weightless Books (weightlessbooks.com)
- ▶ Baen (www.baen.com)

Some of these sites offer ebooks in several formats, so ensure you select carefully and get the EPUB or PDF version.

Perhaps one of the greatest benefits to having an ebook reader that supports the EPUB format is that you can read ebooks from many public libraries. Check with your local library to see if it offers the capability of checking out EPUB ebooks. If it doesn't, you might still get a library card from a nearby library. Check out the Overdrive website at www.overdrive.com. You can enter your ZIP code and it will give you a list of libraries in your area that support Overdrive for checking out EPUB books.

Use Calibre to Search for ebooks

In 2011, Calibre came out with a release that added an ebook search function. One of the great things about Calibre's features is that you can control which locations to look at and get DRM status. Calibre does not let you purchase a book through them, but it can give you a quick look at what's available.

Open Calibre and click Get Books. The Get Books dialog opens (see Figure B.1).

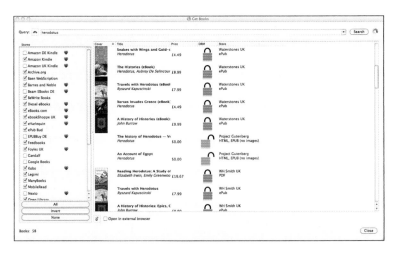

FIGURE B.1   Use Calibre to search for ebooks.

You can adjust which stores to search by clicking the appropriate check boxes in the Store list. In the Query box, type your search criteria. Click Search.

If you double-click a title in the search results, Calibre opens that web page. Alternatively, you can click Open in External Browser, and when you double-click a title, your default browser opens to that web page. As usual, Calibre offers extensive settings options, so feel free to explore.

Libraries and ebooks

Many libraries offer selections of ebooks that you can read on your NOOK. A popular ebook lending service for libraries is Overdrive. If you are curious if your library offers ebook lending services, go to http://www.overdrive.com/ and enter your ZIP code. A list of libraries appears. Select the link to your library to see what they have available.

To check out library ebooks, you first need to have a valid library card from that particular lending library. The specifics can be found at that library. Using the library's website, select the title you want. Most offerings from libraries are either PDF or EPUB, both of which you can read on your NOOK.

Download the file as instructed by the library. Most of the time, you need to open the file using Adobe Digital Editions (**see** the "Using Adobe Digital Editions" section in Appendix A, "Understanding ebook Formats," for information about using that software). You can then sideload the book to your NOOK Simple Touch.

NOTE: Libraries have their own policies, guidelines, and requirements, so be sure to check all the available information on the library's website to understand the options related to ebook lending. You can also contact the library directly and speak to a librarian to get answers.

Can I Read This Here?

With all the devices available for reading NOOK Books, the following should help you distinguish which formats can be read on each device.

	Samsung Galaxy Tab 4 NOOK, NOOK HD, NOOK HD+	NOOK Glow-Light	NOOK for PC/Mac App	NOOK for iOS[1]	NOOK for Android[2]	NOOK for Kids for iPad	NOOK Study	NOOK Tablet	NOOK Color
NOOK Books	Yes	Yes	Yes	Yes	Yes	Yes	Yes	Yes	Yes
NOOK Books for Kids with Read to Me	Yes	No	No	No	No	Yes	No	Yes	Yes
NOOK Books for Kids with Read and Play	Yes	No	No	No	No	No	No	Yes	Yes
NOOK Books for Kids with Read and Record	Yes	No	No	No	No	No	No	Yes	Yes
eTextbooks	No	No	No	No	No	No	Yes	No	No
Newspapers	Yes	Yes	Yes	Yes	Yes	No	Yes	Yes	Yes
Magazines	Yes	Yes[3]	No	Yes[3]	Yes[3]	No	No	Yes	Yes
Enhanced NOOK Books	Yes	No	No	No	No	No	No	Yes	Yes
Supports LendMe	Yes	Yes	Yes	Yes	Yes	No	Yes	Yes	Yes
PagePerfect	Yes	No	No	Yes	No	No	No	Yes	Yes[4]
Comics	Yes	No	No	Yes	Yes	No	No	Yes	Yes[4]
NOOK Video	Yes	No	No	Yes	Yes	No	No	No	No

[1] iPhone, iPad Mini, iPad, and iPod Touch.
[2] Android phones and tablets.
[3] Most magazines are readable—check the magazine's product page at BN.com to verify.
[4] You must update your NOOK Color to 1.4 before reading PagePerfect books.

Index

A

About Device settings (Samsung Galaxy Tab 4 NOOK), 39-40
About menu (NOOK for Web), 332-333
Accessibility panel settings (Samsung Galaxy Tab 4 NOOK), 29
accessories settings (Samsung Galaxy Tab 4 NOOK), 32
Accounts settings (Samsung Galaxy Tab 4 NOOK), 31
ADE (Adobe Digital Editions), 386-388
adjusting font size in Samsung Galaxy Tab 4 NOOK, 69-70
Adobe Digital Editions (ADE), 386-388
adult profiles, 141-145
Airplane Mode setting (Samsung Galaxy Tab 4 NOOK), 21
Android, NOOK app for. *See* NOOK app for Android
application settings (Samsung Galaxy Tab 4 NOOK)
    Link to Social Networking settings, 46-47
    Newspaper/Magazine/Comics/Catalogs Reader settings, 44-45
    NOOK Video settings, 45-46
    Reader settings, 43-44
Applications settings (Samsung Galaxy Tab 4 NOOK), 32-35
apps. *See names of specific apps*
Apps app, 131
archiving ebooks, 214
audio files (Samsung Galaxy Tab 4 NOOK)
    audiobooks, 117-118
    installing, 111-112
    playing, 112-116
    podcasts, 116-117
audiobooks, 117-118
authorizing for ADE DRM, 386-388

B

B&N apps, 131
B&N hotspots, 169-171, 237
B&N Library, browsing (NOOK for Kids app), 285-287
Back key, Samsung Galaxy Tab 4 NOOK, 8
Backup settings (Samsung Galaxy Tab 4 NOOK), 32
balloon tips, 210
battery, 11-12, 196-198
Battery settings (Samsung Galaxy Tab 4 NOOK), 36
Blocking mode setting (Samsung Galaxy Tab 4 NOOK), 21, 29
Bluetooth, 19-23, 112
Book settings (Samsung Galaxy Tab 4 NOOK), 43-44
bookmarks
    NOOK app for Android, 272-273
    NOOK app for iOS, 247-249
    NOOK for Kids app, 292-293
    NOOK for PC app, 308
    NOOK GlowLight, 227
    Samsung Galaxy Tab 4 NOOK, 94-96
Bookmarks screen (web browser), 137-138
Books button (Samsung Galaxy Tab 4 NOOK Library), 55-58
books. *See* ebooks
borrowing ebooks, 110, 223-224
Brightness setting (Samsung Galaxy Tab 4 NOOK), 19
browsing
    B&N Library, NOOK for Kids app, 285-287
    music, 112-114
    My NOOK Library, 241-242, 266-267
    NOOK Store, 163-164, 233-234

NOOK GlowLight, 209-216
NOOK Library, 373-375
online library (NOOK for PC app),
   297-300
web, 131-138
buying
   content from NOOK Store
     from your computer, 168-169
     on NOOK GlowLight, 234-236
     on Samsung Galaxy Tab 4 NOOK,
      164-168
   ebooks
     NOOK app for Android, 277-281
     NOOK app for Windows, 381-384
   music, 174

C

Calibre, 385
   configuring, 335-336
   converting Word/TXT documents, 209
   ebooks
     adding covers, 339-340
     adding to library, 336-337
     converting, 342-343
     editing metadata, 337-339
     reading, 342
     sideloading, 340-342
   news subscriptions in, 342
   searching for ebooks, 390
cameras, 183-189
Caps Lock, 217
Catalog Reader Settings screen (Samsung
   Galaxy Tab 4 NOOK), 44-45
catalogs, reading on Samsung Galaxy Tab 4
   NOOK, 82-84
Catalogs screen (Samsung Galaxy Tab 4 NOOK
   Library), 63-64
Certification Authorities (CA), 39
changing
   font size, 244-247
   screensaver images, 200
   text font and size, 218-219
   themes, 246-247
   wallpaper images, 15-17
charging battery, 11-12, 198
child profiles, 141, 145-148
children's books, NOOK for Kids app, 283
   adding notes/highlights/bookmarks,
     292-293
   browsing B&N Library, 285-287
   Go To menu, 293-294
   installing, 284-285

Parents button, 294-296
   reading ebooks, 287-292
Chrome, 131-138
cleaning touchscreen, 14, 198
clearing searches, NOOK GlowLight, 206
Cloud settings (Samsung Galaxy Tab 4
   NOOK), 31
collaborators, inviting (NOOK Press), 363-366
comics, reading, 393
   NOOK app for Android, 275-276
   NOOK app for iOS, 252-253
   NOOK app for Windows, 380-381
   Samsung Galaxy Tab 4 NOOK, 75-80
Comics Reader Settings screen (Samsung
   Galaxy Tab 4 NOOK), 44-45
comparing Hulu Plus and Netflix, 121-122
configuring
   Calibre, 335-336
   camera settings, 186-189
   NOOK for PC app, 309-310
   NOOK Press, 355-357
   Wi-Fi access, Samsung Galaxy Tab 4
     NOOK, 2-3
connecting
   Bluetooth devices, Samsung Galaxy Tab 4
     NOOK, 23
   Wi-Fi hotspots, 9-11, 195-196
contacts, 205
Contents menu (NOOK for Web), 329
Contents screen, 243-244, 268-269
Contents view (NOOK Study app), 320-322
contextual filenames, 188
controls settings (Samsung Galaxy Tab 4
   NOOK), 29-31
converting
   ebooks with Calibre, 342-343
   Word/TXT files for NOOK, 209, 385
copying screensaver images, NOOK
   GlowLight, 200
courses, creating in NOOK Study app, 314
cover image, uploading (NOOK Press),
   366-367
covers, adding in Calibre, 339-340
custom locations for Calibre library, 335
customizing
   NOOK app for Android, 264-265
   NOOK GlowLight
     changing screensaver images, 200
     copying screensaver images, 200
     creating screensaver images, 199
     decals, 201
     Device Info section (Settings menu),
      201-203
     finding screensaver images, 201

GlowLight section (Settings menu), 201
Screen section (Settings menu), 203-204
Search section (Settings menu), 206
Shop section (Settings menu), 204
Social section (Settings menu), 205-206
Time section (Settings menu), 204
Wireless section (Settings menu), 203
Samsung Galaxy Tab 4 NOOK
   Accessibility panel settings, 29
   Blocking mode settings, 29
   Bluetooth settings, 21-23
   changing wallpaper images, 15-17
   display settings, 24-25
   font settings, 28
   General settings, 31-40
   Link to Social Networking settings, 46-47
   Lock screen settings, 26-28
   Multi Window settings, 26
   Newspaper/Magazine/Comics/ Catalog Reader settings, 44-45
   NOOK Settings screen, 40-43
   NOOK Video settings, 45-46
   Notifications panel settings, 28
   palm motion and Smart Screen settings, 31
   Reader settings, 43-44
   reading options, 71
   Settings screen, 17-21
   sound settings, 24
   voice and input settings, 29-31
   wallpaper settings, 28
NOOK Simple Touch, Reader section (Settings menu), 204

D

The Daily, viewing in NOOK for PC app, 300
Data Usage setting (Samsung Galaxy Tab 4 NOOK), 23
date and time settings (Samsung Galaxy Tab 4 NOOK), 32
DecalGirl skins, 201
decals, NOOK GlowLight, 201
Default Applications settings (Samsung Galaxy Tab 4 NOOK), 35
definitions, looking up, 219
   NOOK app for Android, 269-271
   NOOK app for iOS, 247-249
deleting
   ebooks in Library (Samsung Galaxy Tab 4 NOOK), 58
   highlights in NOOK for PC app, 308
   notes in NOOK for PC app, 308
   notes/highlights, 92, 226-227
   sideloaded content, 216
Details screen, sharing from, 230
Device Administrators, 38
Device Info section (Settings menu), NOOK GlowLight, 201-203
device settings (Samsung Galaxy Tab 4 NOOK), 24-29
dictionaries
   NOOK app for iOS, 247-249
   Samsung Galaxy Tab 4 NOOK, 71-73
digital rights management (DRM), 107, 221, 386
directions, 177-179
disconnecting Wi-Fi hotspots, 11, 197
display settings (Samsung Galaxy Tab 4 NOOK), 24-25
displaying thumbnails, NOOK Books for Kids, 100
double-tap gesture, 193
Download button, 213
downloading content to My NOOK Library, 349-350
drag gesture, 2
drive letters in Windows, 340
DRM (digital rights management), 107, 221, 386. See also ADE
Dual Book view (NOOK Study app), 319

E

ebooks
   adding to Calibre library, 336-337
   adding covers in Calibre, 339-340
   adding to shelf in Library (Samsung Galaxy Tab 4 NOOK), 58
   archiving, 214
   borrowing, 110, 223-224
   buying, 277-281, 381-384
   converting with Calibre, 342-343
   deleting in Library (Samsung Galaxy Tab 4 NOOK), 58
   editing metadata in Calibre, 337-339
   editing, NOOK Press, 359-363
   enhanced NOOK Books, reading on Samsung Galaxy Tab 4 NOOK, 73-75
   in EPUB format, sources for, 389
   file formats, 385-388

importing into NOOK for PC app,
    308-309
inviting collaborators, NOOK Press,
    363-366
lending. *See* LendMe
from libraries, 389-391
organizing, Shelves, 214
publishing, NOOK Press, 367-369
readability by device, 393
reading
    Calibre, 342
    NOOK for Kids app, 287-292
    NOOK for PC app, 303-306
    NOOK for Web, 327-334
    NOOK Study app, 317-322
    NOOK app for Android, 267-272
    NOOK app for iOS, 242-247
    NOOK app for Windows, 376-378
    NOOK GlowLight, 216-218
    Samsung Galaxy Tab 4 NOOK,
    67-69
searching for with Calibre, 390
sideloading with Calibre, 340-342
uploading
    NOOK app for Android, 276-277
    NOOK app for iOS, 257-259
    NOOK Press, 357-359
uploading cover image, NOOK Press,
    366-367
viewing in Library (Samsung Galaxy Tab
    4 NOOK), 56-57
editing
    ebooks, 359-363
    highlights in NOOK for PC app, 308
    metadata in Calibre, 337-339
    notes in NOOK for PC app, 308
    notes/highlights, 92-94, 226
encryption, 37
enhanced NOOK Books, 73-75, 393
EPUBs, 386, 389
    NOOK app for Android, 276-277
    NOOK app for iOS, 257-259

F

Facebook. *See also* social features; social net-
    working features
    accessing, 153
    linking, 331
    linking to, 205
    linking to NOOK HD, 46
    posting to, 155
factory defaults, resetting to, 203

file formats
    ADE (Adobe Digital Editions), 386-388
    for ebooks, converting with Calibre,
        342-343
    EPUB format, 386, 389
    for NOOK, 385
    images, 17
    readability by device, 393
file paths, viewing, 216
Find My Mobile feature, 37
finding screensaver images, NOOK GlowLight,
    201
firmware, reversing updates, 202
font settings (Samsung Galaxy Tab 4
    NOOK), 28
font size
    adjusting, 69-70, 320, 330
    changing, 218-219
        NOOK app for Android, 271
        NOOK app for iOS, 244-247
        NOOK for Kids app, 291-292
forgetting Wi-Fi hotspots, 11
formatting options (NOOK Press), 361-363
friends, 231-232
friends, managing, 206
Friends screen (My NOOK Library), 350-352
Full Screen option (NOOK for Web), 333
Full Screen view (NOOK Study app), 322

G

Gallery app, 138-139
General settings (camera), 188-189
General Settings screen (Samsung Galaxy Tab 4
    NOOK), 31-40
gestures, 1-2, 193-194
GlowLight section (Settings menu), NOOK
    GlowLight, 201
Gmail, linking, 331
Go To menu, NOOK for Kids app, 293-294
Google, linking to, 205
Google Chrome, 131-138
Google Contacts, linking to, 205
Google Hangouts, 190-192
Google Maps, 177-179
Google Play Music app, 112-116
Google Play Store, 173-176
Google+, 179-181
Grid view, 211

H

Hangouts, 190-192
Help setting (Samsung Galaxy Tab 4 NOOK), 22
hiding LendMe books from NOOK Friends, 232
highlights
    adding
        NOOK app for Android, 272-273
        NOOK app for iOS, 247-249
        NOOK GlowLight, 225-226
        Samsung Galaxy Tab 4 NOOK, 90-91
        NOOK for Kids app, 292-293
        NOOK for PC app, 307
        NOOK Study app, 322
    defined, 89, 225
    deleting in NOOK GlowLight, 226-227
    editing in Samsung Galaxy Tab 4 NOOK, 92-94
    editing/deleting with NOOK for PC app, 308
    support for, 89
    viewing, 226, 308
Highlights and Notes app, 93-94
Home button, 14, 194
Home screen, 6-9, 209-210
hotspots, B&N, 169-171, 237. *See also* Wi-Fi, hotspots
HTML files, reading on Samsung Galaxy Tab 4 NOOK, 85
Hulu Plus, 121-127

I

icons in My Library, 212
images
    changing for wallpaper, 15-17
    cover image, uploading to NOOK Press, 366-367
    file formats, 17
    Gallery app, 138-139
    screensavers (NOOK Glowlight), 199-201
importing ebooks into NOOK for PC app, 308-309
installing
    apps, 174
    audio files, 111-112
    microSD cards, 47-50, 206-207
    NOOK Study app, 312
    NOOK app, 239
    NOOK app for Windows, 371
    NOOK for Kids app, 284-285

inviting collaborators, NOOK Press, 363-366
iPad
    NOOK app. *See* NOOK app for iOS
    NOOK for Kids app, 283
        adding notes/highlights/bookmarks, 292-293
        browsing B&N Library, 285-287
        Go To menu, 293-294
        installing, 284-285
        Parents button, 294-296
        reading ebooks, 287-292
iPhone, NOOK app. *See* NOOK app for iOS
iPod Touch, NOOK app. *See* NOOK app for iOS
ISBNdb.com, 337
item options, NOOK for PC app, 301-302

J-K-L

Kids Interactive books, 99
Kids screen (Samsung Galaxy Tab 4 NOOK Library), 62
Kies, 111

Landscape mode (Samsung Galaxy Tab 4 NOOK), switching to Portrait mode, 69
lending ebooks. *See* LendMe
LendMe
    NOOK app for Windows, 384
    NOOK GlowLight, 221-223
    NOOK for PC app, 310-311
    Samsung Galaxy Tab 4 NOOK, 107-110
LendMe books, hiding from NOOK Friends, 232
LendMe feature, NOOK Study app, 325
libraries
    archiving items, 214
    browsing
        Home screen, 209-210
        My Files, 215-216
        My Library, 210-214
        Shelves, 214
    ebooks from, 389-391
    Samsung Galaxy Tab 4 NOOK, 51-55
        Books button, 55-58
        Catalogs screen, 63-64
        Kids screen, 62
        Magazines screen, 60-62
        Movies and TV screen, 62
        My Files screen, 66
        My Shelves screen, 65-66
        Newspapers screen, 63, 65
        View Details screen, 58-60
    NOOK Study app, files, adding to, 325-326

Library screen (My NOOK Library), 345-347
Link to Social Networking Settings screen
    (Samsung Galaxy Tab 4 NOOK), 46-47
List view, 211
live wallpapers, 15-16
Location settings (Samsung Galaxy Tab 4
    NOOK), 19, 23
Lock screen, Samsung Galaxy Tab 4
    NOOK, 5-6
Lock screen settings (Samsung Galaxy Tab 4
    NOOK), 26-28
looking up words. *See* dictionaries
lookup features in NOOK Study app, 324-325

M

Magazine Reader Settings screen (Samsung
    Galaxy Tab 4 NOOK), 44-45
magazines
    buying NOOK app for Android, 277-281
    notes/highlights support, 89
    readability by device, 393
    reading
        NOOK app for Android, 273-275
        NOOK app for iOS, 249-252
        NOOK app for Windows, 380-381
        NOOK GlowLight, 219-220
        Samsung Galaxy Tab 4 NOOK,
            75-80
    sampling, 167-168, 236
Magazines screen (Samsung Galaxy Tab 4
    NOOK Library), 60-62
Manage My NOOK screen (My NOOK
    Library), 352-353
managing subscriptions in My NOOK
    Library, 349
maps, Google Maps, 177-179
metadata, 210, 337-341
metering in camera settings, 187
microSD cards, installing, 47-50, 206-207
Microsoft Office documents, reading on
    Samsung Galaxy Tab 4 NOOK, 84-85
mobile hotspots, 3
modes (camera), 184-186
modifying Home screen, Samsung Galaxy Tab
    4 NOOK, 8-9
More Networks setting (Samsung Galaxy Tab 4
    NOOK), 23
Movies and TV screen (Samsung Galaxy Tab 4
    NOOK Library), 62
Movies screen (Hulu Plus), 125-126
Multi Window setting (Samsung Galaxy Tab 4
    NOOK), 19, 26
music, buying, 174. *See also* audio files

My Files, 215-216
My Files screen (Samsung Galaxy Tab 4
    NOOK Library), 66
My Library, 210-216
My Library screen, NOOK Study app, 314-318
My NOOK Library
    accessing, 345
    browsing
        NOOK app for Android, 266-267
        NOOK app for iOS, 241-242
    content, downloading, 349-350
    Friends screen, 350-352
    Library screen, 345-347
    Manage My NOOK screen, 352-353
    Recommendations screen, 352
    recommending tools, 347-348
    reviewing tools, 347-348
    subscriptions, managing, 349
My Project screen (NOOK Press), 369-370
My Shelves screen (Samsung Galaxy Tab 4
    NOOK Library), 65-66

N

Netflix, 121-124
news subscriptions with Calibre, 342
Newspaper Reader Settings screen (Samsung
    Galaxy Tab 4 NOOK), 44-45
newspapers
    readability by device, 393
    reading
        NOOK app for Android, 273
        NOOK app for iOS, 249
        NOOK app for Windows, 376-378
        NOOK GlowLight, 219-220
    reading on Samsung Galaxy Tab 4
        NOOK, 80-81
    sampling
        on NOOK GlowLight, 236
        on Samsung Galaxy Tab 4 NOOK,
            167-168
Newspapers screen (Samsung Galaxy Tab 4
    NOOK Library), 63-65
NOOK apps
    B&N apps, 131
    formats readable on, 393
    Gallery, 138-139
    installing, 239
    Search, 129-130
    Today, 171
    web browser, 131-138
NOOK app for Android
    comics, reading, 275-276
    Contents screen, 268-269

customizing, 264-265
ebooks
    reading, 267-272
    uploading, 276-277
formats readable on, 393
interface, 262-264
magazines, reading, 273-275
My NOOK Library, browsing, 266-267
newspapers, reading, 273
notes/highlights/bookmarks, adding,
    272-273
profiles, 281-283
shopping from, 277-281
Text Options screen, 271-272
NOOK app for iOS
    comics, reading, 252-253
    Contents screen, 243-244
    ebooks
        reading, 242-247
        uploading, 257-259
    formats readable on, 393
    interface, 240-241
    magazines, reading, 249-252
    My NOOK Library, browsing, 241-242
    newspapers, reading, 249
    notes/highlights/bookmarks, adding,
        247-249
    PagePerfect books, reading, 254
    profiles, 255-257
    Text Options screen, 244-247
NOOK app for Windows, 371
    comics, reading, 380-381
    ebooks
        buying, 381-384
        reading, 376-378
    installing, 371
    interface, 371-373
    LendMe and, 384
    magazines, reading, 380-381
    newspapers, reading, 376-378
    NOOK Library, browsing, 373-375
    PagePerfect books, reading, 376-379
    Text Options screen, 378-379
NOOK Books for Kids
    formats, 99
    Read and Record, 102-105
    reading, 99-102
    thumbnails, displaying, 100
NOOK Color, formats readable on, 393
NOOK for Kids app, 283
    B&N Library, browsing, 285-287
    ebooks, reading, 287-292
    Go To menu, 293-294
    installing, 284-285
    notes/highlights/bookmarks, adding,
        292-293

Parents button, 294-296
readability by device, 393
NOOK for Mac app, shelves, 300
NOOK for PC app
    bookmarks, adding, 308
    configuring, 309-310
    ebooks,
        importing, 308-309
        reading, 303-306
    highlights, 307-308
    item options, 301-302
    LendMe in, 310-311
    notes, 307-308
    online library, 297-300
    viewing the Daily, 300
NOOK for Web, 327-334
NOOK Friends, 231-232
NOOK GlowLight
    archiving items, 214
    B&N hotspots, accessing, 237
    battery, 197-198
    bookmarks in, 227
    borrowing ebooks, 223-224
    browsing
        Home screen, 209-210
        My Files, 215-216
        My Library, 210-214
        Shelves, 214
    buttons, 194
    customizing
        changing screensaver images, 200
        copying screensaver images, 200
        creating screensaver images, 199
        decals, 201
        Device Info section (Settings menu),
            201-203
        finding screensaver images, 201
        GlowLight section (Settings
            menu), 201
        Screen section (Settings menu),
            203-204
        Search section (Settings menu), 206
        Shop section (Settings menu), 204
        Social section (Settings menu),
            205-206
        Time section (Settings menu), 204
        Wireless section (Settings
            menu), 203
    formats readable on, 393
    gestures, 193-194
    LendMe, 221-223
    NOOK Store
        browsing, 233-234
        content, purchasing, 234-236
        content, sampling, 234-236
        searching, 234

notes/highlights, 225-227
reading ebooks, 216-218
reading magazines and newspapers, 219-220
registering, 194-195
social features, 229-231
text, 218-219
touchscreen, cleaning, 198
Wi-Fi hotspots, 195-197
NOOK HD, formats readable on, 393
NOOK Library, browsing (NOOK app for Windows), 373-375
NOOK Press
    collaborators, inviting, 363-366
    configuring, 355-357
    cover image, uploading, 366-367
    ebooks
        publishing, 367-369
        uploading, 357-359
    formatting options, 361-363
    My Project screen, 369-370
    Quick Outline section, 359-361
    terms and conditions, 355-356
    Text Area section, 361
NOOK Profiles. *See* profiles
NOOK Settings screen (NOOK HD), 40-43
NOOK Simple Touch
    customizing Reader section (Settings menu), 204
    formats readable on, 393
    microSD cards, installing, 206-207
    Page Turn buttons, 194
NOOK Store
    browsing on NOOK GlowLight, 233-234
    browsing on NOOK HD, 163-164
    content
        purchasing on NOOK GlowLight, 234-236
        purchasing on Samsung Galaxy Tab 4 NOOK, 164-168
        sampling on NOOK GlowLight, 234-236
        sampling on Samsung Galaxy Tab 4 NOOK, 164-168
    searching on NOOK GlowLight, 234
    shopping from your computer, 168-169
    shopping on Samsung Galaxy Tab 4 NOOK, 161-163
NOOK Study app, 311
    courses, creating, 314
    ebooks, reading, 317-322
    files, adding to library, 325-326
    fonts, adjusting, 320
    formats readable on, 393
    highlights, adding, 322
    installing, 312
    LendMe feature, 325

lookup features, 324-325
My Library screen, navigating, 314-318
navigating, 313
notes, adding, 322-323
page turning, 320
NOOK Tablet, formats readable on, 393
NOOK Today, 171
NOOK-Look, 201
NOOK Video app, 259-262, 393
NOOK Video Settings screen (Samsung Galaxy Tab 4 NOOK), 45-46
notes
    adding
        NOOK GlowLight, 225-226
        NOOK app for Android, 272-273
        NOOK app for iOS, 247-249
        NOOK for Kids app, 292-293
        NOOK for PC app, 307
        NOOK Study app, 322-323
        Samsung Galaxy Tab 4 NOOK, 90-91
    defined, 89, 225
    deleting in NOOK GlowLight, 226-227
    editing
        NOOK GlowLight, 226
        NOOK for PC app, 308
        Samsung Galaxy Tab 4 NOOK, 92-94
    support for, 89
    viewing, 226, 308
Notifications panel settings (Samsung Galaxy Tab 4 NOOK), 28

O

online library (NOOK for PC app), 297-300
options, NOOK for PC app, 301-302
Options menu (Reading Tools bar), 73
organizing ebooks, Shelves, 214
orientation, changing in Samsung Galaxy Tab 4 NOOK, 69
Overdrive, 389-391
overwriting metadata, 341

P

Page Turn buttons, 194
page turning in NOOK Study app, 320
PagePerfect, readability by device, 393
PagePerfect books, 97
    NOOK app for iOS, 254
    NOOK app for Windows, 376-379
    Samsung Galaxy Tab 4 NOOK, 86-87

palm motion settings (Samsung Galaxy Tab 4 NOOK), 31
Parents button, 294-296
passwords, 38
PDF files, 85-87, 257-259
Photo settings, 186
photos, cameras, 183-189
pinch gesture, 2
Play Music app, 112-116
Play Store, 173-176
playing
    audio files, 112-116
    audiobooks, 117-118
    podcasts, 116-117
podcasts, playing (Samsung Galaxy Tab 4 NOOK), 116-117
Portrait mode (Samsung Galaxy Tab 4 NOOK), switching to Landscape mode, 69
posting to Facebook wall, 155
Power button, 13, 194
Power Saving Mode settings (Samsung Galaxy Tab 4 NOOK), 36
Power Saving setting (Samsung Galaxy Tab 4 NOOK), 21
press-and-hold gesture, 2
Primary profile, 141
printing to NOOK Study app, 325
profiles
    adult profiles, 142-145
    child profiles, 145-148
    managing content visibility, 149-151
    NOOK app for Android, 281-283
    NOOK app for iOS, 255-257
    types of, 141
publishing ebooks, 367-369
purchasing. *See* buying

Q-R

Queue screen (Hulu Plus), 126-127
Quick Outline section (NOOK Press), 359-361

Read and Play books, 99-101
Read and Record (NOOK Books for Kids), 102-105
Read to Me books, 99-100
Reader section (Settings menu), 204
Reader Settings screen (Samsung Galaxy Tab 4 NOOK), 43-44
reading
    catalogs on Samsung Galaxy Tab 4 NOOK, 82-84
    comics
        NOOK app for Android, 275-276
        NOOK app for iOS, 252-253

    NOOK app for Windows, 380-381
    on Samsung Galaxy Tab 4 NOOK, 75-80
ebooks
    with Calibre, 342
    NOOK app for Android, 267-272
    NOOK app for iOS, 242-247
    NOOK app for Windows, 376-378
    NOOK GlowLight, 216-218
    NOOK for Kids app, 287-292
    NOOK for PC app, 303-306
    NOOK Study app, 317-322
    NOOK for Web, 327-334
    Samsung Galaxy Tab 4 NOOK, 67-69
enhanced NOOK Books on Samsung Galaxy Tab 4 NOOK, 73-75
HTML files on Samsung Galaxy Tab 4 NOOK, 85
magazines
    NOOK app for Android, 273-275
    NOOK app for iOS, 249-252
    NOOK app for Windows, 380-381
    on Samsung Galaxy Tab 4 NOOK, 75-80
magazines and newspapers, NOOK GlowLight, 219-220
Microsoft Office documents on Samsung Galaxy Tab 4 NOOK, 84-85
newspapers
    NOOK app for Android, 273
    NOOK app for iOS, 249
    NOOK app for Windows, 376-378
    Samsung Galaxy Tab 4 NOOK, 80-81
NOOK Books for Kids, 99-102
PagePerfect books
    NOOK app for iOS, 254
    NOOK app for Windows, 376-379
    Samsung Galaxy Tab 4 NOOK, 86-87
PDF files on Samsung Galaxy Tab 4 NOOK, 85-87
reading options (Samsung Galaxy Tab 4 NOOK), customizing, 71
Reading Tools, 67-70, 73, 217
Reading Tools toolbar, 157-158, 230
Received Files setting (Samsung Galaxy Tab 4 NOOK), 22
Recent Drawer, Samsung Galaxy Tab 4 NOOK, 7-8
Recent key, 7-8
Recommend screen (Samsung Galaxy Tab 4 NOOK), 154-155

Recommendations screen (My NOOK
    Library), 352
recommending tools (My NOOK Library),
    347-348
recording, 102-105
registering
    NOOK GlowLight, 194-195
    Samsung Galaxy Tab 4 NOOK, 2-5
Rename Devices setting (Samsung Galaxy Tab
    4 NOOK), 22
requirements for NOOK for Web, 327
resetting
    to factory defaults, 203
    Samsung Galaxy Tab 4 NOOK, 40
reversing firmware updates, 202
reviewing tools, My NOOK Library, 347-348

S

sampling content from NOOK Store
    on NOOK GlowLight, 234-236
    on Samsung Galaxy Tab 4 NOOK,
        164-168
Samsung Galaxy Tab 4 NOOK
    audio files, 111-116
    audiobooks, 117-118
    B&N hotspots, accessing, 169-171
    Back key, 8
    battery, 11-12
    bookmarks in, 94-96
    borrowing ebooks, 110
    buttons, 13-14
    cameras, 183-189
    catalogs, reading, 82-84
    comics, reading, 75-80
    customizing
        Accessibility panel settings, 29
        Blocking mode settings, 29
        Bluetooth settings, 21-23
        changing wallpaper images, 15-17
        display settings, 24-25
        font settings, 28
        General settings, 31-40
        Link to Social Networking settings,
            46-47
        Lock screen settings, 26-28
        Multi Window settings, 26
        Newspaper/Magazine/Comics/
            Catalog Reader settings, 44-45
        NOOK Settings screen, 40-43
        NOOK Video settings, 45-46
        Notifications panel settings, 28

        palm motion and Smart Screen
            settings, 31
        Reader settings, 43-44
        Settings screen, 17-21
        sound settings, 24
        voice and input settings, 29-31
        wallpaper settings, 28
enhanced NOOK Books, reading, 73-75
font size, adjusting, 69-70
formats readable on, 393
gestures, 1-2
Home screen, 6-9
HTML files, reading, 85
lending ebooks, 107-110
Library, 51-55
    Books button, 55-58
    Catalogs screen, 63-64
    Kids screen, 62
    Magazines screen, 60-62
    Movies and TV screen, 62
    My Files screen, 66
    My Shelves screen, 65-66
    Newspapers screen, 63-65
    View Details screen, 58-60
linking Facebook to, 46
linking Twitter to, 47
Lock screen, 5-6
magazines, reading, 75-80
microSD cards, installing, 47-50
Microsoft Office documents, reading,
    84-85
newspapers, reading, 80-81
NOOK Store
    browsing, 163-164
    content, purchasing, 164-168
    content, sampling, 164-168
    shopping, 161-163
notes/highlights, 90-94
PagePerfect books, reading, 86-87
PDF files, reading, 85-87
Podcasts, playing, 116-117
profiles, 141-151
reading
    ebooks, 67-69
    options, customizing, 71
    orientation, changing, 69
Reading Tools bar, Options menu, 73
Recent Drawer, 7-8
registering, 2-5
resetting, 40
social networking features, 153
    Recommend screen, 154-155
    Share button (Reading Tools tool-
        bar), 157-158

*Share button (Text Selection tool-
bar), 158-160*
View Details screen, 155-157
touchscreen, cleaning, 14
transferring Calibre books, 336
Twitter support, 160
video, 119-127
Wi-Fi access, configuring, 2-3
Wi-Fi hotspots, 9-11
word definitions, looking up, 71-73
Screen Rotation setting (Samsung Galaxy Tab 4
NOOK), 19
Screen section (Settings menu), 203-204
screensavers (NOOK GlowLight), 199-201
scroll gesture, 2, 194
Search app, 129-130
Search button, 210
Search feature (NOOK Study app), 322
Search section (Settings menu), 206
searching
for ebooks with Calibre, 390
in NOOK Study app, 324-325
music, Samsung Galaxy Tab 4
NOOK, 114
NOOK Store on NOOK GlowLight, 234
Security settings (Samsung Galaxy Tab 4
NOOK), 37-39
selecting text, 218
setting up. *See* configuring
settings, camera, 186-189
Settings menu (NOOK GlowLight), 201-206
Settings screen (Samsung Galaxy Tab 4
NOOK), 17-21
Accessibility panel settings, 29
Blocking mode settings, 29
Bluetooth settings, 21-23
display settings, 24-25
font settings, 28
General settings, 31-40
Link to Social Networking settings, 46-47
Lock screen settings, 26-28
Multi Window settings, 26
Newspaper/Magazine/Comics/Catalog
Reader settings, 44-45
NOOK Settings screen, 40-43
NOOK Video settings, 45-46
Notifications panel settings, 28
palm motion and Smart Screen
settings, 31
Reader settings, 43-44
sound settings, 24
voice and input settings, 29-31
wallpaper settings, 28
Share button, 157-160

Share menu (NOOK for Web), 330-332
sharing. *See also* social networking features
from Details screen, 230
from Reading Tools toolbar, 230
from Text Selection toolbar, 231
shelf, 58, 65-66, 300
Shop section (Settings menu), NOOK
GlowLight, 204
shopfront, 233
shopping
NOOK app for Android, 277-281
NOOK app for Windows, 381-384
NOOK Store, 161-169
sideloaded content, 215-216, 340-342, 388
Simple View feature (NOOK for Web), 333-334
size of text, changing, 218-219
sleep mode, 13, 198
sleep timer, NOOK GlowLight, 203
Smart Screen settings (Samsung Galaxy Tab 4
NOOK), 31
Smart Stay setting (Samsung Galaxy Tab 4
NOOK), 21
social features, NOOK GlowLight, 229-232
social media accounts, linking, 331
social networking, Google+, 179-181
social networking features, 153-160
social networking settings (Samsung Galaxy
Tab 4 NOOK), 46-47
Social section (Settings menu), NOOK
GlowLight, 205-206
Sort button, 211
sorting online library (NOOK for PC app),
299-300
Sound setting (Samsung Galaxy Tab 4 NOOK),
19, 24
sources for ebooks in EPUB format, 389
Storage settings (Samsung Galaxy Tab 4
NOOK), 36
streaming video to Samsung Galaxy Tab 4
NOOK, 122-127
streaming video services, 121-122
subscription content
with Calibre, 342
sampling
on NOOK GlowLight, 236
*on Samsung Galaxy Tab 4 NOOK,
167-168*
subscriptions, managing in My NOOK
Library, 349
Surface, NOOK app for. *See* NOOK app for
Windows
surge suppressors, 11, 198
sweep gesture, 2

swipe gesture, 2, 193
Sync button, 210
Sync setting (Samsung Galaxy Tab 4 NOOK), 21

T

tap gesture, 1, 193
terms and conditions, NOOK Press, 355-356
text, 218-219
Text Area section (NOOK Press), 361
Text menu (NOOK for Web), 330
Text Options screen
    NOOK app for Android, 271-272
    NOOK app for iOS, 244-247
    NOOK app for Windows, 378-379
Text Selection toolbar, 68
    on Samsung Galaxy Tab 4 NOOK, Share button, 158-160
    sharing from, 231
themes, changing, 246-247, 272
thumbnails (NOOK Books for Kids), displaying, 100
Time section (Settings menu), NOOK GlowLight, 204
Title Details screen, 213-214
Today app, 171
touchscreen, cleaning, 14, 198
Transferring Calibre books to Samsung Galaxy Tab 4 NOOK, 336
trial subscriptions, 167-168, 236
troubleshooting lending ebooks, 222-223
turning pages in NOOK Study app, 320
TV screen (Hulu Plus), 125-126
Twitter, 47, 160, 205, 331. *See also* social features; social networking features
TXT files, converting for NOOK, 209, 385
Type button, 210

U

UltraViolet, 45
Unarchive button, 213
unpinch gesture, 2
updates, reversing (firmware), 202
uploading
    cover image, NOOK Press, 366-367
    ebooks
        NOOK app for Android, 276-277
        NOOK app for iOS, 257-259
        NOOK Press, 357-359
Users settings (Samsung Galaxy Tab 4 NOOK), 35

V

vendor accounts (NOOK Press), creating, 356
video
    NOOK Video app, 259-262
    on Samsung Galaxy Tab 4 NOOK, 119-121
    streaming to NOOK HD, 122-127
    YouTube, 181-182
video chatting, Google Hangouts, 190-192
Videos screen, 62
Videos settings, 188
View Details screen (Samsung Galaxy Tab 4 NOOK Library), 58-60, 155-157
visibility of content, managing in profiles, 149-151
Visibility Timeout setting (Samsung Galaxy Tab 4 NOOK), 22
voice and input settings (Samsung Galaxy Tab 4 NOOK), 29-31
volume buttons (Samsung Galaxy Tab 4 NOOK), 14
Volume setting (Samsung Galaxy Tab 4 NOOK), 19

W-X-Y-Z

wallpaper, changing images (Samsung Galaxy Tab 4 NOOK), 15-17
wallpaper settings (Samsung Galaxy Tab 4 NOOK), 28
web browser app, 131-138
websites, MP3 audiobooks, 117
white balance, 188
Wi-Fi, hotspots (B&N), 169-171, 237
Wi-Fi access, configuring Samsung Galaxy Tab 4 NOOK, 2-3
Wi-Fi hotspots, 9-11, 195-196
Wi-Fi setting (Samsung Galaxy Tab 4 NOOK), 19
Windows, drive letters, 340
Windows, NOOK app for. *See* NOOK app for Windows
Wireless section (Settings menu), NOOK GlowLight, 203
Word documents, converting for NOOK, 219, 385
words, looking up. *See* dictionaries

YouTube, 181-182

zooming with pinch gesture, 2